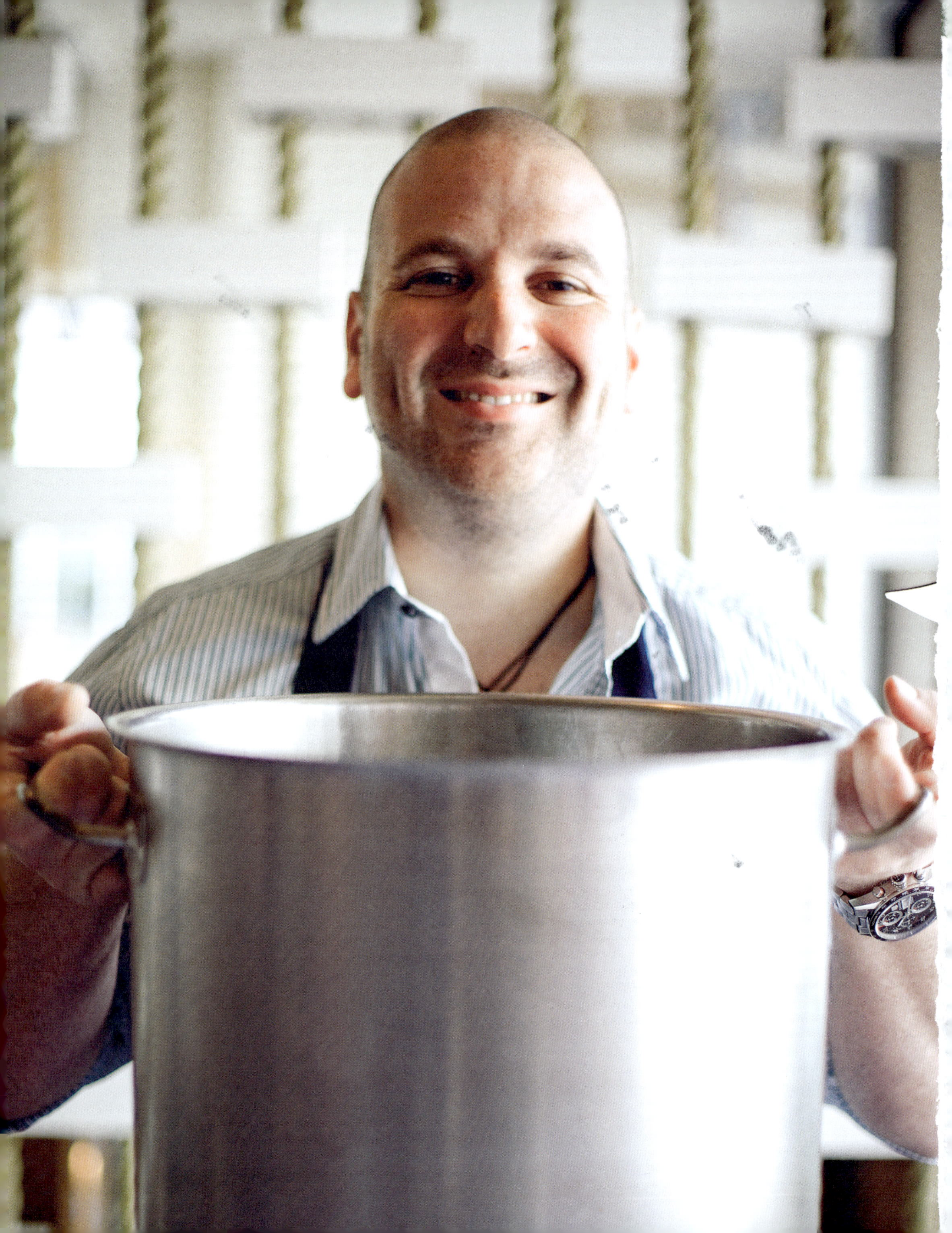

George Calombaris was voted one of the 'Top 40 chefs of Influence in the World' in 2004 by *The Global Food and Wine Magazine*, and he continues to live up to this acclaim. He owns six restaurants in Melbourne, The Press Club, Maha, Hellenic Republic, P M 24, St Katherine's and Mama Baba, as well as consulting for The Belvedere Club restaurant in Mykonos, Greece. George is the co-author of *Your Place or Mine?* and *Cook with Us*, and author of *Greek Cookery from the Hellenic Heart* and *The Press Club: Modern Greek Cookery*. He is also a judge on *MasterChef Australia* and *Junior MasterChef Australia*.

Georgie Porgie

FOR KIDS AGED 8 TO 80

George Calombaris

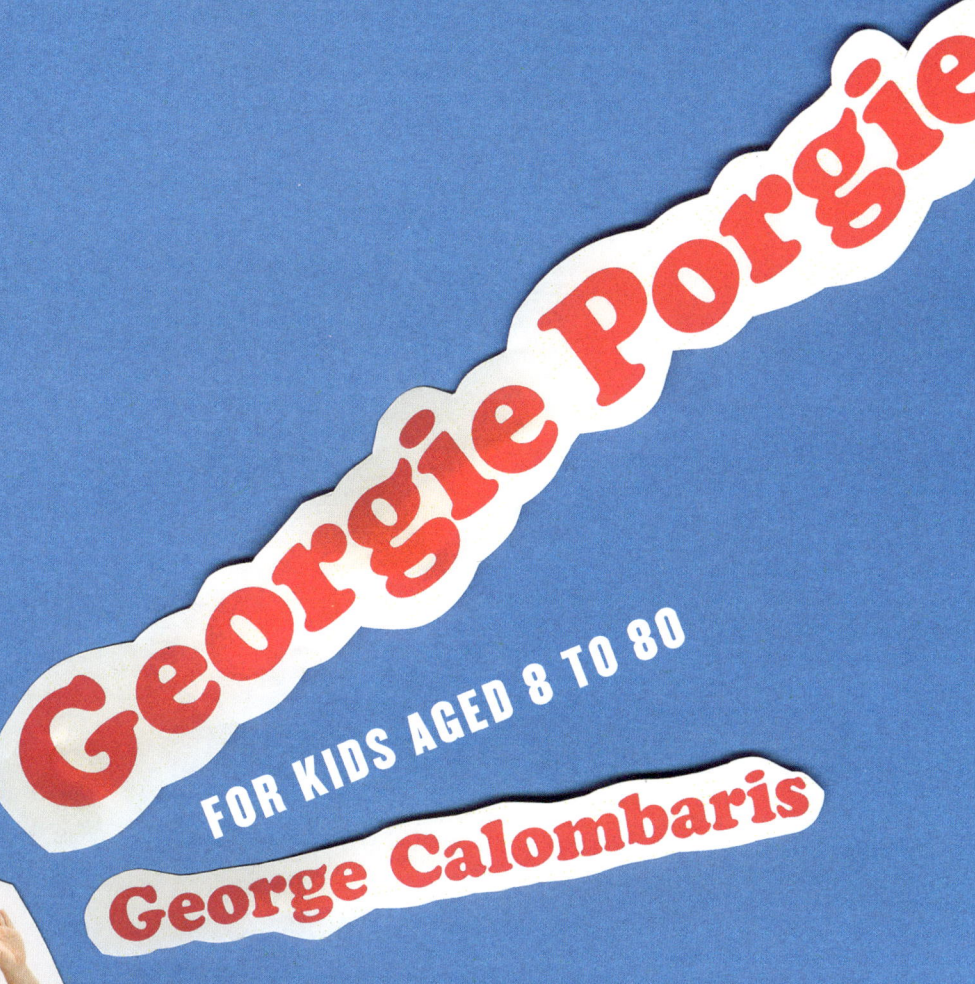

Photography by **Mark Chew**

LANTERN
an imprint of
PENGUIN BOOKS

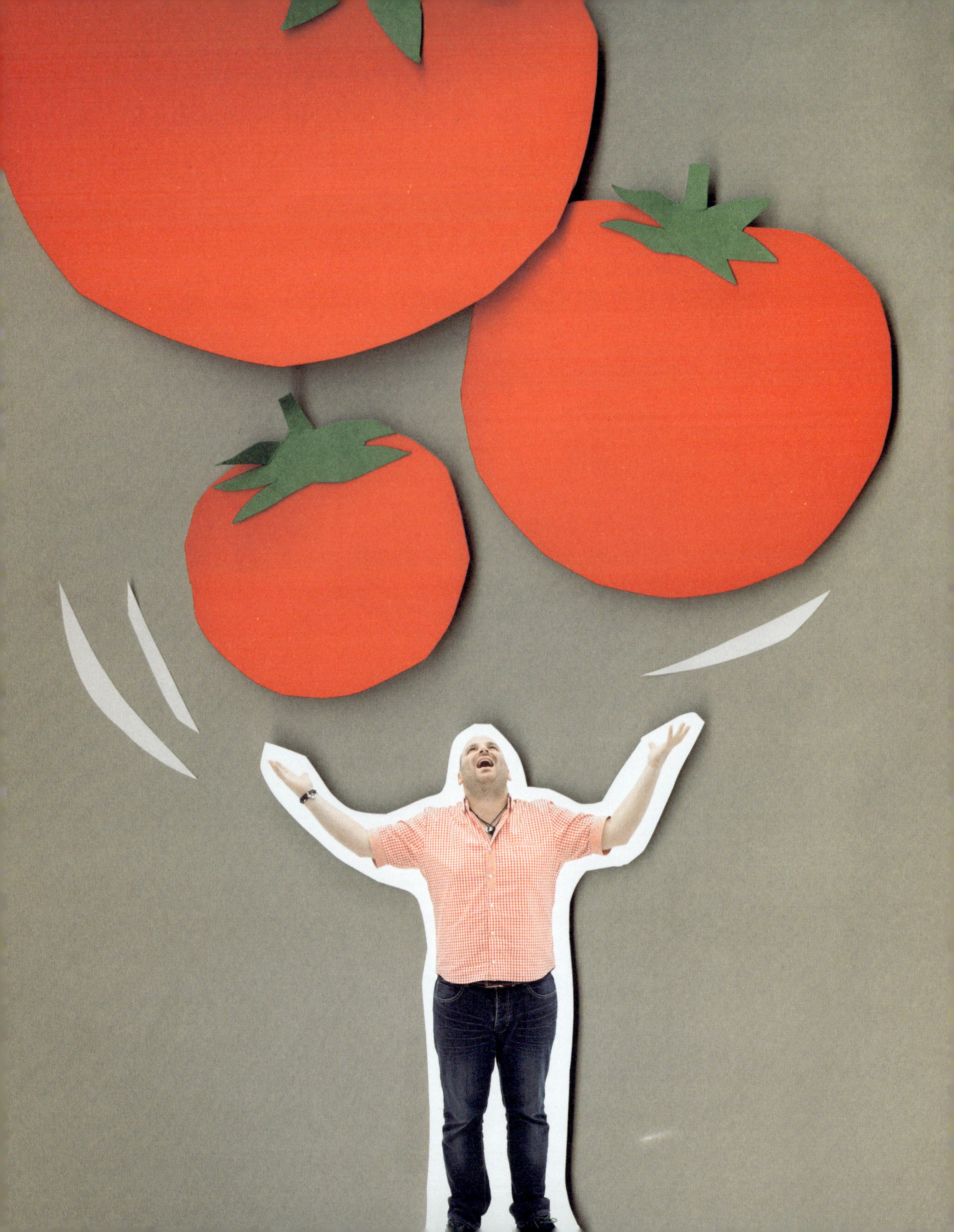

Contents

Introduction vii	Potato 115
	Prawns 123
Apples 1	Quick dinners 131
Bread 9	Rice 139
Chicken 17	Soup 147
Dips 27	Treats 155
Eggs 35	Vegetables 163
Fritters 43	Wraps 171
Guilty pleasures 51	Yoghurt 179
Healthy salads 59	Zucchini 187
Ice cream 67	
Jelly 75	Kitchen basics 195
Lamb 83	
Mince 91	Glossary 201
On a stick 99	Thank you 205
Pasta 107	Index 207

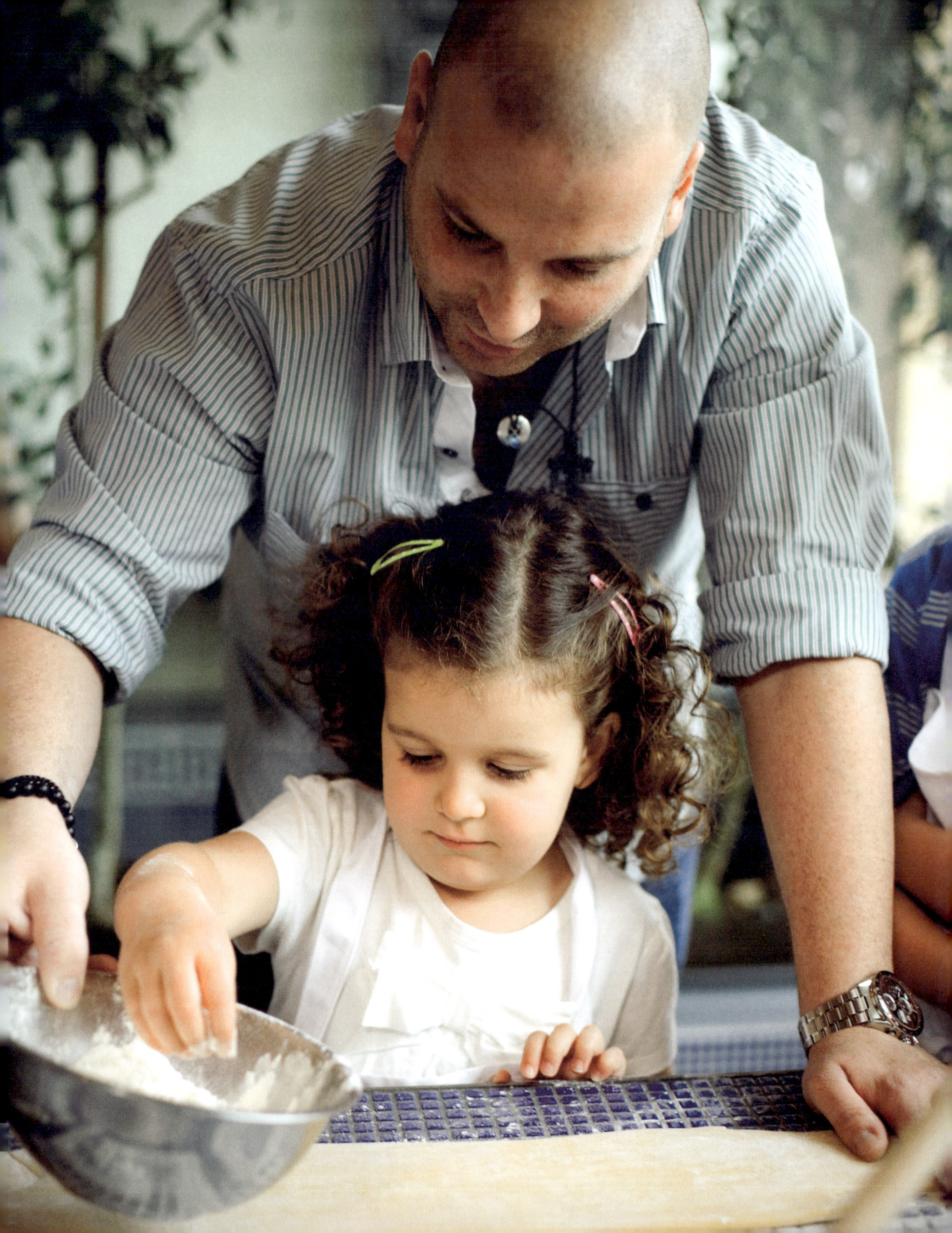

Introduction

As a kid I used to sit at the end of the kitchen bench while my mum cooked. It was during these times that I learnt about the wonderful flavours of our family food. I'd watch as she skilfully knotted Greek biscuits. She'd let me help, even though my own knots looked clumsy compared to hers. I used to taste, smell and touch everything. I was always getting into trouble for eating raw dough. My passion followed me to kindergarten, where I'd hang out in the little play kitchen area, in my own imaginary world, cooking.

Food formed the basis of our family life. It drew us to the table and taught us the joy of sharing a meal with loved ones. Food was part of our many celebrations. I remember watching my dad line the bathtub with a black plastic sheet, which he then used to marinate a whole lamb. Later he showed me how to skewer the lamb and put it on the spit. I remember everyone coming home after midnight mass and sharing bowls of soup, not because we were hungry, but because it was an important part of our family ritual.

These experiences made me realise food was about something more than simply satisfying hunger and providing nutrition. Food was a part of who we were. It was linked to our family stories and interwoven with our memories. It was an integral part of my experience of growing up.

My mum was not my only inspiration. Both my grandmothers were wonderful cooks. Their influence is evident in several of the recipes in this book. My Nonna (Grandma) Nicoletta was Italian, and she introduced us to the food of her homeland. When I eat dishes such as the simple pasta with ricotta and parmesan (see page 108 for the recipe), I'm transported back to her table. She'd follow this dish with more fresh ricotta for dessert, which she'd dust with icing sugar and cinnamon. It was absolutely delicious.

Yia Yia (Grandma) Kaili had a Greek-Cypriot background, and she cooked many Turkish-style dishes, which had lots of spices. I remember her making filo pastry and rolling it out with a narrow rolling pin, which she told me helped make the dough thin. I remember a funny story she told me about arriving in Australia, of how the customs officers took away her treasured mortar and pestle because they thought it was a weapon. Of course, we all know now that this is a very useful piece of kitchen equipment, but things were different back then.

When I was fifteen, my parents sent me to Greece to stay with my great-uncle Chris. I remember eating wonderfully simple food, such as freshly made yoghurt that was set in a ceramic pot, drizzled with delicious Greek honey and scattered with fresh walnuts. We ate it for breakfast. I still make this dish and, in fact, I love it so much that I have included a recipe here (see page 180) for you to try.

Travelling to Greece gave me more of an understanding of my heritage and helped cement my desire to become a professional chef. I wanted to start my apprenticeship the minute I turned sixteen, but my father made me finish school. At the time, I wasn't happy, but now realise this was the right decision. I would give the same advice to young people today.

There's so much to learn about cooking and it's never too late – or too early – to start. These recipes will help you get going, but you also need to learn by doing. You have to get into the kitchen and touch, smell and taste the food – just like I did as a kid. Learning about food in this way makes you a more instinctive cook. I don't remember my mother or grandmothers using recipes at all when I was growing up. But recipes are important in their own way, and it's good to follow a recipe at first so that you get to understand the techniques and ingredients. Once you're familiar with a dish, you can then start improvising by using different ingredients depending on what you have in your fridge or pantry at home. This is the very best path to home cooking.

Everyone makes mistakes when starting out – this is true not just of cooking, but of life. Making mistakes is how you learn. You have to stop and think about why something went wrong, and then work out how to fix it. Cooking is about learning skills and practising them over and over. Not everyone wants to become a professional chef, but everyone should know how to cook for their health and their happiness, and, of course, because it's great fun.

I've written the recipes in this book for kids aged eight years and up, but also for the kid in all of us. Some recipes are really simple and some are more complex – perfect for those of you who want a bit of a challenge. Many are based on my memory of the tastes and aromas that came from the kitchens of my mother and grandmothers. Others are versions of dishes from my restaurant menus. There are sweet and savoury treats, as well as the sort of meals that will encourage you to experiment with different flavours and textures and, of course, develop your skills in the kitchen.

I hope this book will inspire all of you, not only to cook but also to try new dishes and share and enjoy meals around the table with your family, as I did with my family and hope to do some day with my kids.

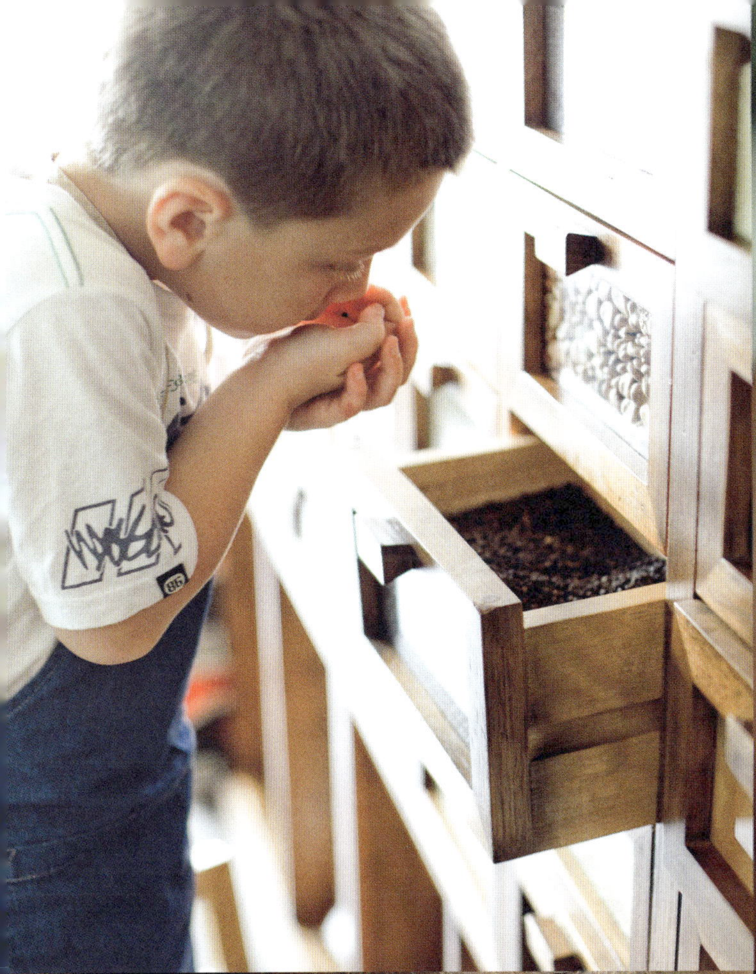

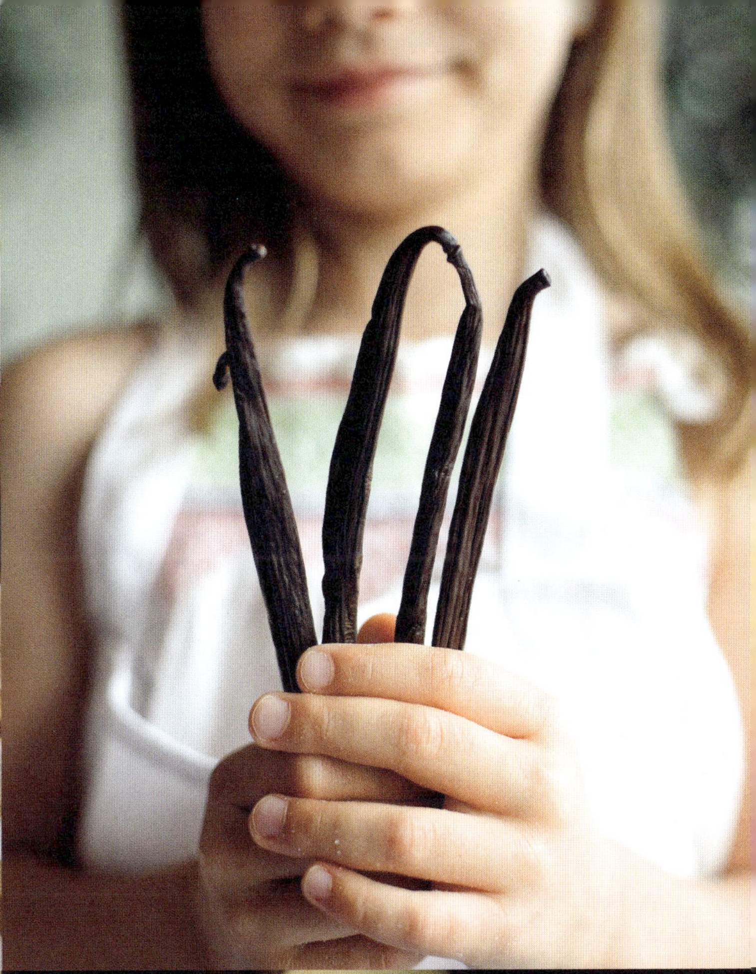

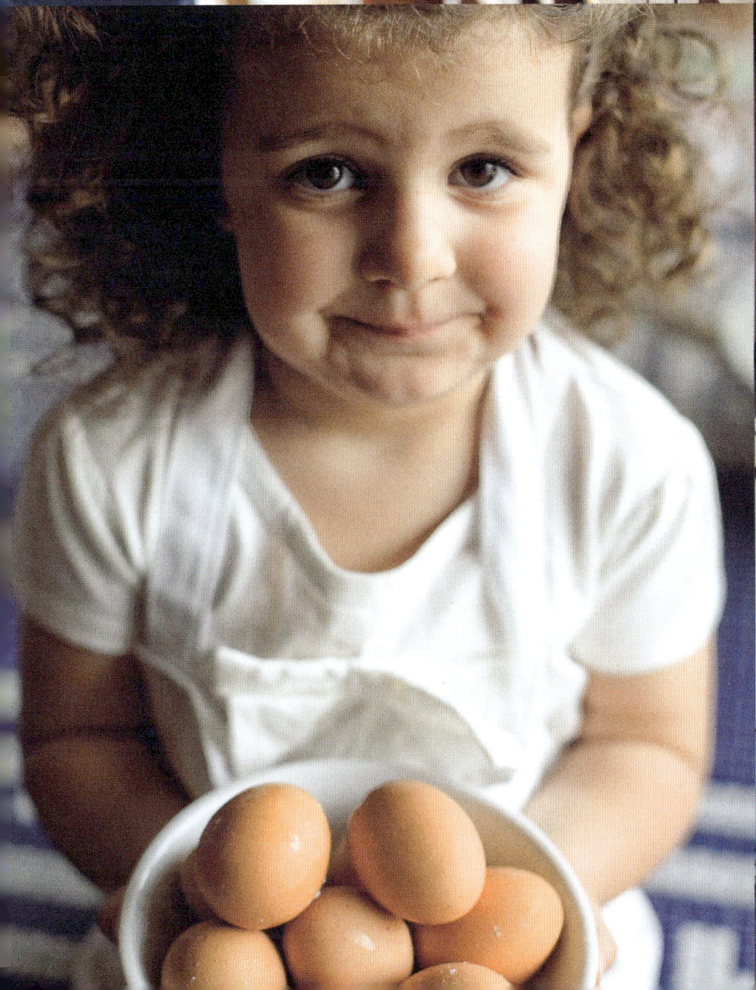

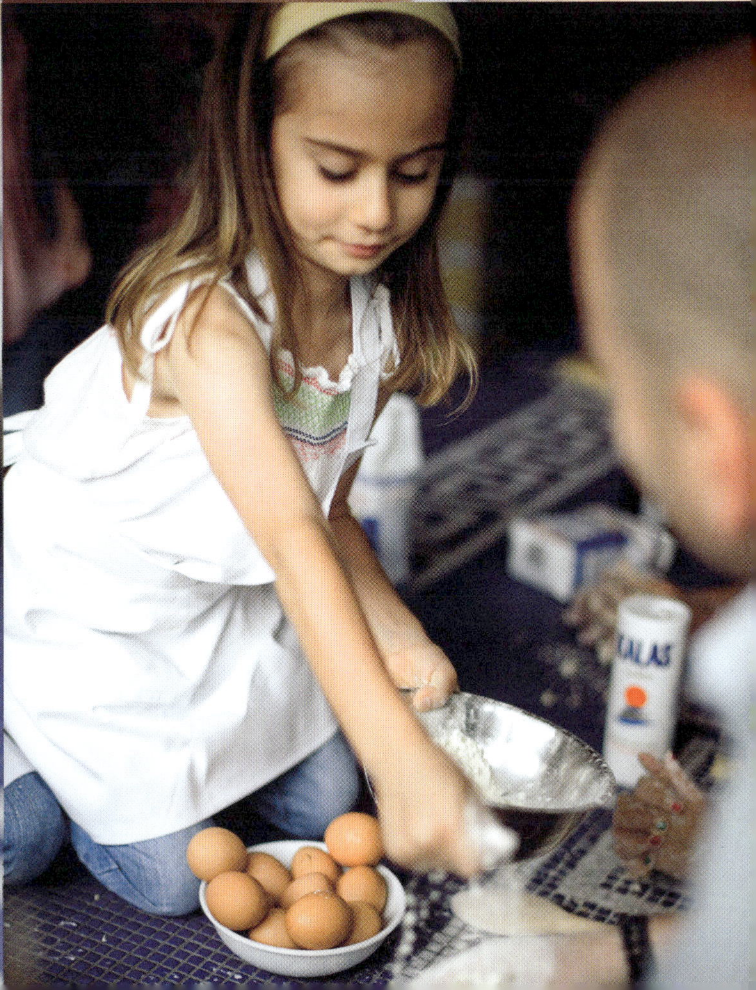
KALAS

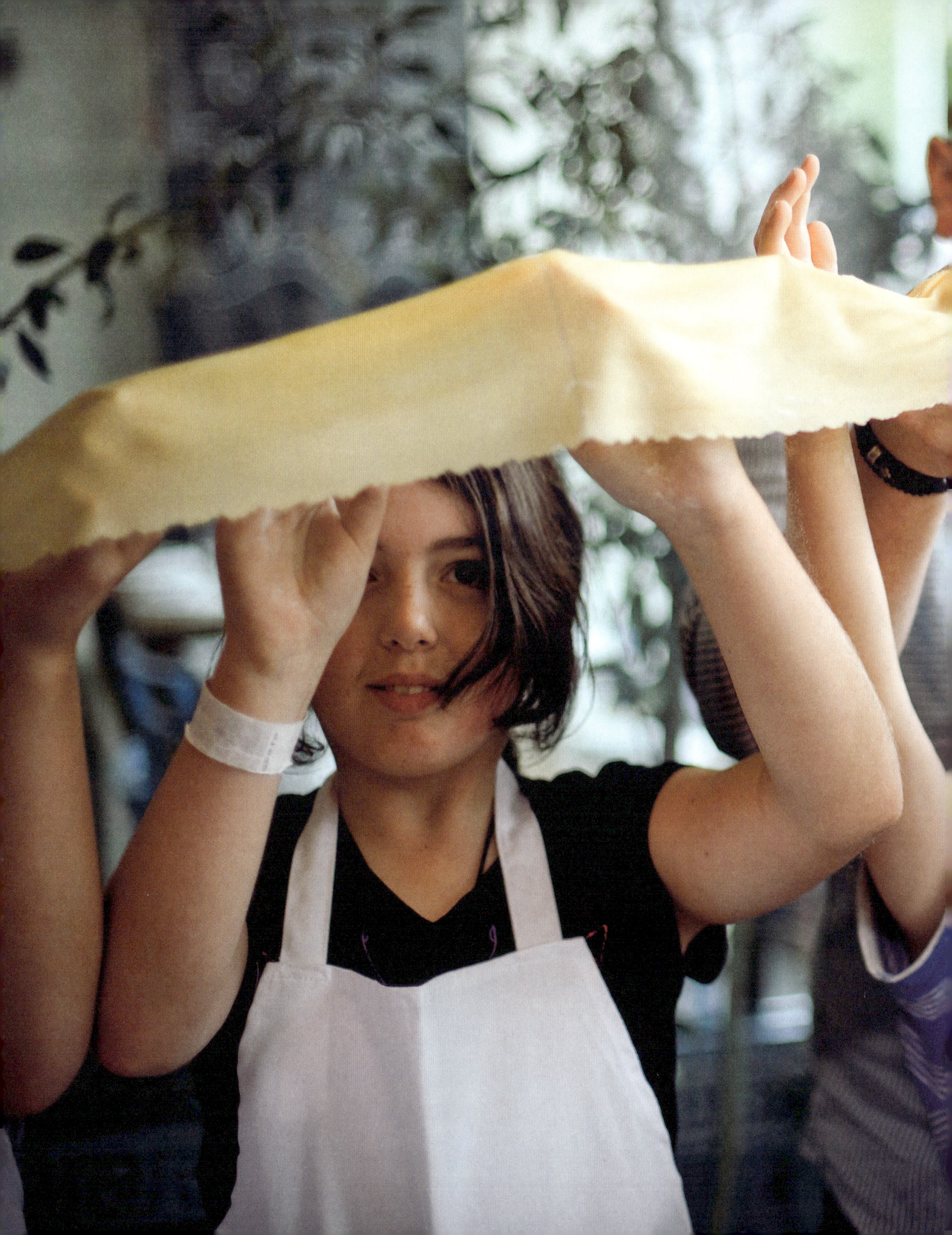

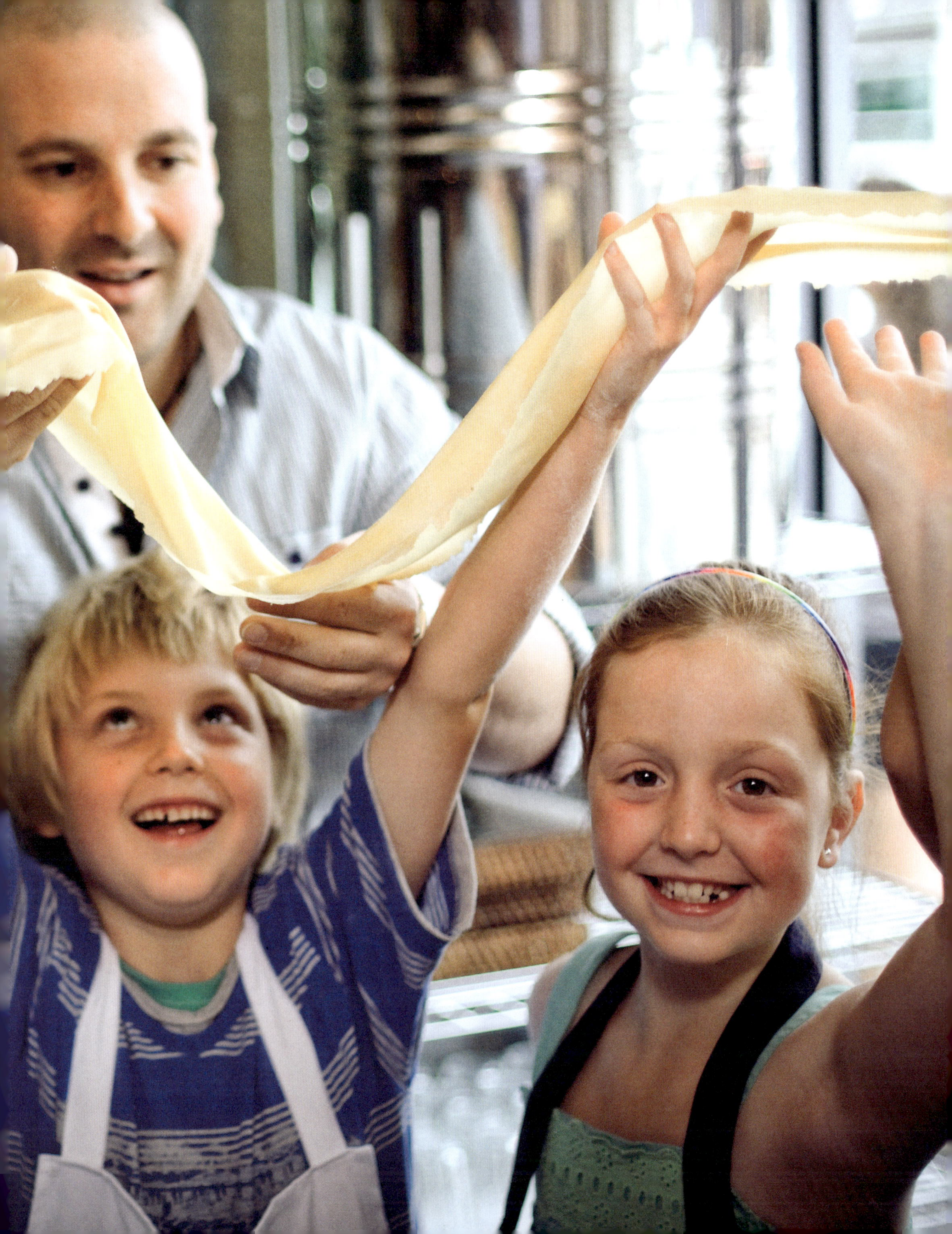

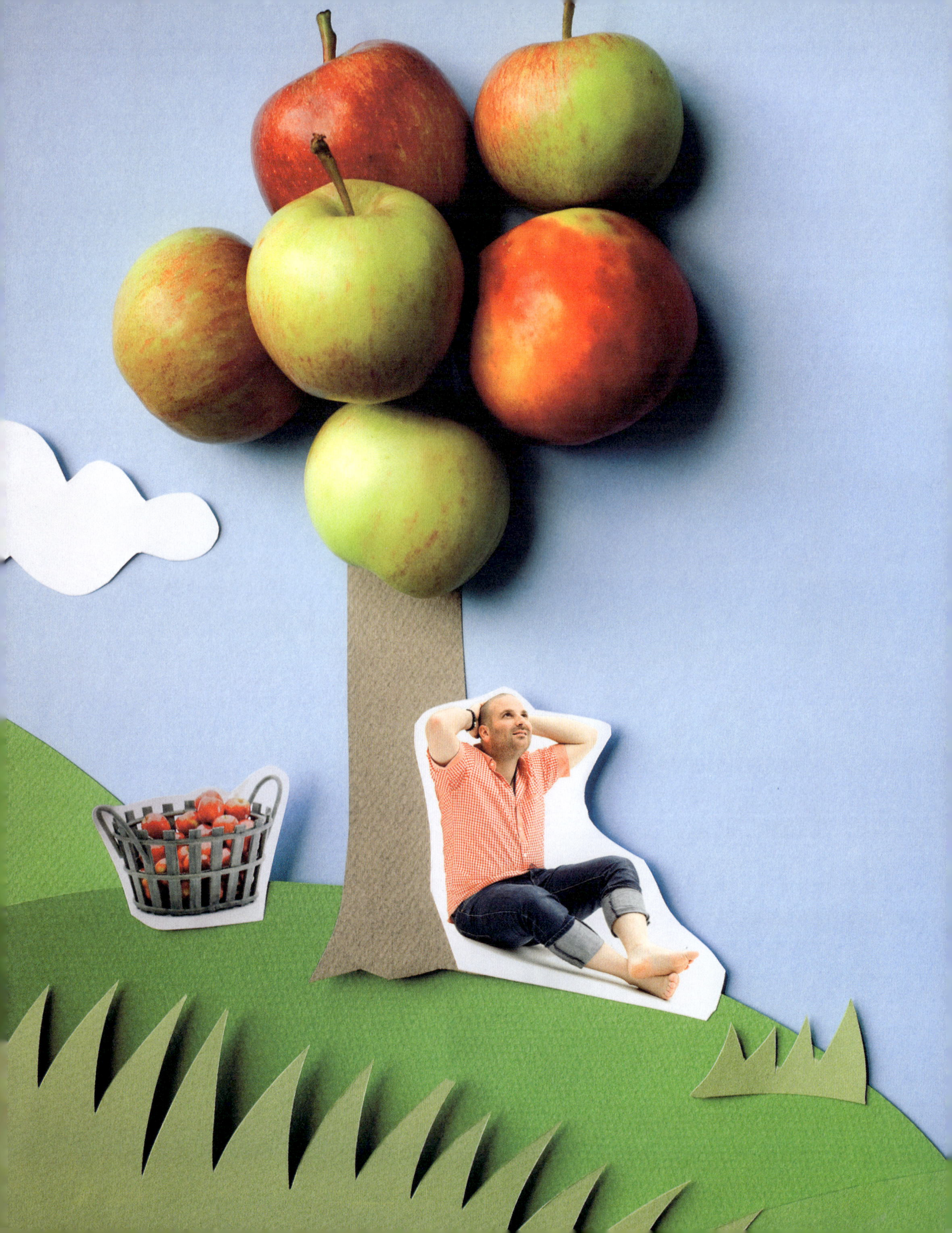

apples

Australia's favourite cooking apple varieties are the Granny Smith and Jonathan. These are also good for eating. Cooking apples tend to be larger, hold their shape better when cooked and taste sourer than eating apples.

When selecting apples, choose ones that are firm and free of bruises, punctures or brown spots. Be aware of the different tastes of each apple variety, and try different ones to find your favourite.

Apples like to be cool so keep them chilled in the vegetable crisper drawer of your refrigerator. When cooking with apples, wash them to remove any contaminants on the skin and cut out any bruised or softer sections.

Fresh apples are a great snack and have important health benefits. As apples contain vitamins A and C, potassium, pectin and fibre, an apple a day really does keep the doctor away. Apples are best eaten with the peel, as this is where most of the fibre and antioxidants are found.

Apples are an important ingredient in many desserts, such as pies, crumbles and cakes. They are often baked, stewed or pureed. Apples are also made into apple butter, apple jelly, apple cider and apple juice.

Did you know?

- Currently, there are more than 7500 known apple varieties worldwide.
- The heaviest known apple was grown in Japan in 2005, weighing 1.849 kg!
- Apples ripen 6–10 times faster at room temperature than they do in the fridge.
- Apples contain 80–85 per cent water.
- Fresh apples float because 25 per cent of their volume is air. Hooray for apple bobbing!
- To protect sliced apple from browning, dip it in a solution of one part citrus juice to three parts water.

Apple and rhubarb puree

This delicious fruit puree is great for infants, so you can help out in the kitchen if you have a baby brother or sister. Older people love it too, especially if you serve it alongside a really good cheese. This puree is delicious on muesli for breakfast or served with a dollop of homemade yoghurt (see page 180), as a simple dessert. Although rhubarb is technically a vegetable, it's most often used as a fruit. It tastes very tart, so you need to add sugar. Remember, don't ever eat rhubarb leaves as they are poisonous!

Makes 3½ cups (875 ml)

4 (about 500 g) Granny Smith apples

1 bunch rhubarb (about 400 g), leaves discarded and stalks washed

juice of 1 orange

½ cup (110 g) white sugar, plus extra if needed

* SPECIAL EQUIPMENT
corer (optional)
stick blender

---

1 Peel the apples, then cut into quarters and remove the core. Cut the quarters in half. Trim the rhubarb and cut it into 5 cm lengths.

2 Place the apple, rhubarb, orange juice and sugar in a saucepan over medium heat. When the mixture comes to the boil, reduce the heat to low. Cover the saucepan with the lid and cook over low heat for 10 minutes until the fruit softens and breaks down. Remove the pan from the heat. Puree the apple mixture with a stick blender, then taste and adjust the sweetness by adding extra sugar, if necessary.

3 Store in an airtight container in the fridge for up to 1 week.

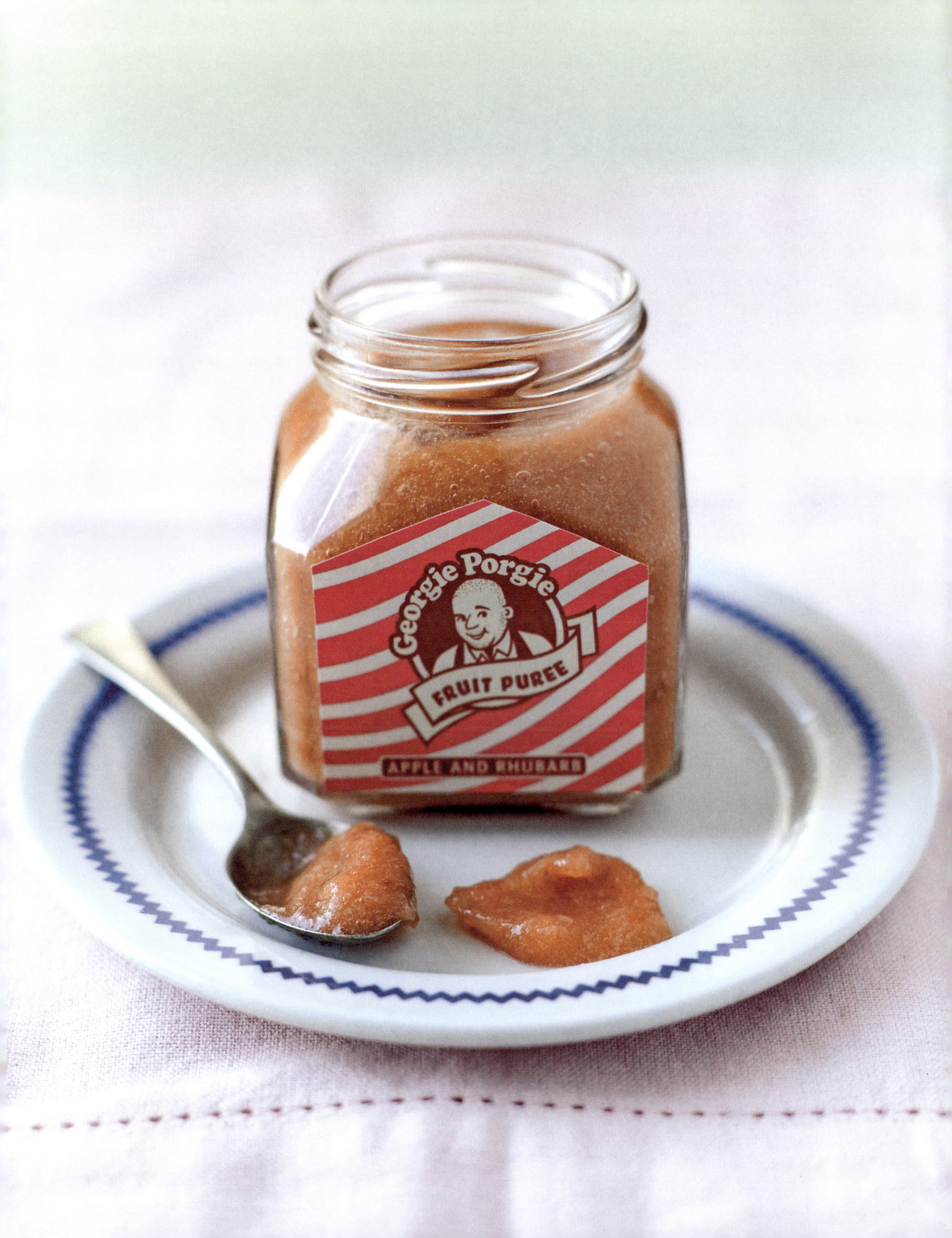

Georgie Porgie
FRUIT PUREE
APPLE AND RHUBARB

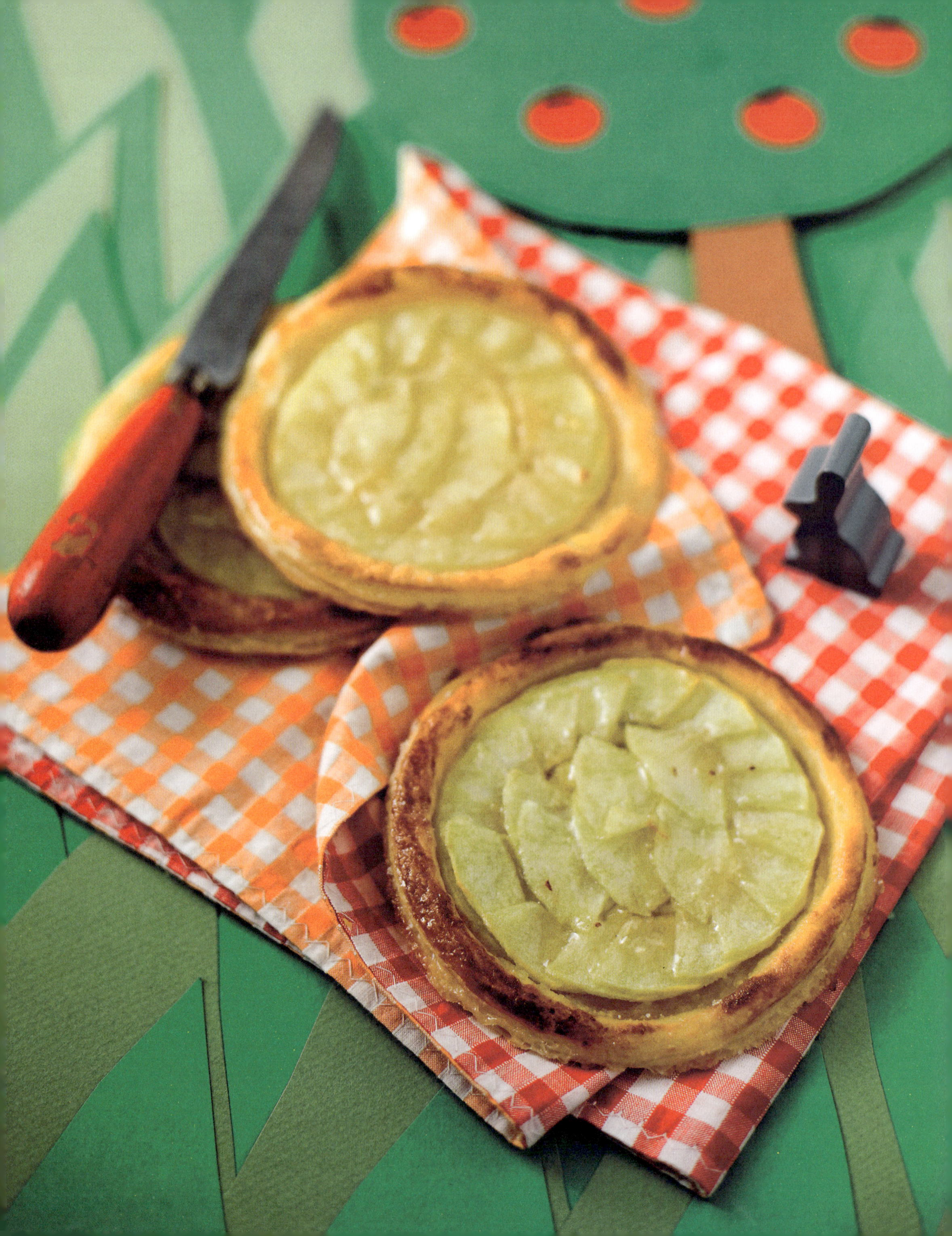

Apple tarts with frangipane cream

I once brought home an apple pie that I'd cooked in my home economics class in high school. I can still remember how proud I was to show it to my mum and dad. This tart is a little more flash, but it's still achievable. Frangipane is a rich pastry cream flavoured with almonds. The puff pastry base must be cooked at a very high temperature so that the air trapped between the layers expands and causes the pastry to rise. The fat content separates the layers, giving the pastry a crisp texture.

Makes 8

2 sheets frozen butter puff pastry, thawed

1 egg yolk, lightly beaten

2 small red apples, cored, quartered and thinly sliced

⅓ cup (115 g) orange marmalade (optional)

FRANGIPANE CREAM

100 g softened unsalted butter

100 g caster sugar

100 g ground almonds

1 egg

½ teaspoon vanilla extract

✱ SPECIAL EQUIPMENT
food processor
10 cm round pastry cutter (optional)
pastry brush

1 To make the frangipane cream, place the butter, sugar and ground almonds in a food processor and blend well. Add the egg and the vanilla extract and process until well mixed. Set aside.

2 Preheat the oven to 180°C fan-forced (200°C conventional).

3 Cut each pastry sheet into 4 small rounds (10 cm diameter), using a 10 cm pastry cutter or saucer as a guide. Place the pastry rounds on two baking trays lined with baking paper. Score a 1 cm border around the edge with a sharp knife, taking care not to cut all the way through the pastry. Brush the pastry with the egg yolk to glaze. Place 2 teaspoons of frangipane cream onto the centre of each piece of pastry and spread to the border to form a 5 mm-thick layer.

4 Place the apple slices on top of the frangipane cream.

5 Bake the tarts for 10 minutes, then reduce the heat to 160°C fan-forced (180°C conventional) and bake for a further 15–20 minutes or until the pastry is golden brown and puffed around the edges. Remove the tarts from the oven and transfer to a wire rack to cool.

6 Place the marmalade (if using) in a microwave-safe bowl and heat on medium power for 20 seconds to warm. Brush the tarts with warmed marmalade to glaze, if desired.

Compressed apple with slow-roasted pork belly

Even now I get so excited when I know my family is coming to one of my restaurants for dinner. I want to spoil them and, of course, show off what I am doing. There's no reason why kids can't cook a dinner party for their family at home, say, once a week. This dish is perfect for a dinner party – it's a real conversation stopper when it arrives at the table. Compressing the apple in ziplock bags is like doing a science experiment in the kitchen. The citric acid acts to preserve the apple slices. Citric acid occurs naturally in citrus fruits and is used mainly to add a tangy sour flavour. When you buy the pork belly ask the butcher for the thicker end as this will cook more evenly and be beautiful and moist.

Serves 4–6

1 × 1.5 kg piece pork belly, bones removed and skin scored (ask your butcher to do this)

2 tablespoons ground cinnamon

1 tablespoon ground star anise

2 tablespoons sea salt

2 tablespoons olive oil

freshly ground black pepper

thyme flowers (optional), to serve

COMPRESSED APPLES

4 Granny Smith apples

2 tablespoons caster sugar

2 teaspoons citric acid (see page 201)

✱ SPECIAL EQUIPMENT
4 small ziplock bags

1 Preheat the oven to 120°C fan-forced (140°C conventional).

2 Place the pork belly on a chopping board. Mix the cinnamon, star anise and salt together in a small bowl and rub all over the pork belly.

3 Drizzle a large roasting pan with olive oil. Put the pork belly in the pan, skin side down, then drizzle with a little more olive oil.

4 Roast the pork belly for 2½ hours. Carefully turn the pork belly over so the skin-side is facing up. Increase the oven temperature to 170°C fan-forced (190°C conventional) and roast for another 30 minutes or until the skin is crisp and crunchy.

5 Meanwhile, for the compressed apples, peel the apples and slice widthways into 1 cm-thick rounds. Mix the sugar and citric acid together in a small bowl, then sprinkle over the apple slices. Place each apple in a ziplock bag and squeeze out the air. Refrigerate for at least 2 hours.

6 Remove the pork belly from the oven. Do not cover as this makes the crackling soft. Set aside to rest for 15 minutes.

7 Remove the apple from the ziplock bags. Slice the pork belly, scatter with thyme flowers (if using), and serve with the compressed apple.

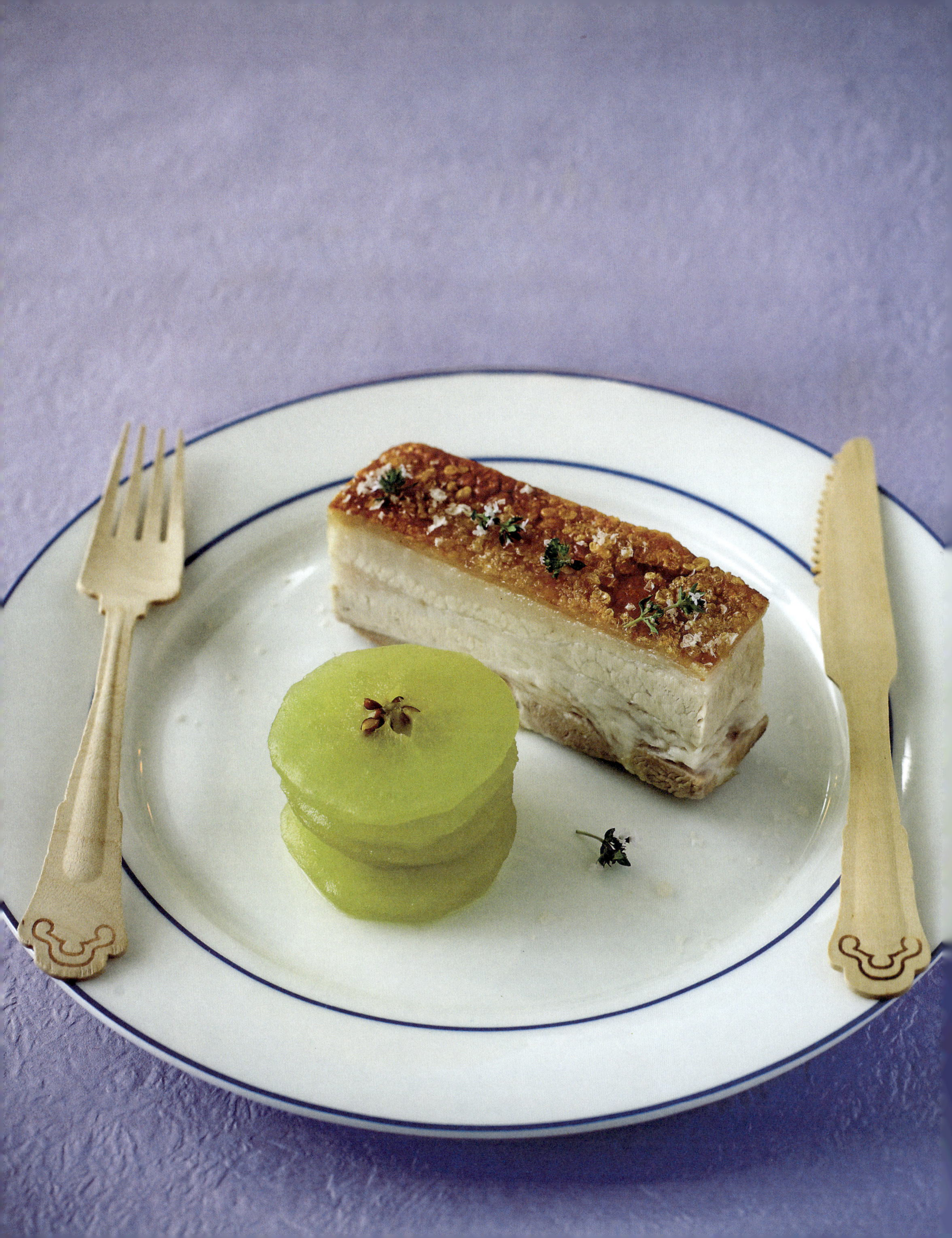

Did you know?

- There have been professional breadmakers since 2000 B.C. (or earlier).
- Bread can be leavened or unleavened, meaning risen or unrisen. Regular sandwich bread is risen, whereas lavosh bread is not.
- Why is money called dough? Because we all knead it!
- During World War II, sliced bread was banned in the U.S.A. because it becomes staler faster than uncut loaves (wasting wheat), and the metal needed to repair bread-slicing machines was diverted to producing weapons.
- You don't need to throw away stale bread. Use it to make breadcrumbs, stuffing or croutons.

BREAD

Bread is one of the oldest prepared foods and is now eaten as a staple food in many countries around the world. Bread is made by cooking a dough made of flour and water. It's usually baked, but it can also be steamed or fried.

A leaven causes a foaming action, which lightens and softens the bread as it cooks by making carbon dioxide. This is then trapped in the structure of the dough, causing it to rise. Yeast is the most commonly used natural leavening agent and can be purchased either fresh or dried. When you use fresh yeast, you need twice the amount as dried yeast. Baking powder and bicarbonate of soda are other well known and widely available raising agents, and are used to make breads such as Irish soda bread. Beer, buttermilk and yoghurt are also used as leavening agents. Sourdough starters, made from feeding a mixture of airborne yeasts, lactobacillus, sugar and flour with flour, are the basis of sourdough breads available from specialist bakeries. The lactobacillus produces lactic acid, which gives the classic sour taste in sourdough bread.

Different flours can be used to make bread, including wheat, rye, barley, spelt, maize (corn) and oat. Bread can either be savoury or sweet.

In colonial times, Australian stockmen, drovers and swagmen made a simple bread called damper, which was baked directly on an open fire. To re-create this at home, combine 450 g self-raising flour with a pinch of salt, then rub in 80 g chopped cold butter until the mixture resembles fine breadcrumbs. Add 180 ml water, then mix together with a dinner knife to form a dough – add a splash of extra water if necessary. Knead on a lightly floured bench for a couple of minutes, then form into an 18 cm disc. Bake on a baking tray lined with baking paper at 180°C fan-forced (200°C conventional) for 30 minutes or until cooked through – the base should sound hollow when tapped.

Pita bread

My mum would make this homemade bread as an afternoon snack. I would sit at the breakfast bench and watch her roll out the dough. I believe there is a real pleasure in combining water and flour to create something special. This dough can also be used as a base for pizza (see page 52). Pita bread can be cooked in a char-grill pan or on a barbecue flat or grill plate.

Makes 8

4 cups (600 g) strong '00' plain flour (see page 203), plus extra for dusting the bench

3 teaspoons salt

1 × 7 g sachet dried yeast

300 ml lukewarm water (approximately)

2 tablespoons olive oil

1 tablespoon honey

1 tablespoon natural Greek-style yoghurt

olive oil spray

1 cup (180 g) semolina (see page 203)

* SPECIAL EQUIPMENT
electric mixer with dough hook
rolling pin

1 Mix the flour, salt and yeast in the bowl of an electric mixer with a dough hook.

2 Mix the water, oil, honey and yoghurt in a jug until combined.

3 Pour the yoghurt mixture into the flour mixture and knead with the dough hook for 5 minutes until the dough is smooth.

4 Turn the dough onto a floured bench and shape into a ball. Transfer the dough to a large oiled bowl, then cover with plastic film and set aside in a warm place to rise for 1 hour. The dough should double in size.

5 Sprinkle some of the semolina onto the bench. Place the dough on the bench, then knock down and knead again to remove any air.

6 Use a sharp knife to divide the dough into 8 pieces, then shape into balls. Sprinkle the bench with more semolina and roll the balls with a rolling pin until they are 4 mm thick. Prick each piece of dough all over with a fork and spray with olive oil.

7 Preheat a non-stick frying pan over low–medium heat. Cook one pita bread at a time for about 1 minute on each side or until lightly coloured.

8 Serve immediately. (Reheat in a frying pan for best results.)

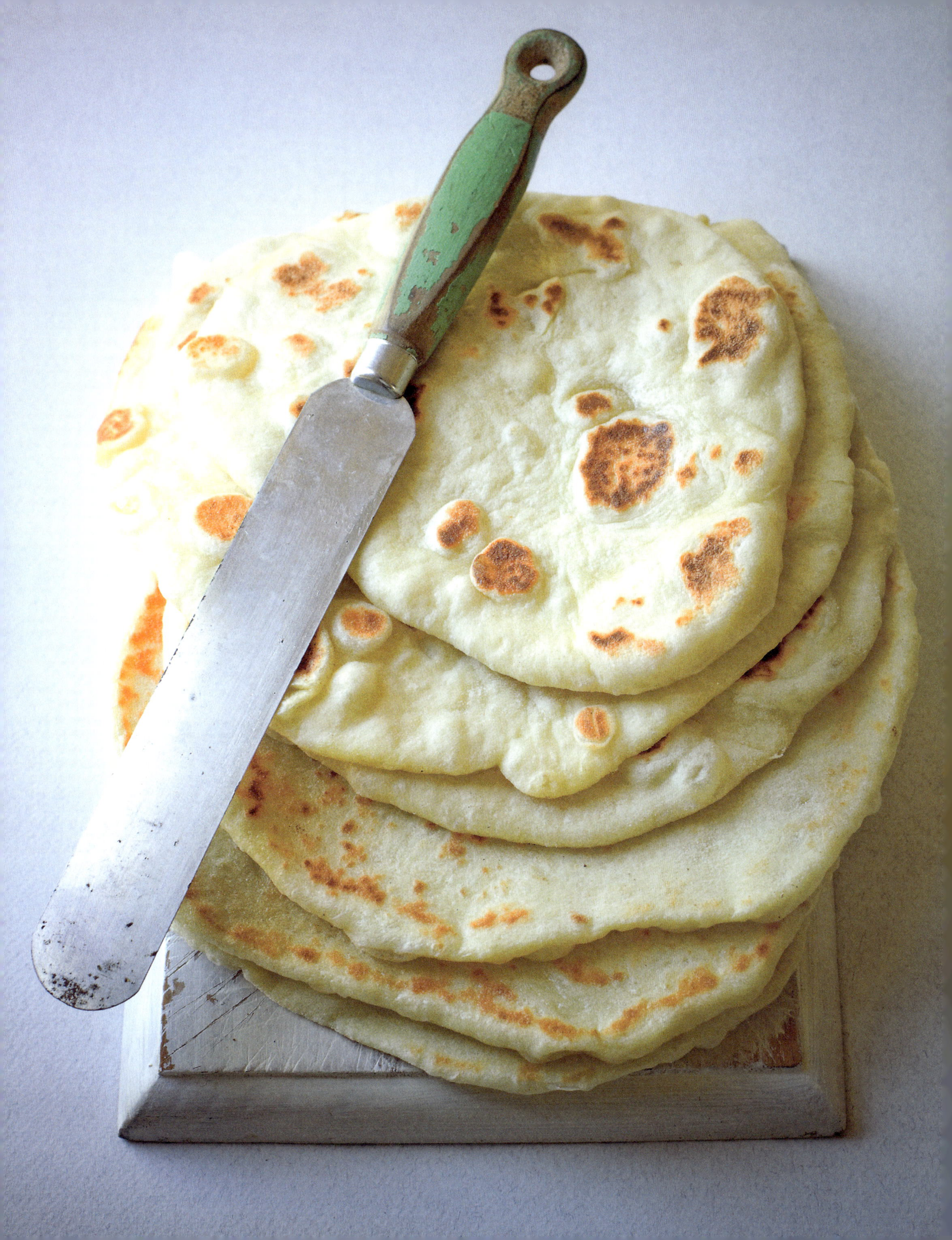

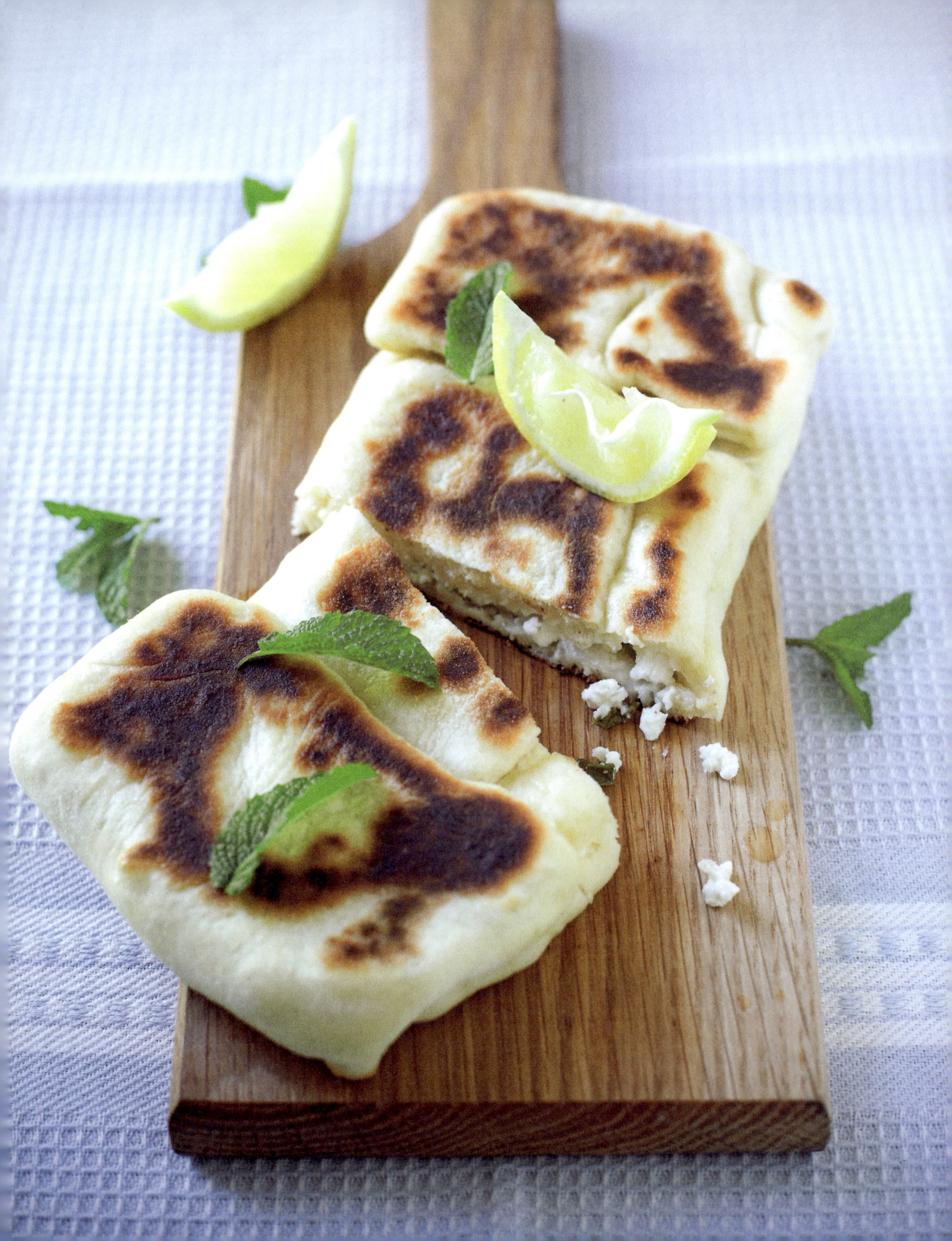

Flatbread filled with feta and mint

Simple and inexpensive dishes such as this would make a regular appearance on the menu at home when I was growing up. I love this sort of food. Crunchy, bread-y, salty and yummy, it's fit for a king! The dough needs to be rolled out until it's quite thin, so make sure it doesn't stick to the bench.

Serves 4

300 ml warm water

1 × 7g sachet dried yeast

a pinch of salt

1 teaspoon caster sugar

3 cups (450 g) strong '00' plain flour, plus extra for dusting the bench

⅓ cup (80 ml) olive oil

lemon wedges and mint leaves, to serve

FETA AND MINT FILLING

200 g feta, crumbled

1 tablespoon chopped mint or dried mint

sea salt and freshly ground black pepper

✶ **SPECIAL EQUIPMENT**
  rolling pin
  pastry brush

1 Combine the water, yeast, salt and sugar in a measuring jug. Stir with a fork and set aside to stand for 5 minutes or until bubbles form on the surface.

2 Sift the flour into a large bowl. Add the yeast mixture and 2 tablespoons of the olive oil. Mix to form a soft dough. Turn the dough onto a lightly floured bench and knead for 5 minutes or until it feels elastic.

3 Use a sharp knife to divide the dough into 4 pieces and roll into balls. Place the dough balls on a greased baking tray. Cover with a clean tea towel and place in a warm spot for 20 minutes or until the dough has doubled in size.

4 Sprinkle a little flour onto the bench. Roll each piece of dough with a rolling pin into a thin, rough 30 cm square.

5 Sprinkle one quarter of the crumbled feta and mint over the centre of one piece of the dough and season to taste with salt and pepper. Fold the bottom edge of dough towards the centre to cover the filling. Fold the top edge of the dough in, then fold in each side, until you have created a neat parcel. Press the edges to seal. Repeat this process with the remaining dough and filling to make 4 filled flatbreads.

6 Preheat a barbecue grill plate or heavy-based non-stick frying pan to high heat. Use a pastry brush to brush one side of each flatbread with some of the remaining olive oil, then cook for 2–3 minutes or until the base is golden. Brush the uncooked side with olive oil, then turn over and cook until golden and crisp. Remove and repeat with the remaining filled flatbreads.

7 Scatter with mint leaves, then serve hot with lemon wedges.

Mini chocolate tsoureki

This is my take on tsoureki, the traditional sweet brioche-style Greek Easter bread. I love chocolate. When I was ten years old, my parents owned a supermarket and it was my job to sweep the aisles. I'd snaffle dark chocolate bars and hide behind the big bins at the back to eat them. My parents never caught me, but I reckon my dad always knew. If not, he'll know now!

Makes 6

- 10 g dried yeast
- 90 g caster sugar
- 100 ml milk, warmed
- 250 g (1⅔ cups) strong '00' plain flour (see page 203)
- ⅓ cup (30 g) dutch-process cocoa (see page 202)
- 1 teaspoon salt
- 2 eggs
- 50 g soft unsalted butter, chopped
- ½ cup (95 g) dark couverture chocolate buttons (see page 202)
- olive oil, for greasing

HOT CHOCOLATE

- 100 ml milk
- 400 ml pouring cream
- 300 g dark couverture chocolate buttons (see page 202)

* SPECIAL EQUIPMENT
electric mixer
6 mini loaf tins
(10 cm × 6 cm)

1 Mix the yeast with 1 teaspoon of the sugar and the warm milk in a medium-sized bowl. Sift the flour and cocoa into another bowl. Add ½ cup (75 g) of the flour mixture to the milk mixture. Cover with plastic film and stand in a warm place for 15 minutes or until it is spongey.

2 Place the remaining flour mixture, sugar and salt in the bowl of an electric mixer with a dough hook. Add the yeast mixture and eggs. Mix on low speed for 6 minutes. Add the butter, piece by piece, then beat until smooth. Place the dough in an oiled bowl, cover with plastic film and leave in a warm place for 1½ hours or until doubled in size.

3 Turn the dough out onto a floured bench, then knock it back with your fists to remove any air. Add the chocolate chips and knead to incorporate.

4 Use a sharp knife to divide the dough into 6 pieces, then roll into balls. Transfer the balls to 6 greased mini loaf tins (mine are 10 cm × 6 cm). Cover the loaf tins with a damp tea towel and set aside in a warm place for 30 minutes or until doubled in size.

5 Preheat the oven to 190°C fan-forced (210°C conventional).

6 Place the bread tins on a baking tray and bake for 20 minutes or until a skewer inserted into the centre comes out clean. Remove each loaf from its tin and leave to cool on a wire rack.

7 For the hot chocolate, heat the milk and cream in a small saucepan over medium heat until warm. Add the chocolate and remove the pan from the heat. Stir until the chocolate has melted. Serve with the tsoureki.

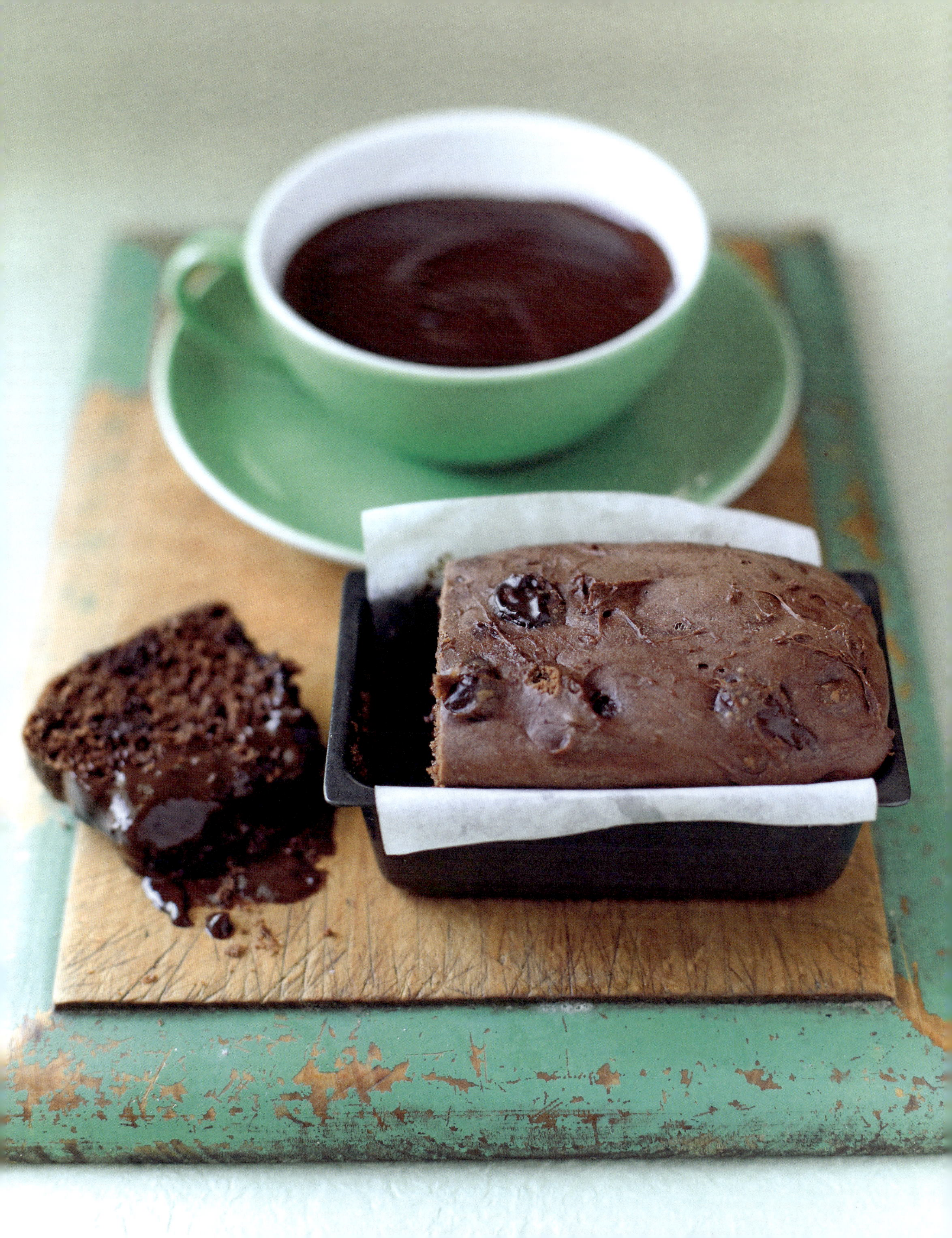

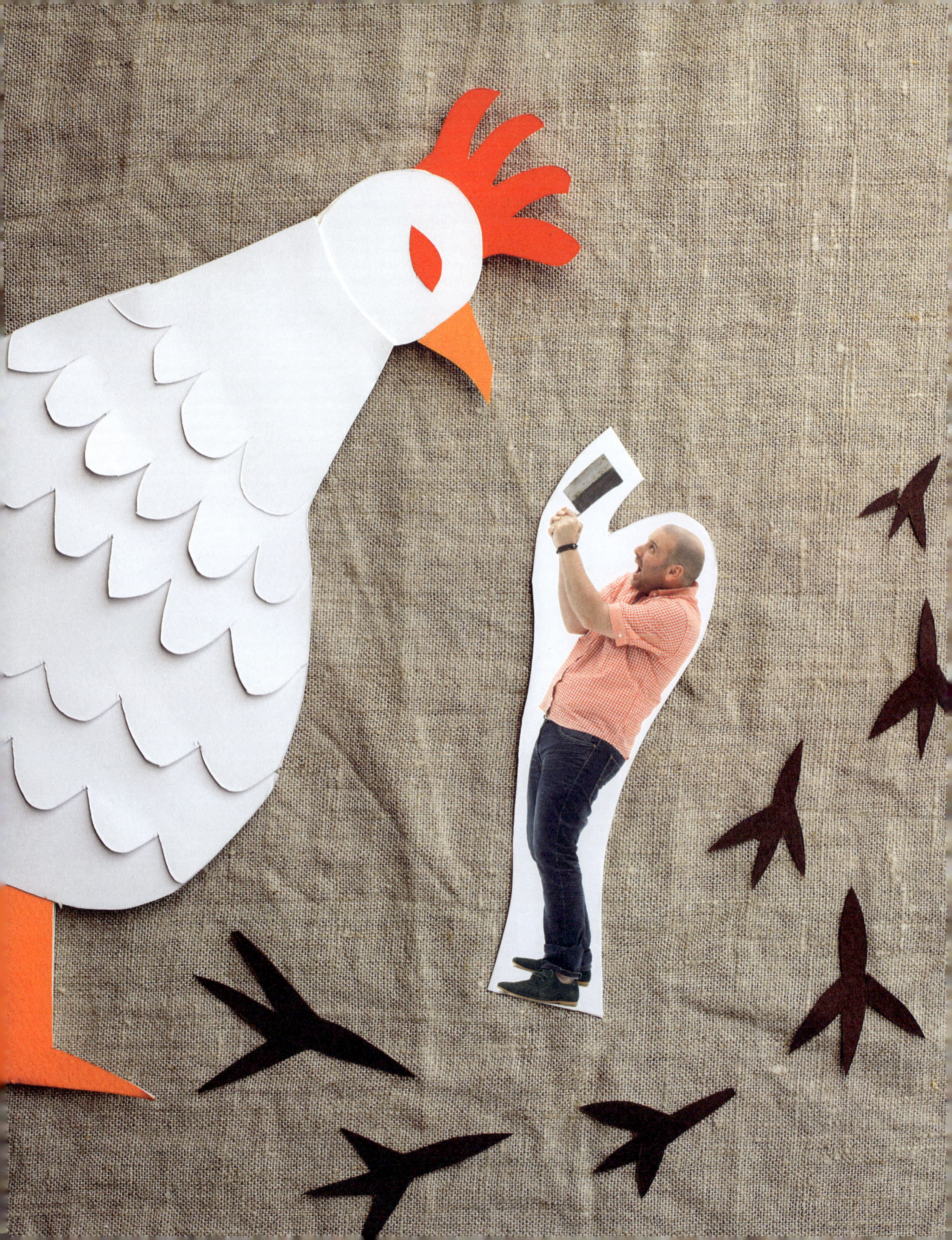

CHICKEN

There are more chickens in the world than any other species of bird. It's hard to count them, but there are estimated to be around 43 billion chickens worldwide!

Adult male chickens are called roosters. They have long feathers on their tail, a crest on their head called a comb and skin hanging under their beaks called wattles. Adult female chickens are called hens. Some hens can lay up to 300 eggs per year. Hens cluck to let their chicks know where to find food. Younger females are called pullets and their eggs are called pullet eggs.

Poussin and spatchcock are words used to describe young chickens, although spatchcock is also the term used to describe a chicken that has been split down the back with the backbone removed and opened flat for grilling.

Chickens are omnivores – they eat both meat and vegetables, usually worms, insects, seeds and vegetable scraps.

How to joint a chicken

1 Place the chicken breast-side up, legs towards you.

2 Use poultry shears to snip through the breast bone, from the cavity at the base towards the neck end.

3 Turn the chicken over and cut along either side of the backbone. You will now have two halves.

4 Cut through the line dividing the leg from the breast. Separate the leg from the thigh by finding the white line at the centre of the joint. Cut through it with a sharp knife.

5 Cut the breast in half. You now have 8 pieces.

Chicken drumettes with homemade barbecue sauce

Wings are the tastiest part of the chook. With a little bit of technique you can make the drummette portion of the wings look like little drumsticks – it's a cool way to present them. This homemade barbecue sauce is great with this dish – the flavour rocks.

Serves 4

1 kg chicken drummettes (if unavailable, use 1.5 kg chicken wings)

2 tablespoons olive oil

1 tablespoon thyme leaves

40 g unsalted butter, chopped

sea salt and freshly ground black pepper

BARBECUE SAUCE

2 tablespoons olive oil

2 turnips (about 600 g), peeled and coarsely grated

4 golden shallots, finely chopped

2 cloves garlic, crushed

1 cup (220 g) white sugar

1 tablespoon kecap manis (see page 202)

1 tablespoon wholegrain mustard

1 teaspoon tomato paste

1 teaspoon sesame oil

1 cup (250 ml) malt vinegar

* SPECIAL EQUIPMENT
stick blender

1 Preheat the oven to 180°C fan-forced (200°C conventional).

2 If you are using whole chicken wings, cut the tips from each chicken wing and keep for making chicken stock (see page 201), then divide in half at the joint into wings and drummettes. Use a small, sharp knife to cut around the thin tip of each chicken drumette. Using the back of the knife, push the flesh to the bottom of the drumette, scraping the bone clean and removing any flesh left on the bone with paper towel.

3 Place the chicken on a baking tray, then drizzle with the olive oil, scatter with the thyme leaves and butter and season with salt and pepper. Bake the chicken for 20–30 minutes or until golden and cooked through.

4 While you are waiting, make the barbecue sauce. Heat the olive oil in a saucepan over medium heat and cook the turnip, shallots and garlic for 10 minutes or until softened and golden. Add the sugar and stir to dissolve. Add the kecap manis, mustard, tomato paste, sesame oil and malt vinegar and cook over low–medium heat for 20 minutes, stirring occasionally until the sauce has thickened.

5 Remove the pan from the heat and puree the sauce with a stick blender until smooth.

6 Serve the chicken drumettes with barbecue sauce to the side.

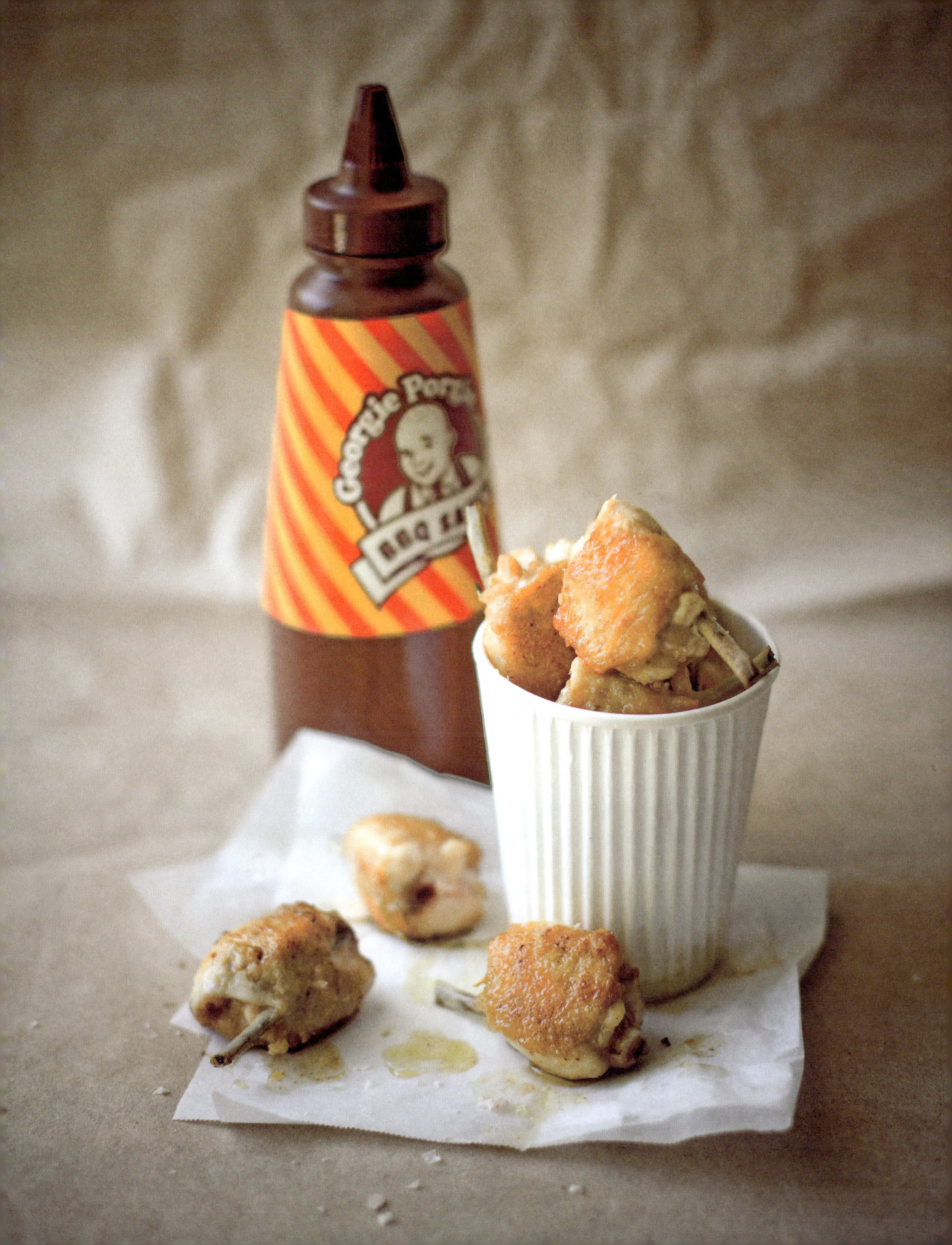
Georgie
BBQ

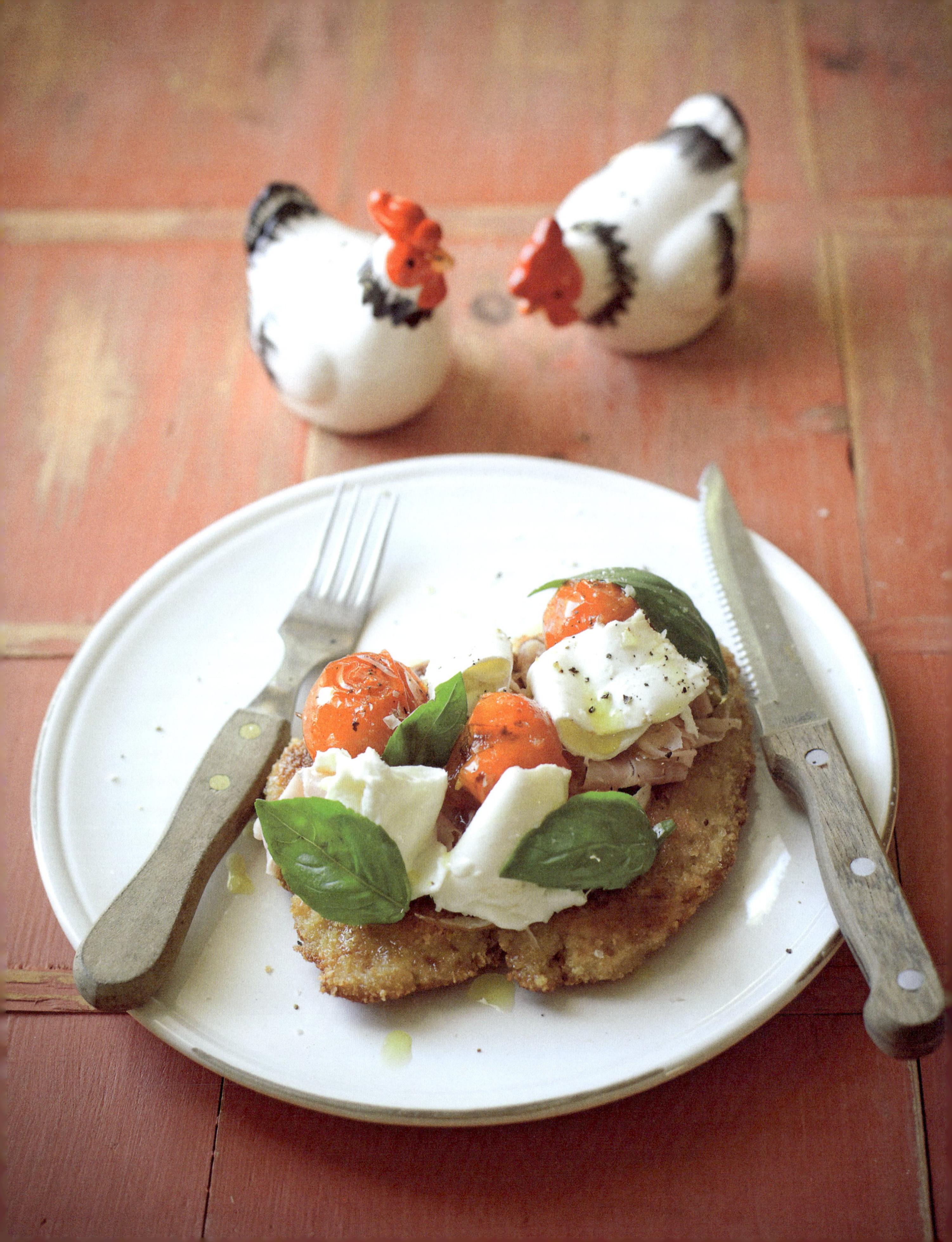

Real chicken parma

I love a good 'parma' and this one qualifies. Tasty chicken with tomatoes that have been kissed by the sun, some real cheese (not the square plastic stuff) and ham cut from the bone – there's no other way to do it.

Serves 4

250 g (1 punnet) small mixed cherry tomatoes

4 stalks basil, leaves picked, stalks reserved

½ cup (125 ml) olive oil, plus 1 tablespoon extra

sea salt and freshly ground black pepper

4 skinless chicken thigh fillets (about 440 g)

200 g sourdough bread, crusts removed and discarded, diced

1 egg

2 tablespoons milk

¼ cup (35 g) plain flour

40 g unsalted butter

4 slices leg ham off-the-bone (about 100 g)

2 balls buffalo mozzarella (about 200 g, see page 201), torn

✻ SPECIAL EQUIPMENT
  meat mallet
  food processor

1 Preheat the oven to 180°C fan-forced (200°C conventional).

2 Place the tomatoes and basil stalks on a baking tray. Drizzle with 1 tablespoon of the olive oil and season with salt and pepper. Bake the tomatoes for 25 minutes or until the skins have blistered and burst. Set aside.

3 Place the chicken thighs in one layer between 2 sheets of plastic film on a chopping board and lightly pound with the flat side of a meat mallet to flatten (this helps them to cook more evenly). Set aside.

4 Place the sourdough in a food processor and process to make fine breadcrumbs. Transfer the breadcrumbs to a plate and season with salt and pepper.

5 Whisk the egg and milk together in a wide shallow bowl. Sprinkle the flour on a plate. Lightly dust each chicken piece in flour, then dip in the beaten egg and coat with breadcrumbs.

6 Heat half the remaining olive oil in a large frying pan over medium heat. Cook the chicken in two batches for 4–5 minutes on each side or until golden and tender. Reduce the heat to low and add half the butter, then continue to cook until the butter is golden and bubbling and the chicken is crisp and cooked through. Remove the chicken from the pan and place on paper towel to drain off any excess oil. Return the pan to medium heat and repeat with the remaining oil, chicken and butter.

7 Divide the chicken among 4 serving plates, then top each piece with a slice of ham, some roasted tomatoes, torn pieces of mozzarella and basil leaves.

Chicken and sweetcorn pie

To make a quick version of this pie, simply fill individual ramekins – little oven-proof dishes available from kitchen shops – with the chicken filling, then top with the ready-made puff pastry and bake.

Serves 4–6

25 g unsalted butter

1 kg skinless chicken thigh fillets, cut into 2 cm pieces

2 leeks, white part only, well washed and thinly sliced

1 clove garlic, finely chopped

4 sprigs thyme

¼ cup (35 g) plain flour

1 cup (250 ml) Chicken Stock (see page 201)

1½ cups (240 g) corn kernels

⅓ cup (4 tablespoons) chopped flat-leaf parsley

sea salt and freshly ground black pepper

1 egg, beaten

1 sheet frozen butter puff pastry, thawed

MAGGIE BEER'S SOUR-CREAM PASTRY

200 g chilled butter, chopped

250 g plain flour, plus extra for dusting the bench

½ cup (125 ml) sour cream

1 egg yolk

✴ SPECIAL EQUIPMENT
   food processor
   pastry brush

1 To make the pastry, place the butter, flour, sour cream and egg yolk in a food processor and pulse until a dough forms. Remove from the food processor, form into a ball and flatten slightly. Wrap in plastic film and refrigerate for 20 minutes.

2 Melt the butter in a large frying pan over medium heat. Cook the chicken in batches for 2–3 minutes on each side. Remove from the pan and set aside. Add the leek and cook over low heat for 2–3 minutes. Add the garlic and thyme and stir. Sprinkle in the flour, stirring well to combine, then add the stock and bring to a gentle simmer. Cook for 2–3 minutes, stirring well so there are no lumps. Return the chicken to the pan and simmer for 4–5 minutes or until cooked through. Add the corn and parsley, then season to taste with salt and pepper and mix well. Remove from the heat and refrigerate until completely cold.

3 Roll out the pastry on a bench lightly dusted with flour until 5 mm thick. Use the pastry to line the base and sides of a 1 litre-capacity baking dish, then trim around the edge with the back of a sharp knife. Patch any tears and holes with pastry off-cuts. Spoon the cooled filling into the pie dish. Wet the edges of the pastry base with some of the beaten egg, then gently put the puff pastry over the top of the pie and trim around the edge, allowing a little overhang. Push the edges together with a fork and brush with beaten egg. Cut a small cross in the top of the pie with a small, sharp knife to help steam escape (this helps the pastry to rise so it isn't soggy). Refrigerate the pie for 30 minutes. Brush the pastry with beaten egg one last time.

4 Preheat the oven to 200°C fan-forced (220°C conventional). Bake the pie for 40 minutes or until golden brown.

5 Serve slices of the pie hot, warm or cold.

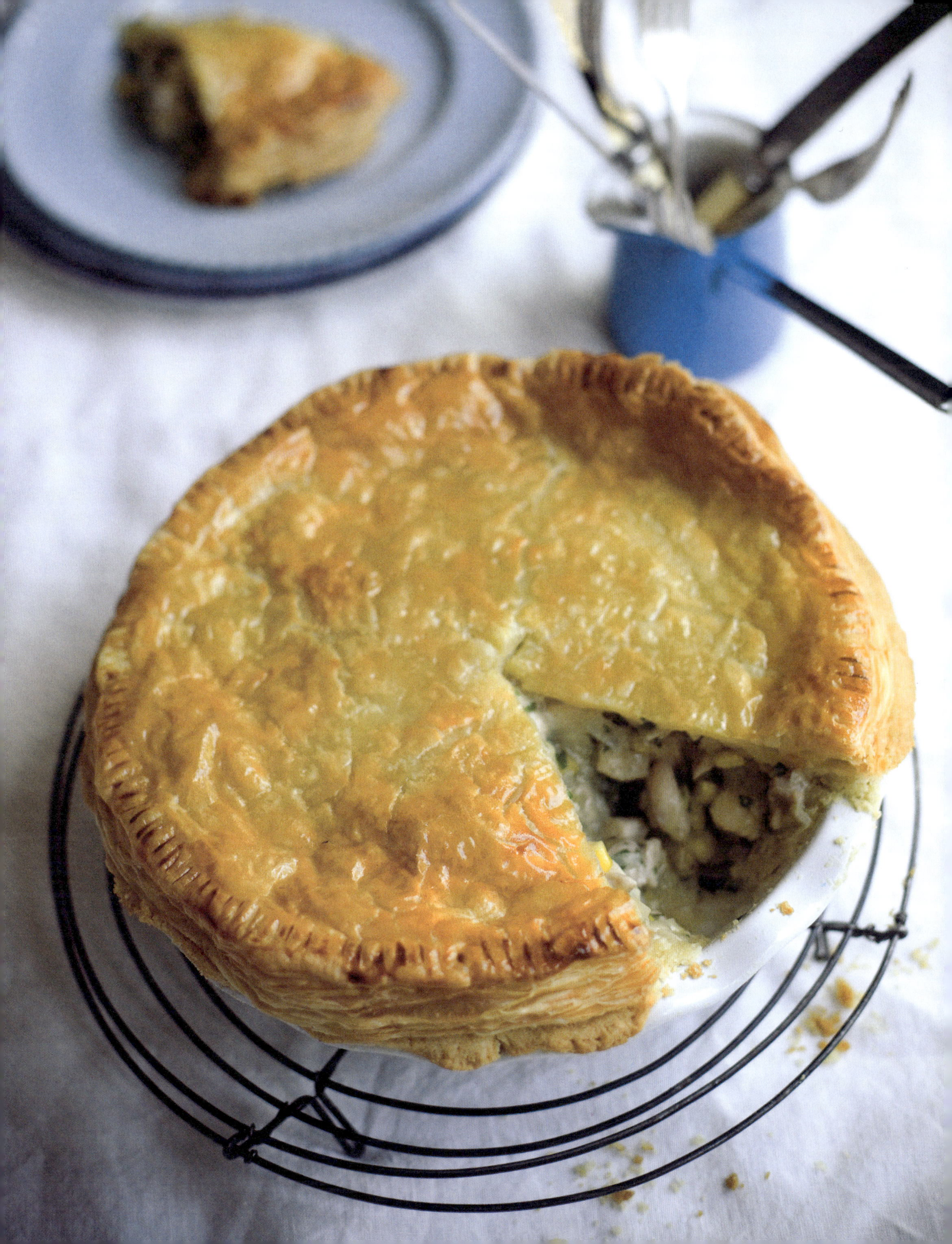

Braised chicken with potato, tomatoes and cinnamon

Matching chicken with cinnamon might sound a bit odd, but in Greek cooking the use of cinnamon is very common in traditional savoury dishes. I even add a little to my spaghetti bolognese (see page 92). Cinnamon was introduced to me at a young age by my mum. I am so lucky to have grown up with a mother who loved to cook with so much heart and soul. That's how you must cook, whether you're fifteen or fifty.

Serves 4–6

1 teaspoon cumin seeds

1 teaspoon coriander seeds

100 ml olive oil

4 chicken marylands (about 1.2 kg), thighs and drumsticks separated by cutting through the joint

2 onions, thinly sliced

2 cloves garlic, finely chopped

1 stick cinnamon

3 Nicola potatoes (about 600 g), thinly sliced

finely grated zest of 1 lemon

sea salt

200 ml Chicken Stock (see page 201)

500 g cherry tomatoes

freshly ground black pepper

flat-leaf parsley (optional), to garnish

✱ SPECIAL EQUIPMENT
mortar and pestle

1 Preheat the oven to 180°C fan-forced (200°C conventional).

2 Place the cumin and coriander seeds in a small frying pan over medium heat and cook for 30 seconds or until they are fragrant. Remove the pan from the heat and crush the seeds with a mortar and pestle. Set aside.

3 Heat the oil in a large heavy-based frying pan over high heat, then add the chicken and cook for 5 minutes on each side until browned. Remove and set aside.

4 Add the onion, garlic, cinnamon and crushed spices to the pan, then reduce the heat to medium and cook for 5 minutes, stirring until the onion is soft. Add the potato and cook for a further 5 minutes.

5 Spread the potato slices over the base of a baking dish large enough to hold the chicken in a single layer (mine is 36 cm × 24 cm). Place the browned chicken, skin-side up, over the potato, then scatter over the onion mixture and lemon zest and season with a little salt.

6 Add the stock and tomatoes, then cover with foil and roast for 45 minutes. Remove the foil and continue to cook for another 20 minutes or until the chicken is golden and cooked through. Season to taste with pepper.

7 Scatter with parsley (if using) and serve.

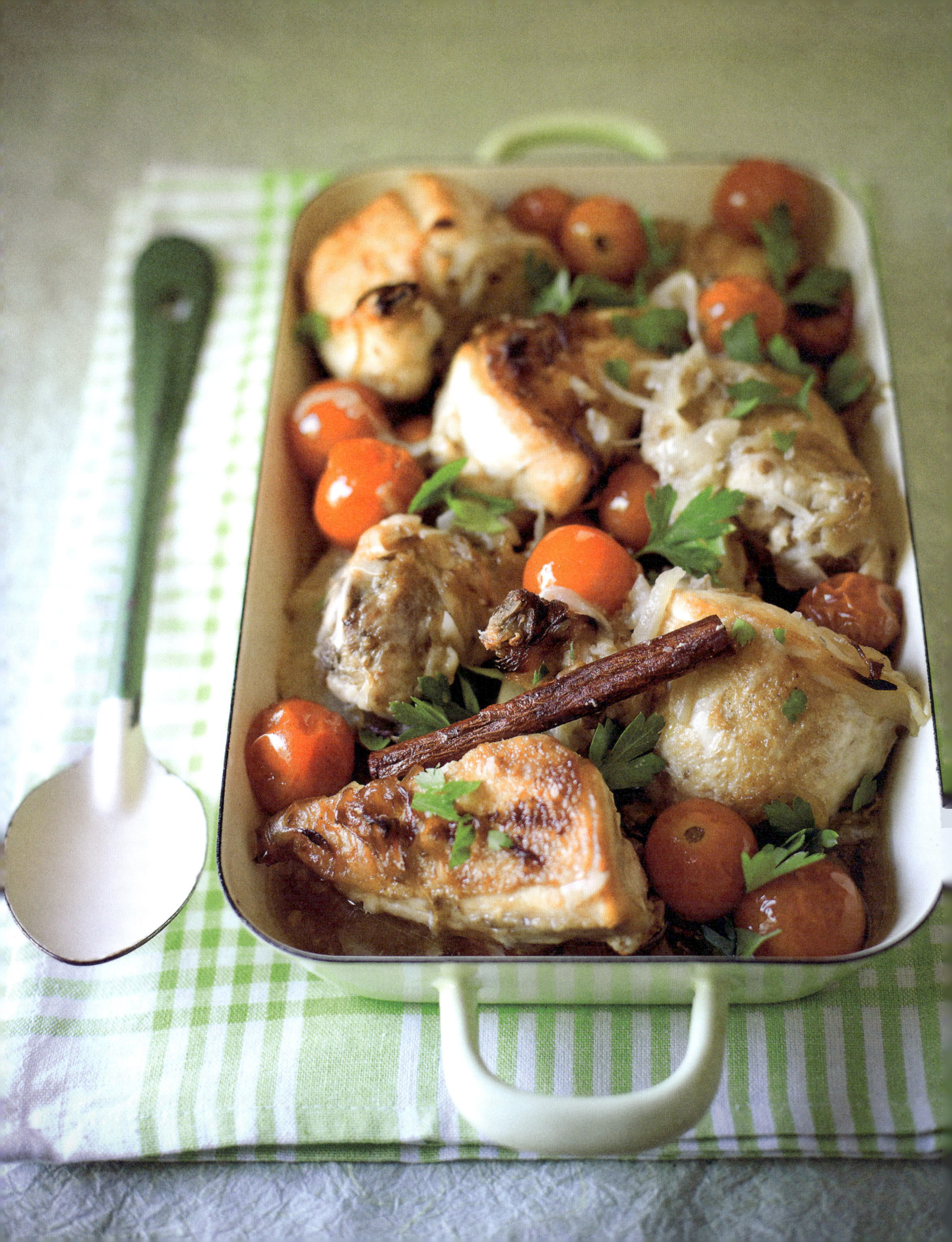

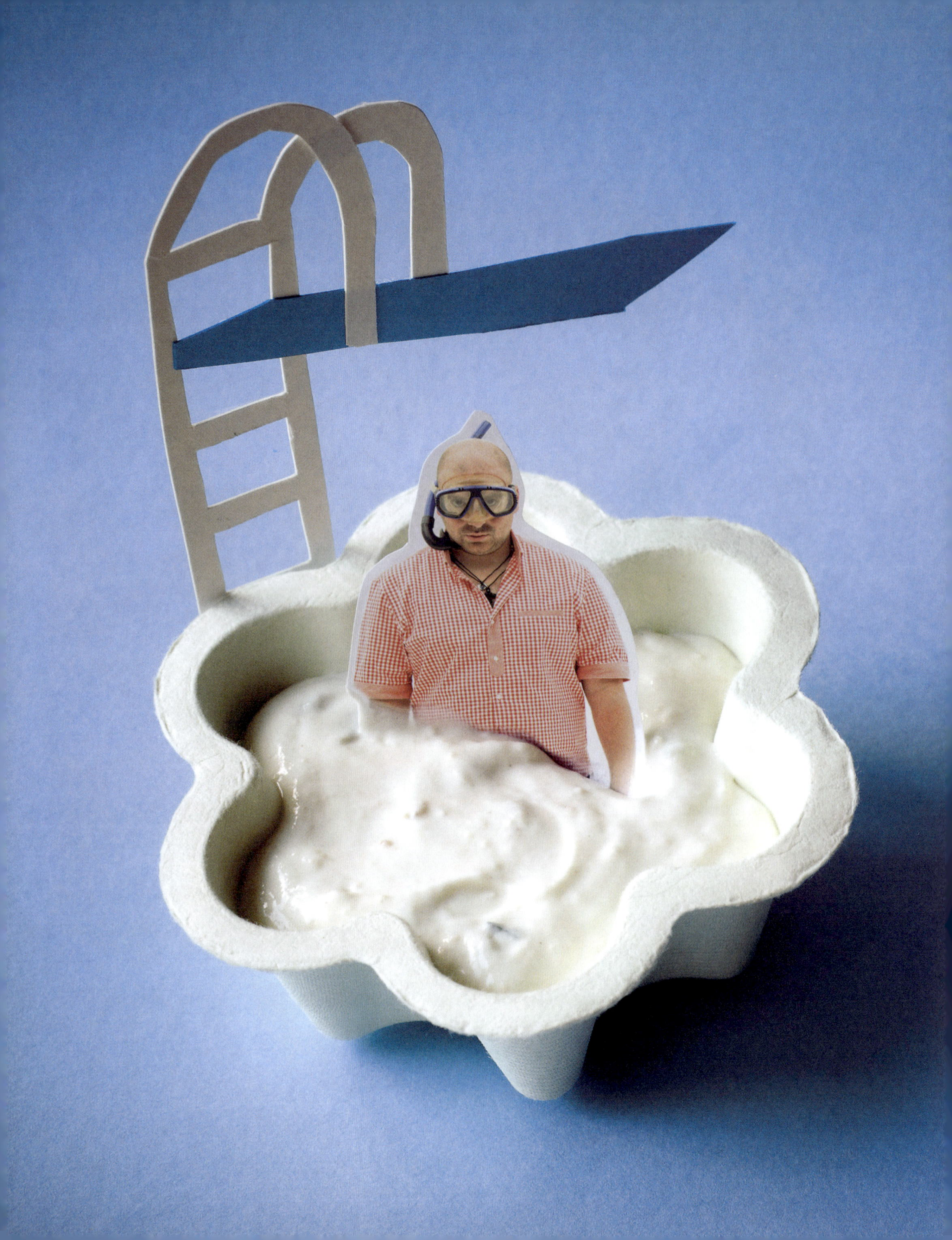

DIPS

Dips come from all over the world and in all sorts of flavours and textures. Dips can be thick or thin, chunky or smooth, sweet or savoury. You can serve a dip as a snack, a starter or a meal. In some countries, dips are served as a part of a selection of small dishes. This is known as mezedes in Greece, antipasti in Italy and meze in the Middle East.

A dip is about eating one sort of food with another sort of food. You have to dip into a dip in order to eat it! A 'dipper' is what you use to dip. You can use bread-y things such as pita, crostini or lavosh. Or you can use cracker-like things such as tortillas, potato chips or crackers. Or you can go for vegetable sticks, which the French call crudites. Try carrot, celery, capsicum, asparagus, green beans, baby zucchini, broccoli or cauliflower.

Make your own dippers by cutting up some pita bread into triangles and baking them in the oven at 160°C fan-forced (180°C conventional) for 5 minutes or until crisp.

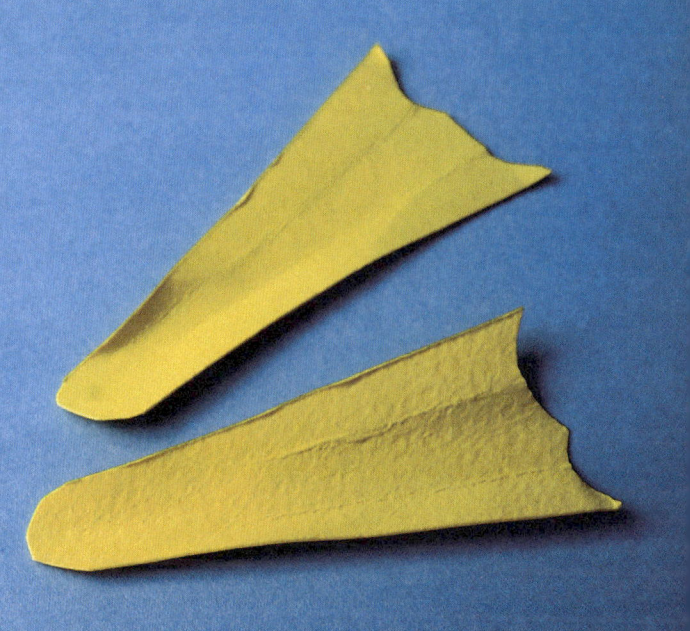

Taramosalata

This is the real stuff, not pink, but white – that's how it must be. My brother-in-law Dave recently rang me to tell me my godson, Michael, who means the world to me, was in the garage dipping popcorn into a tub of taramosalata. How cool is that? I am so proud! You can buy salted cod roe from a Greek deli.

Makes 2 cups (500 ml)

4 slices white bread, crusts removed and discarded

300 ml water, to cover

½ small onion, roughly chopped

100 g salted white cod roe paste (see page 203)

2 tablespoons lemon juice

550 ml olive oil, plus extra for drizzling

sea salt

sourdough bread, to serve

* SPECIAL EQUIPMENT
food processor

1 Put the bread into a bowl, then cover with water and soak for 15 minutes. Remove the bread and squeeze out any excess water. Set aside.

2 Blend the onion in a food processor until smooth. Add the squeezed bread and blend until smooth.

3 Add the cod roe and lemon juice to the food processor and blend once again until smooth. While the motor is running, slowly drizzle in the olive oil, a little at a time. The aim is to create an emulsion with the consistency of mayonnaise. Taste to check the seasoning and add a little salt if necessary.

4 Place in a bowl, drizzle with extra olive oil, then serve with bread for dipping. (Leftover taramosalata will keep in an airtight container in the fridge for up to 1 week.)

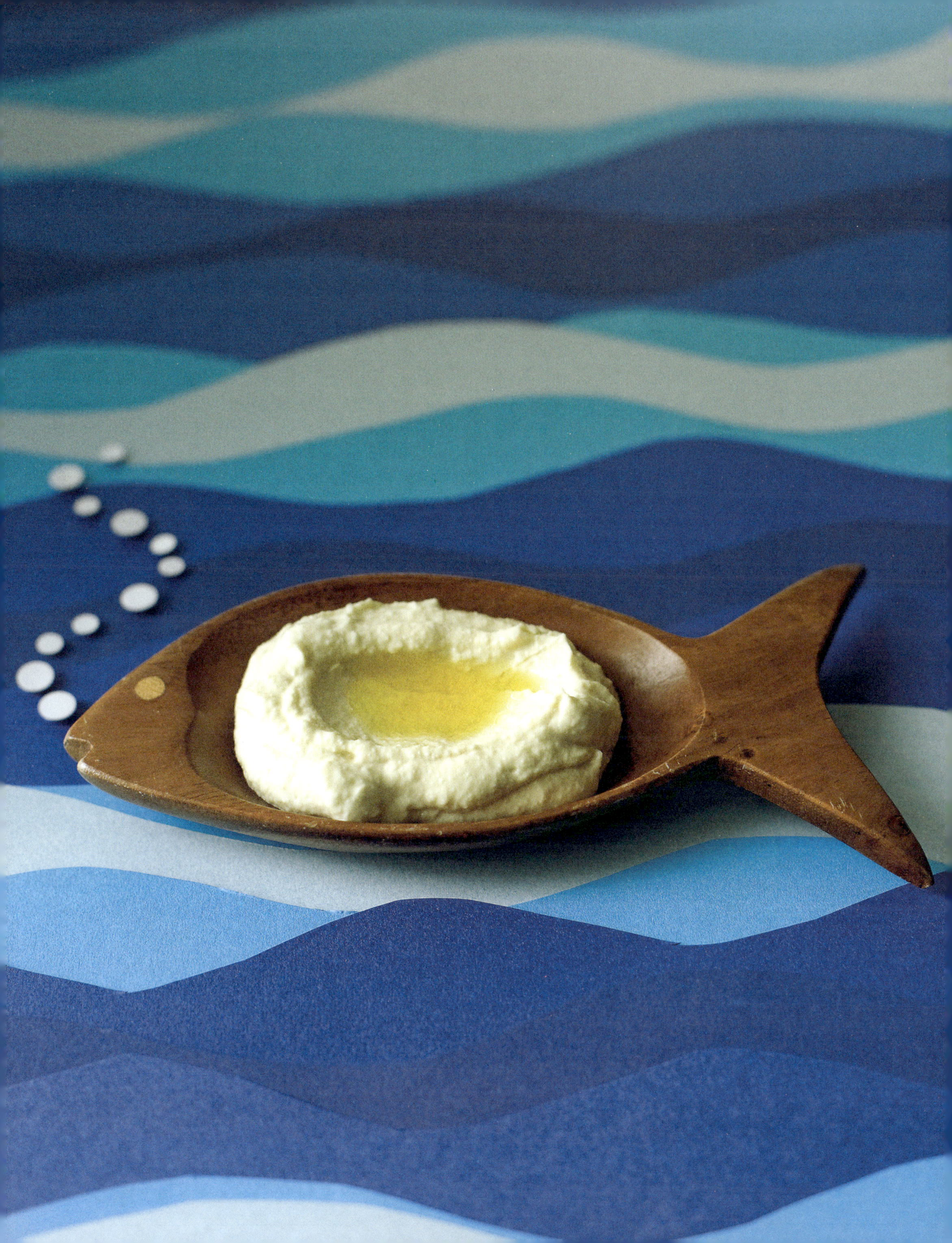

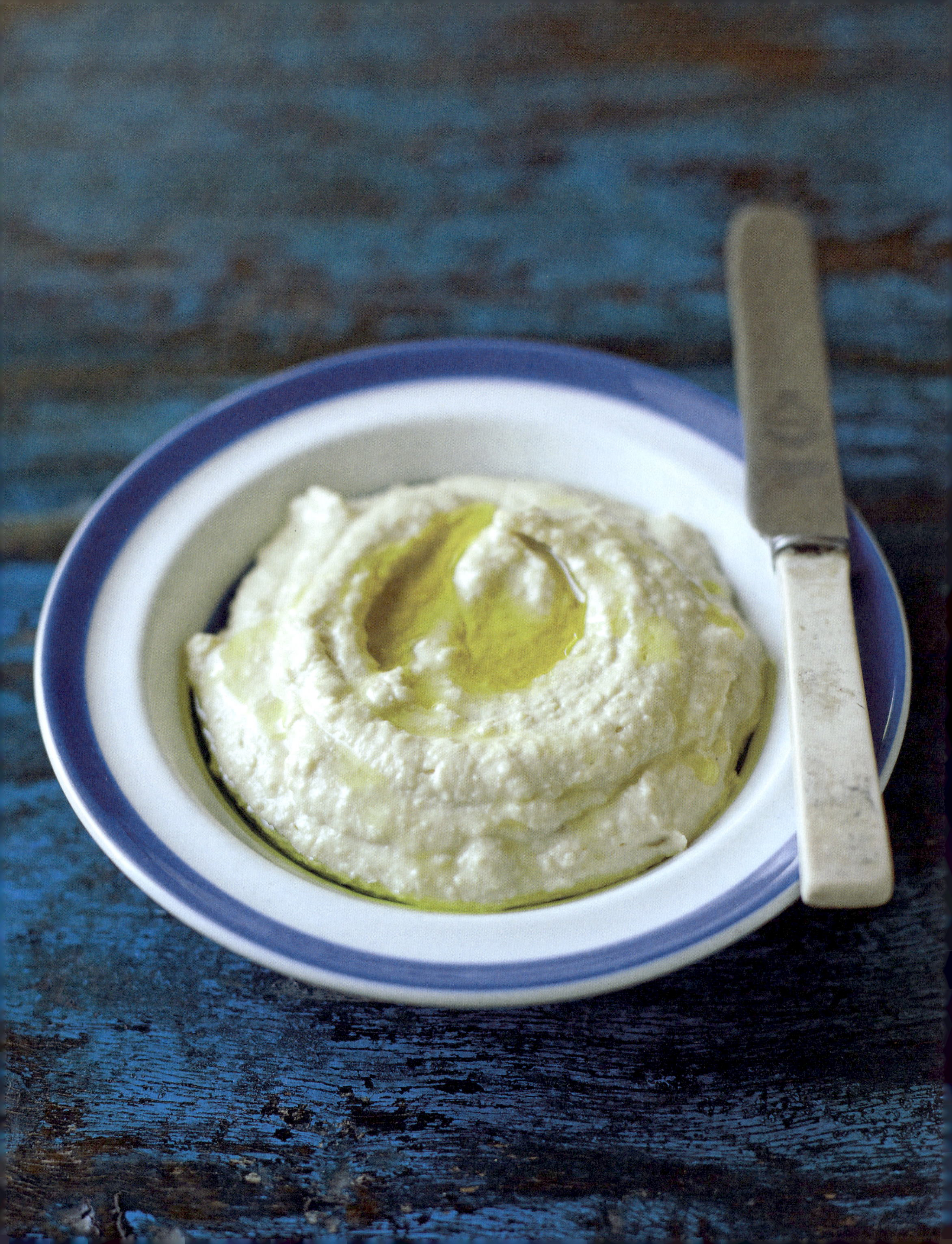

Hummus

I can't believe people buy dips with all those preservatives in them. Don't be lazy, make them yourself! Hummus is so easy and it makes a great lunchbox filler with some vegetable sticks and toasted flatbread. Tahini is made from ground sesame seeds and it's what gives hummus its unique delicious flavour. Serve this dip with the pita bread (see page 10) or carrot and celery sticks (crudites) or add it to sandwiches. I use good-quality tinned chick peas and suggest that you do too as they achieve consistently creamy results. I find soaked dried chick peas can vary in quality, depending on how old they are.

Makes 2 cups (500 ml)

2 × 400 g tins chick peas

2 cloves garlic, crushed

juice of 2 lemons

2 tablespoons tahini (see page 203)

1/3 cup (80 ml) extra virgin olive oil, plus extra for drizzling

sea salt and freshly ground black pepper

Pita Bread (optional, see page 10), to serve

✱ SPECIAL EQUIPMENT
   fine-mesh sieve
   food processor

1 Drain the chick peas in a fine-mesh sieve and rinse under cold water.

2 Place the chick peas, garlic, lemon juice, tahini, olive oil and salt and pepper to taste in a food processor and blend until smooth.

3 Transfer to a bowl, drizzle with extra olive oil and serve with pita bread, if desired.

Avocado tzatziki

I never understand it when people say that kids don't eat green stuff. What does that mean? I had to eat everything growing up as a kid. I had no choice. I'm lucky that I ate the sort of food that trained my palate and helped me appreciate freshness and tastiness. This dip is made by emulsifying flavoured oil with avocado. Make the flavoured oil beforehand, so it can infuse overnight. The dip is delicious served with tiny crisp fried whitebait, and is great spooned over barbecued or grilled chicken or fish.

Serves 4 as a starter

1 teaspoon ground cumin

1 teaspoon ground turmeric

100 ml extra virgin olive oil

3 avocados

juice of ½ lemon

1 clove garlic, crushed

¼ cup (70 g) natural Greek-style yoghurt

sea salt

FRIED WHITEBAIT (OPTIONAL)

vegetable oil, for deep-frying

500 g whitebait

plain flour, for dusting

✻ SPECIAL EQUIPMENT
  coffee filter paper or paper towel
  food processor
  deep-fryer (optional)

1 Place the ground cumin and turmeric in a small frying pan over low heat and gently heat for 30 seconds or until the spices start to smell toasted. Remove the pan from the heat, then add the olive oil and set aside to infuse for 30 minutes. Strain the oil through filter paper (you can use strong paper towel) placed over a bowl. Set aside.

2 Halve the avocados, then carefully remove the seeds. Remove the flesh from the avocadoes and place it in a food processor. Add the lemon juice and garlic and blend until smooth. With the motor running, slowly add the flavoured oil and blend to a puree.

3 Remove the avocado puree from the food processor and fold in the yoghurt with a flexible spatula. Season to taste with salt and set aside.

4 If making the fried whitebait, preheat oil for deep-frying in a deep-fryer to 180°C.

5 Toss the whitebait in flour to coat, then carefully fry in batches for 2 minutes or until crisp. Remove the whitebait from the deep-fryer and drain on paper towel.

6 Serve the avocado tzatziki with the fried whitebait, if desired.

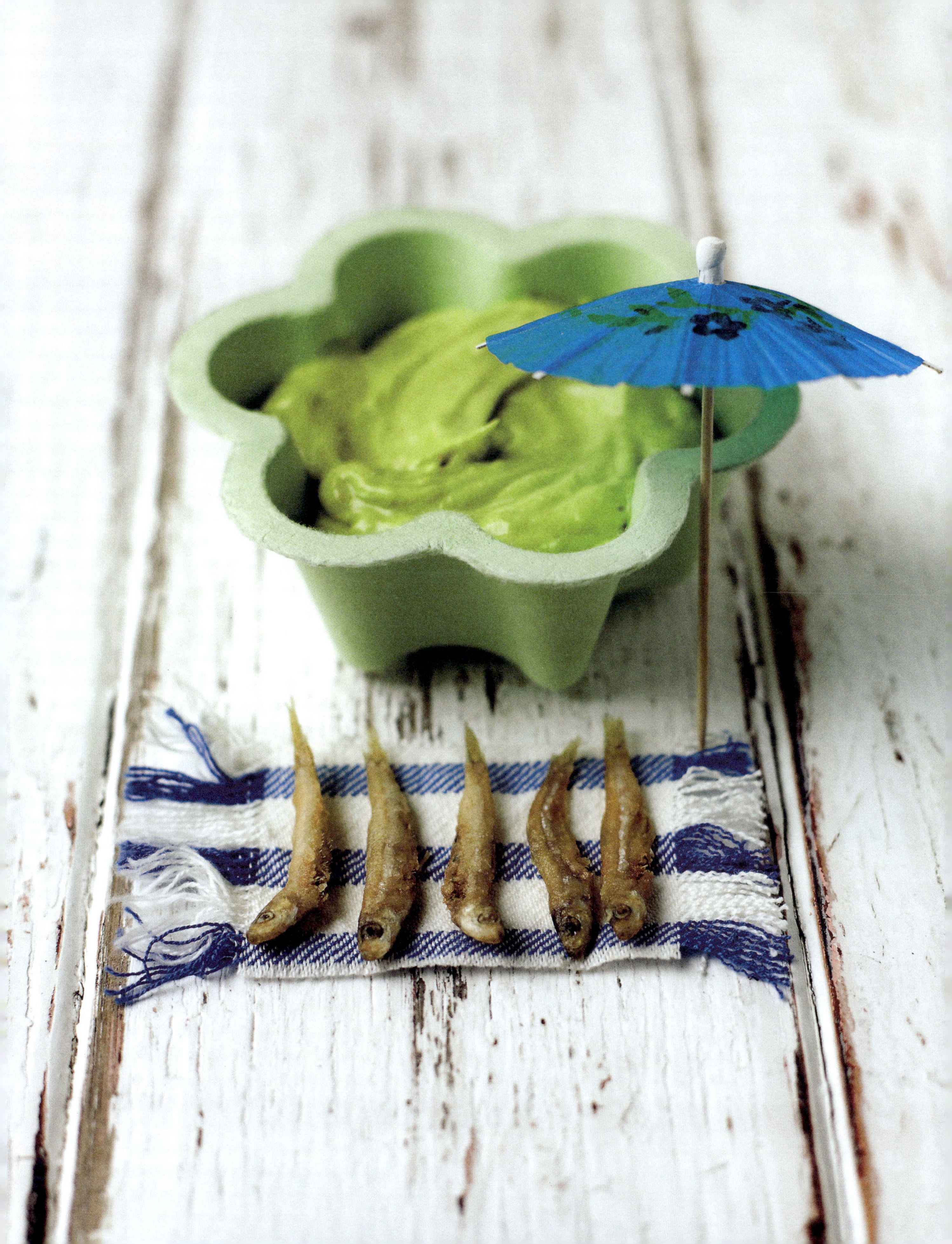

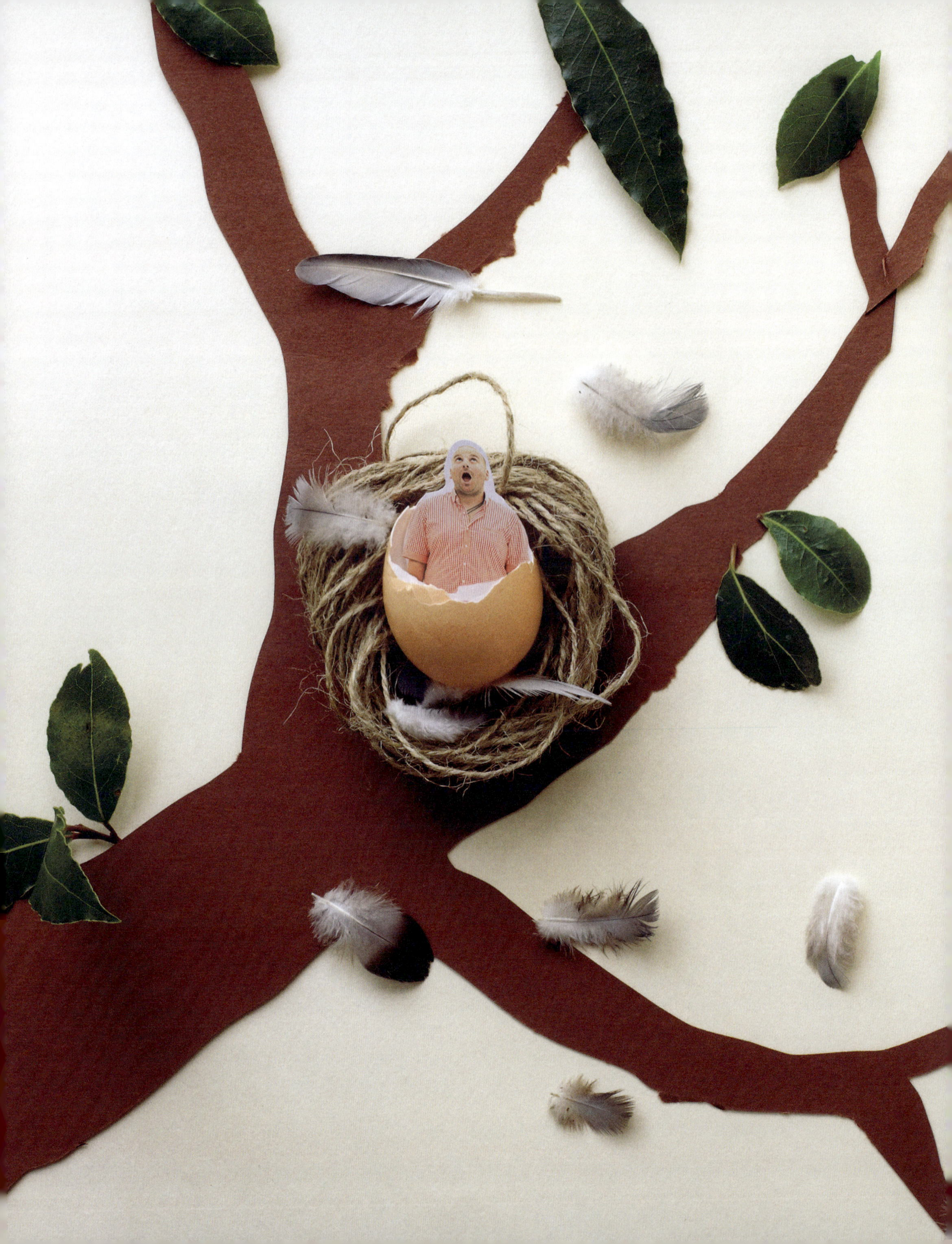

EGGS

If you have a carton of eggs in your fridge you'll never go hungry. Eggs are one of the most versatile foods around. They make a delicious meal in their own right and are an essential ingredient in many baked goods and sauces. Eggs can be scrambled, fried, poached, soft- and hard-boiled or pickled.

The most commonly eaten eggs come from chickens. Eggs from ducks, geese, quail, pheasants, emus, ostriches and gulls are all edible and even considered delicacies. Eggs for eating are unfertilised. However, fertilised eggs are eaten in some parts of South-East Asia.

Egg yolks act as an emulsifier in sauces to combine liquids. Mayonnaise is a good example of this (see page 203). Egg yolks are also used to thicken sauces and custards. The colour of the egg yolk depends on the hen's diet – the yolks of eggs from hens that eat a lot of grass can even be orange.

Egg whites can be whipped to incorporate air. They are used in desserts such as souffles (see page 40), meringues (see page 160) and mousse. The larger the egg, the more egg white it contains.

To test for freshness, place an egg in a bowl of water. A fresh egg will sink. A stale egg will have a larger air cell, which causes it to float.

Store eggs in the fridge for up to one month (or their use-by date) in their original carton. The pointed end should face downward.

Eggs with soldiers

It doesn't matter how old you are, there's nothing better than having soft-boiled free-range eggs with toasted 'soldiers' for breakfast. They make you feel all warm and fuzzy inside when you eat them. Every Saturday morning you should wake up and cook eggs with soldiers for your family. This recipe shows you how to make soft-boiled eggs. If you prefer hard-boiled eggs, simply boil the eggs for ten minutes instead of four.

4 eggs, straight from the fridge

sea salt and freshly ground white pepper

4 slices bread

butter, to spread

* **SPECIAL EQUIPMENT**
  slotted spoon

1 Bring a small saucepan of water to the boil. Gently place the eggs in the pan, using a large spoon. (Make sure the water covers the eggs completely.) Use a timer to boil the eggs for 4 minutes.

2 Turn off the heat and remove the eggs from the water with a slotted spoon.

3 Place the eggs in egg cups and cut the tops off with an egg cutter or sharp knife. Season to taste with salt and pepper.

4 Meanwhile, toast some bread, then spread with butter and cut into soldiers (long strips). Serve the boiled eggs with the toast soldiers.

Did you know?

- The fresher the egg, the harder it is to peel when boiled.

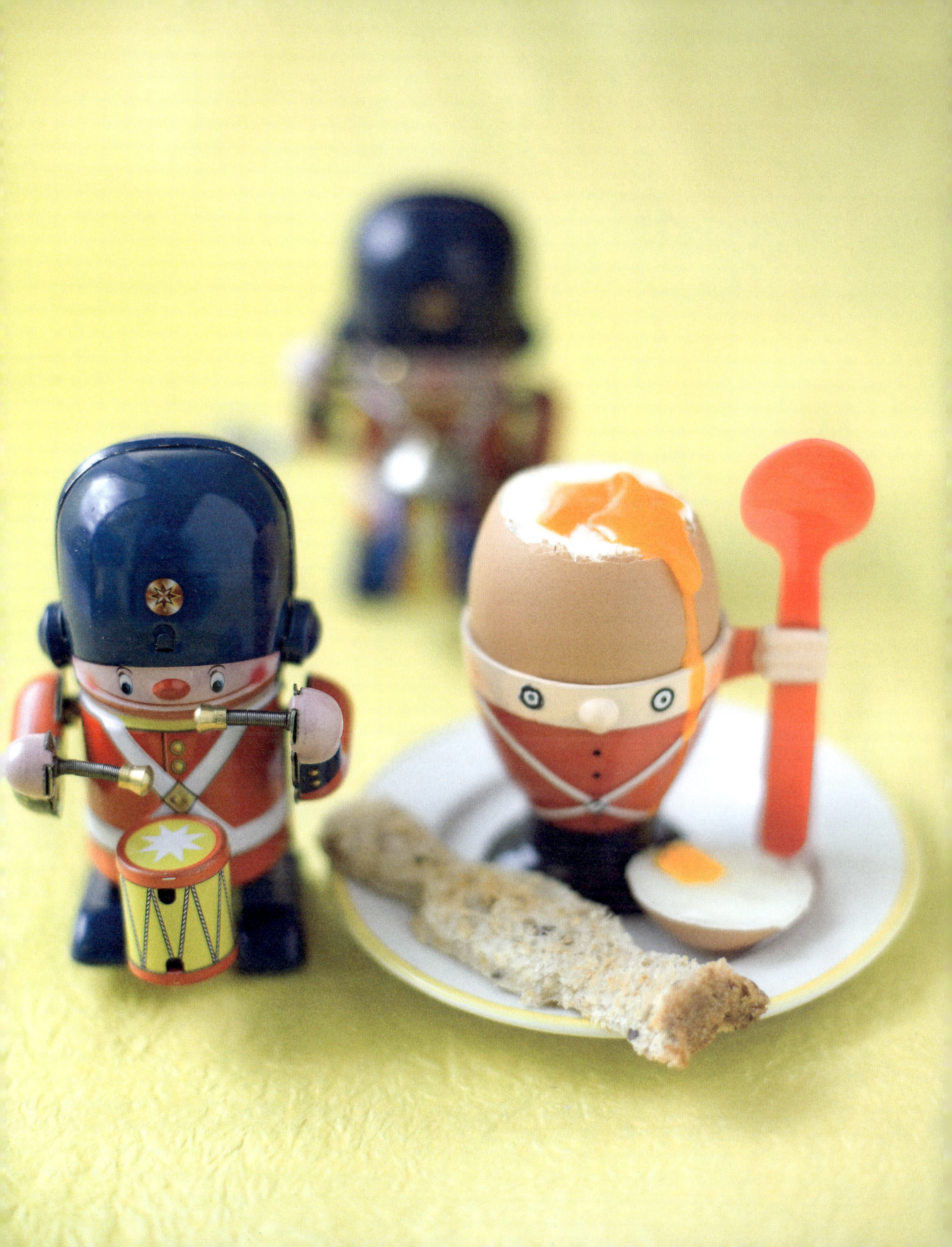

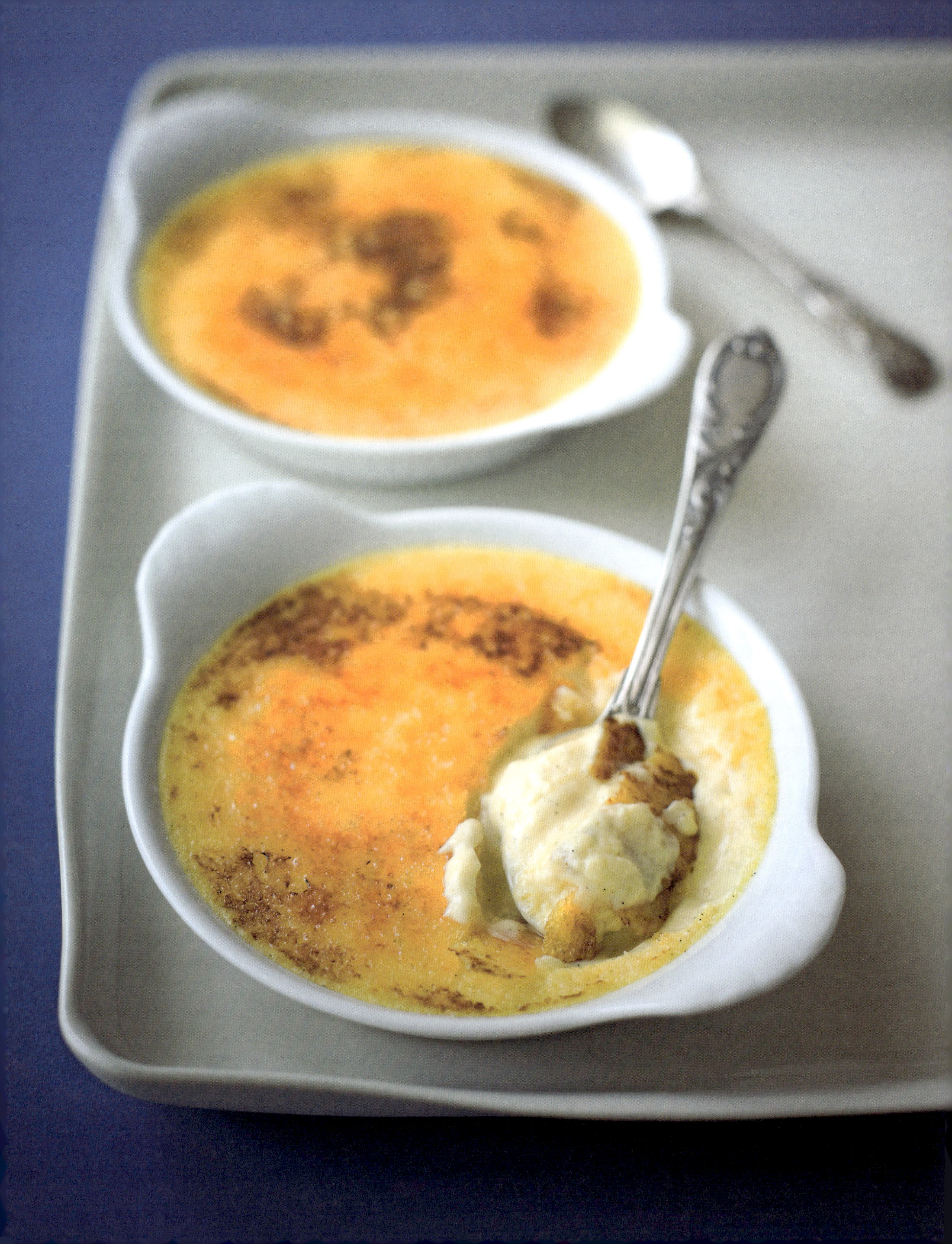

Creme brulee

This is a recipe I will never forget. It was one of the basics I had to master when I started my classical chef training. My apprenticeship was one of the most important parts of my career, because it taught me how to be disciplined. Discipline is the first thing I look for in a new chef. Then it's just a matter of teaching them how to cook, which is the easy bit.

Serves 6

600 ml thickened cream

1 vanilla pod, split lengthways and seeds scraped

6 egg yolks

¼ cup (55 g) caster sugar, plus extra for topping

boiling water

* SPECIAL EQUIPMENT
electric mixer
fine-mesh sieve
6 × 125 ml-capacity gratin dishes or ramekins
kitchen blowtorch (optional)

1 Preheat the oven to 120°C fan-forced (140°C conventional).

2 Heat the cream, vanilla pod and seeds in a small saucepan over medium heat until hot. Remove the pan from the heat before the cream boils. Remove the vanilla pod.

3 Whisk the egg yolks and caster sugar in the bowl of an electric mixer until thick and pale yellow. With the motor running, slowly add the hot cream and continue to whisk until combined.

4 Strain the mixture through a fine-mesh sieve into a jug (this removes any bubbles so the surface of the brulee is smooth), then pour into 6 shallow 125 ml-capacity moulds standing in a large deep roasting pan. Pull out the oven shelf and place the pan on the shelf. Carefully add boiling water from the kettle to the roasting pan to come halfway up the sides of the ramekins. Cover loosely with foil.

5 Bake the brulees for 45 minutes or until the custard has just set (wobble a ramekin gently to check that the liquid has set). Carefully remove the roasting pan from the oven and place on the bench. Taking care, use an egg slide to remove the moulds from the pan of hot water. Refrigerate the brulees for at least 1 hour.

6 Just before serving, sprinkle extra sugar evenly over the custards. Place under a preheated griller for a few minutes to melt the sugar and caramelise the tops. (Alternatively, carefully use a kitchen blowtorch to caramelise the sugar.)

Chocolate marshmallow souffles

Making a souffle is so rewarding. There's a sense of achievement, especially when it rises nicely and is soft and gooey in the middle. Don't be upset if it doesn't work the first time, because it takes practice. To be a great cook or chef you have to practise all the time. The key is repetition. Lots of people feel scared when it comes to making souffles, but once you've mastered the technique, they're pretty easy to whip up. The trick is not to overbeat the whites, and to use a large metal spoon to gently fold the whites into the rest of the mixture. The resulting souffle will be lovely and light.

Serves 4

softened butter, for greasing

2 tablespoons caster sugar, plus extra for dusting

200 g dark couverture chocolate buttons (see page 202)

2 tablespoons milk or pouring cream

3 eggs, separated

2 egg whites

⅓ cup (4 tablespoons) mini marshmallows, plus extra to serve (optional)

icing sugar, for dusting

✱ SPECIAL EQUIPMENT
4 × 200 ml-capacity souffle moulds or ramekins
electric mixer
large metal spoon

1 Preheat the oven to 200°C fan-forced (220°C conventional).

2 Grease the insides of four 200-ml capacity souffle moulds with softened butter, then dust with a little caster sugar. Shake out any excess sugar, then wipe the top inside edge of each mould clean with paper towel or a clean tea towel. Set aside on a baking tray.

3 Place the chocolate in a medium–large microwave-safe bowl. Heat on medium power for 2 minutes, then remove and stir with a metal spoon. Leave for a few minutes; the residual heat will continue to melt the chocolate. Set the chocolate aside to cool slightly, then stir in the milk or cream and the egg yolks.

4 Whisk the 5 egg whites in the bowl of an electric mixer until soft peaks form, then gradually add the sugar, whisking continuously until firm white peaks form. Do not over-beat. Using a large metal spoon, fold one-third of the beaten egg whites into the chocolate mixture to help loosen the mix. Fold in the remaining beaten egg whites.

5 Place 1 tablespoon of mini-marshmallows in the base of each souffle mould. Spoon in the chocolate mixture and wipe around the inside edge to make sure it is clean (this helps the souffles to rise). Bake the souffles for 14 minutes or until risen and cooked through.

6 Dust the souffles with icing sugar and serve immediately with extra marshmallows (if using).

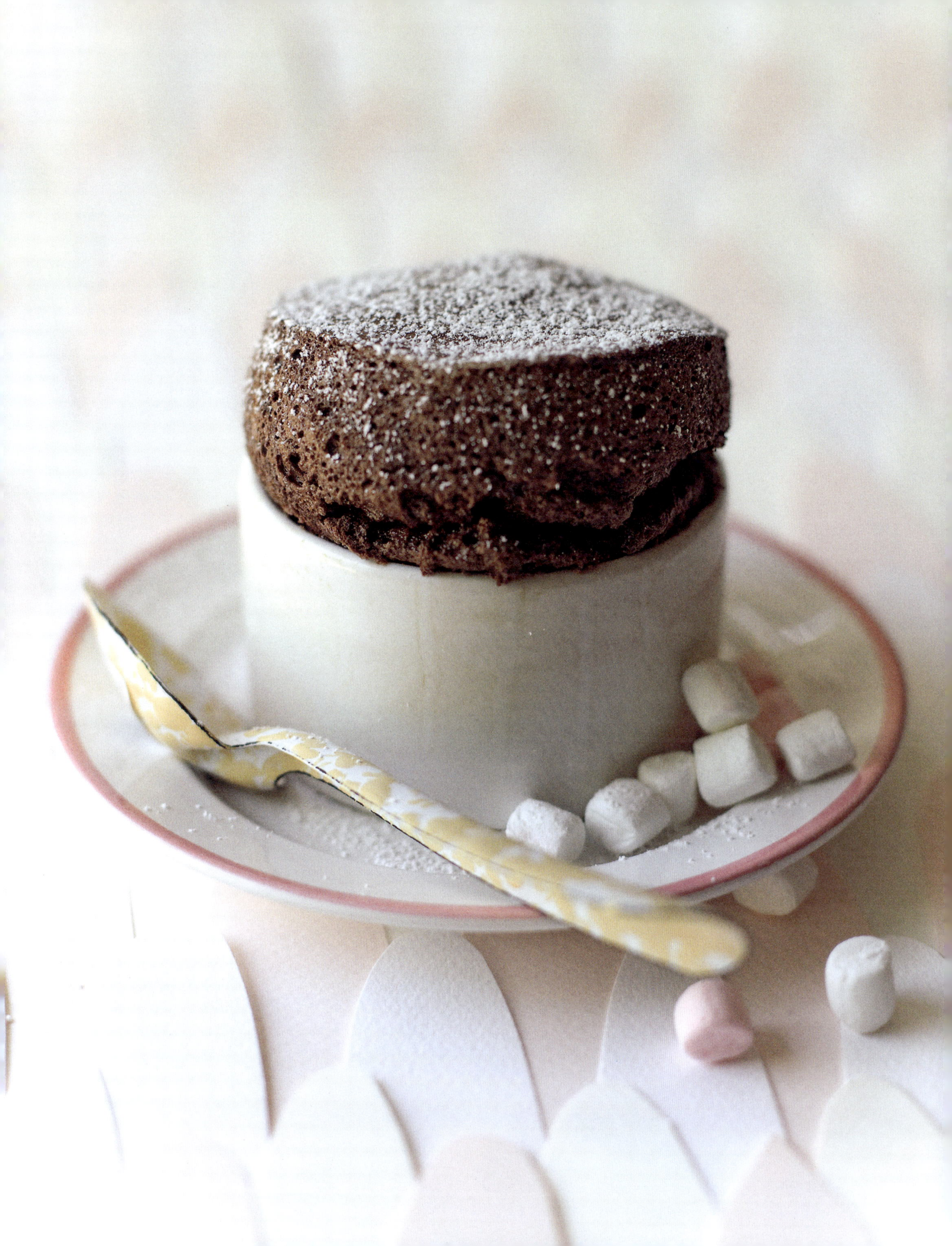

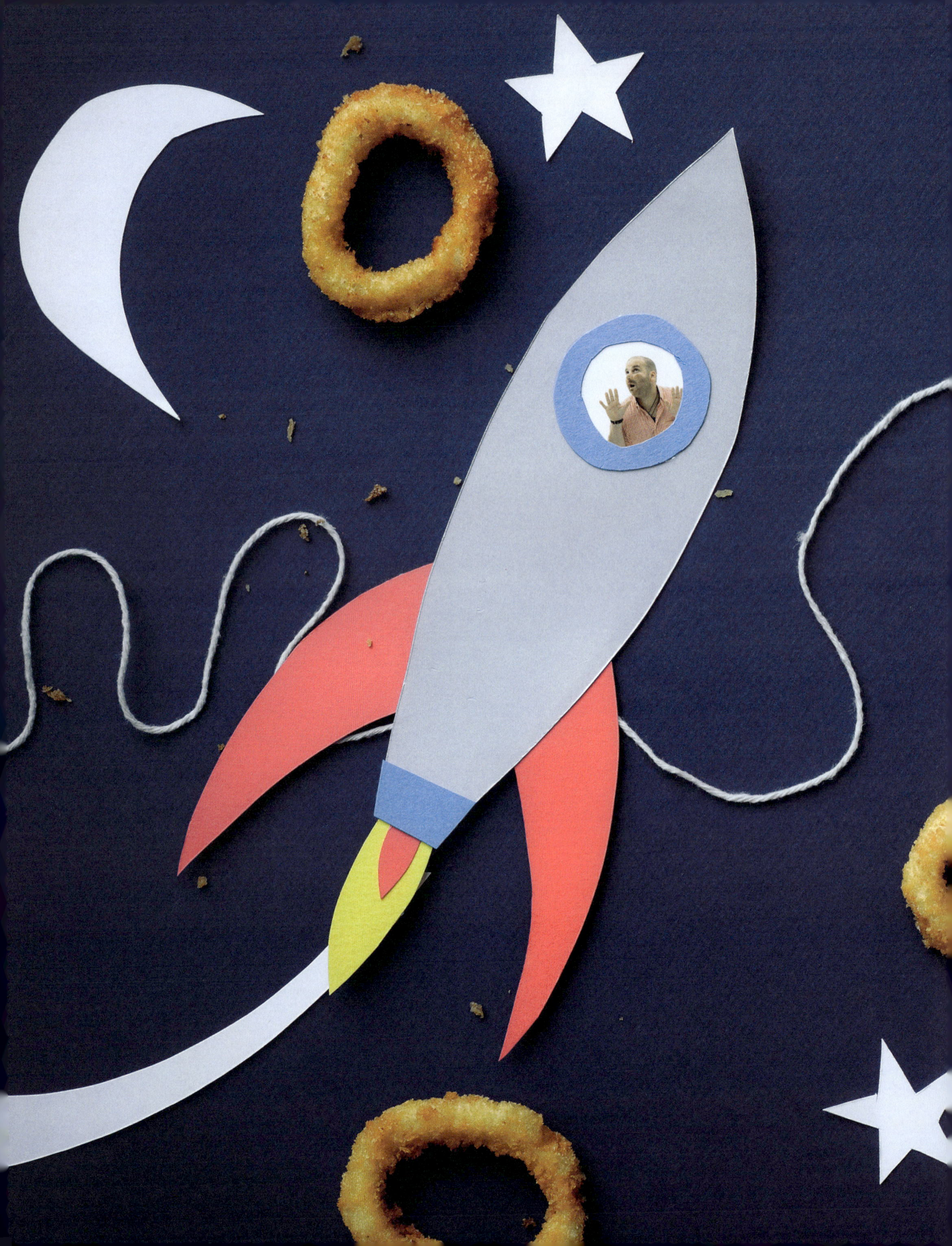

fritters

A fritter is any food coated in or mixed with breadcrumbs or batter and then fried. The breadcrumbs can either be fresh or dried. The flavour and texture of the coating will depend on the bread used. I like to use panko crumbs, which are a large, flaky breadcrumb used in Japanese cuisine. They are made from bread without crusts and have a crisper, airier texture than most other breadcrumbs. Fresh breadcrumbs can be made in the food processor, using leftover bread. To make homemade dried breadcrumbs, place fresh crumbs on a baking tray in a 160°C fan-forced (180°C conventional) oven for 5 minutes or until they dry out.

Batters are made by mixing flour with liquid such as water, milk or eggs. You can fluff up your batter – aerate it – by adding beaten egg whites or by adding soda water, beer or baking powder. Food is dipped into the batter to coat it completely, then deep-fried. The batter protects the food. Batters are also used to make pancakes, waffles and doughnuts.

Crispy fried lamb's brains

When my brother and I were little, Mum fed us crispy fried lamb's brains but told us they were chicken nuggets, and we loved them! At the time we'd never eaten chicken nuggets so we didn't know better.

Serves 4

4 sets of brains

sea salt

¼ cup (35 g) plain flour

1 egg

1 tablespoon milk

½ cup (50 g) dried breadcrumbs

vegetable oil, for deep-frying

COURT BOUILLON

1 litre water

¼ cup (60 ml) white vinegar

1 carrot, sliced

1 onion, sliced

a sprig thyme

1 bay leaf

a few stalks flat-leaf parsley

2 teaspoons salt

1 teaspoon black peppercorns

STAR-ANISE MAYONNAISE

3 star anise

1 cup (250 ml) Mayonnaise (see page 203) or whole-egg mayonnaise

1 tablespoon lemon juice

✱ SPECIAL EQUIPMENT
   deep-fryer
   slotted spoon

1 Soak the brains overnight in the fridge in a bowl of water with a pinch of salt. Remove and carefully peel off the membrane. Soak the brains again in a bowl of fresh water with a pinch of salt for another 1 hour.

2 To make the star-anise mayonnaise, toast the star anise in a small frying pan over medium heat for 30 seconds or until fragrant. Place in a spice (or coffee) grinder and blend to a powder (or use a mortar and pestle). Combine the ground star anise with the mayonnaise and lemon juice. Cover the surface closely with plastic film and refrigerate until required. (Makes 250 ml.)

3 To make the court bouillon (poaching liquid), place the water, vinegar, carrot, onion, thyme, bay leaf, parsley, salt and pepper in a saucepan and slowly bring to the boil over medium heat. Reduce the heat to low and simmer for 30 minutes. Strain through a fine-mesh sieve into a clean saucepan.

4 Bring the court bouillon to the boil, then add the brains and poach over medium heat for 5 minutes; make sure they are covered with the liquid (add a little more water if you need to). Remove the brains with a slotted spoon and drain on paper towel.

5 Separate the 2 lobes of each set of brains and lightly dust with flour. Whisk the egg and milk in a shallow bowl. Place the breadcrumbs in a separate shallow bowl. Dip the brains into the beaten egg, then roll in breadcrumbs to coat well.

6 Preheat oil for deep-frying in a deep-fryer to 180°C. Deep-fry the brains for 3–4 minutes until golden and crisp. Carefully remove with a slotted spoon and drain on paper towel.

7 Serve the crumbed brains with star-anise mayonnaise.

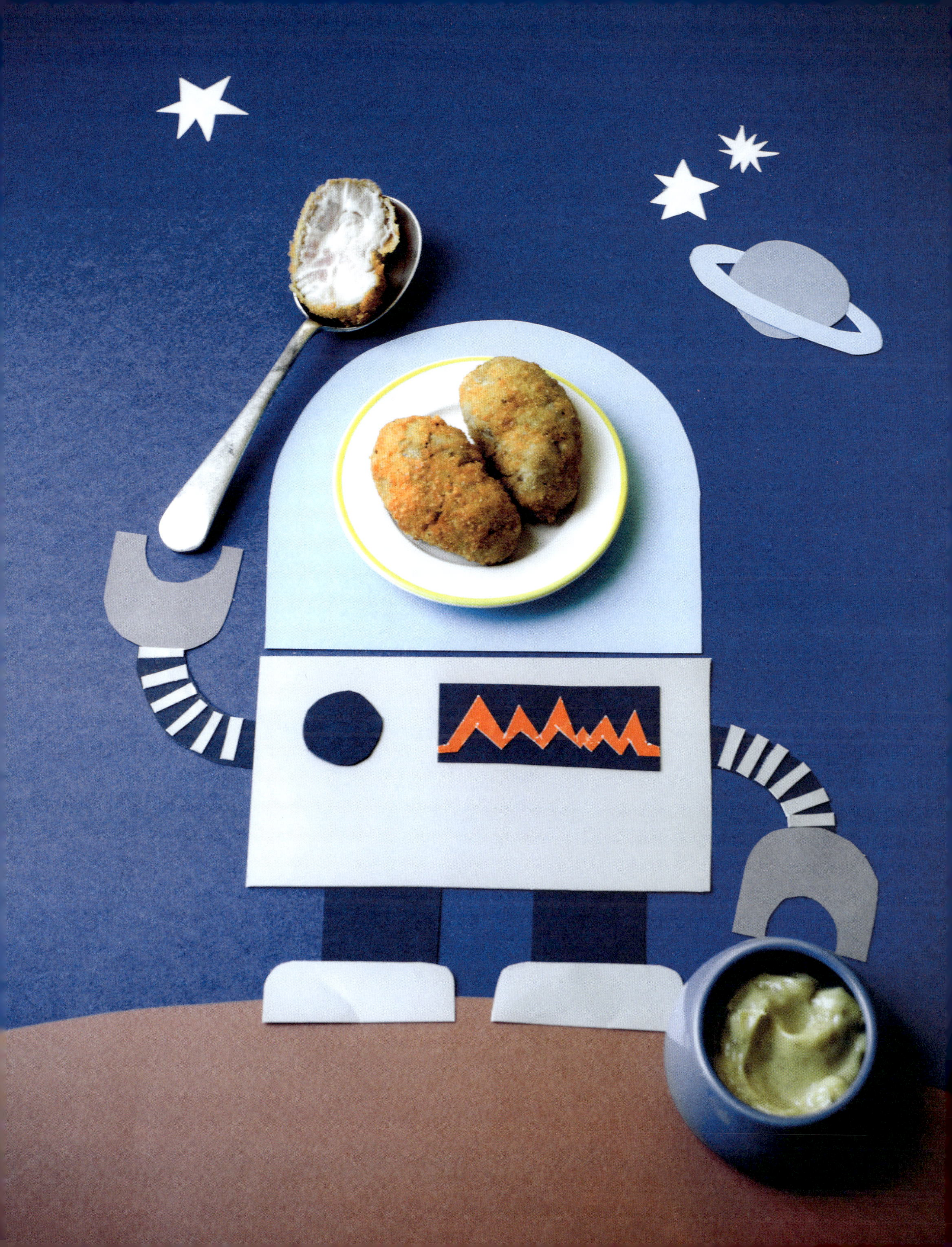

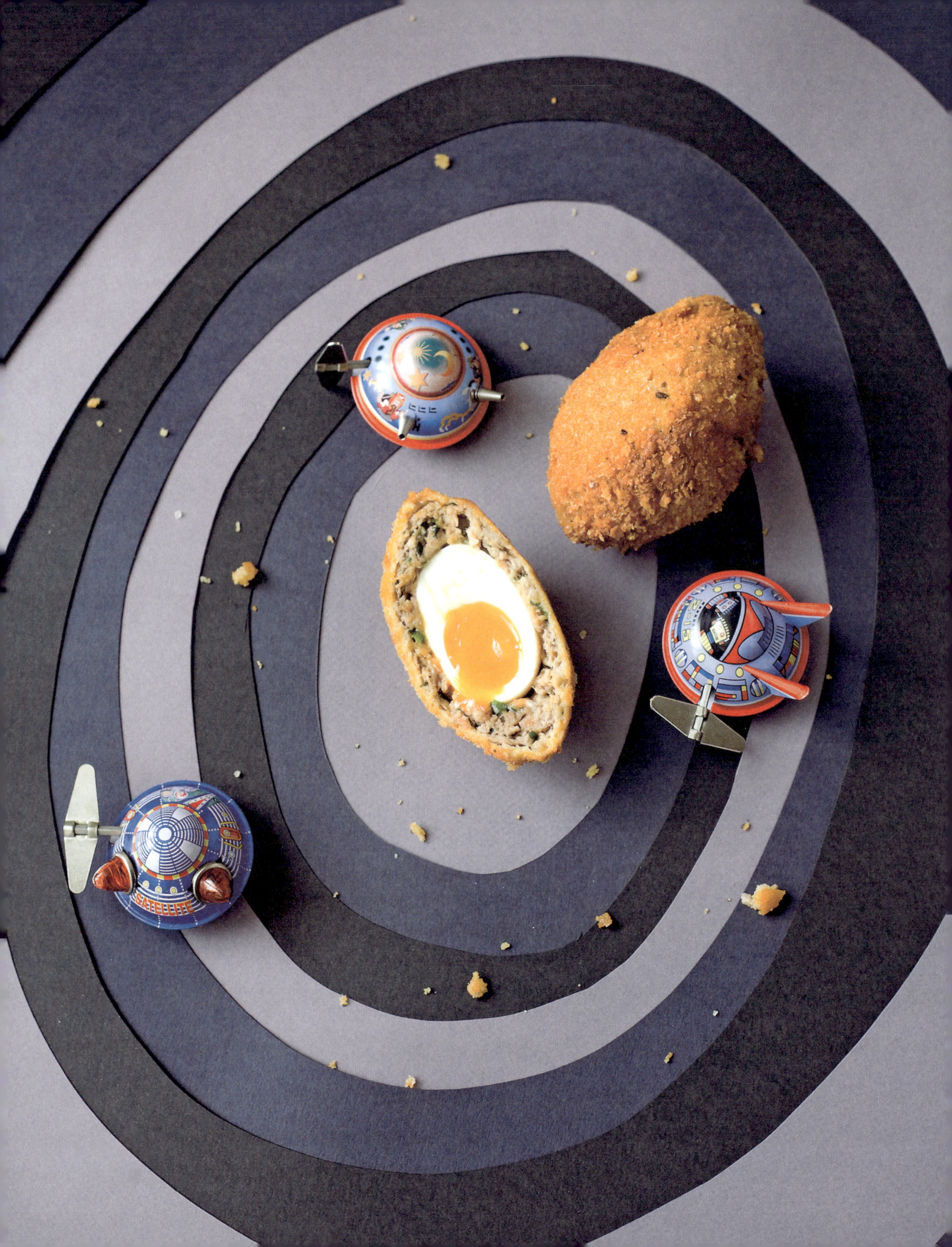

Greek-style Scotch eggs

Here is my version of the Greek-style Scotch eggs called rolo. They taste great! Make sure you soft-boil the eggs to start with. If the yolks are too hard you'll overcook them further when you fry them in the coating.

Serves 4

4 eggs, straight from the fridge, plus 1 egg, beaten

ice cubes

400 g minced lamb

2 tablespoons Dijon mustard, plus extra to serve

2 teaspoons chopped rosemary

2 teaspoons chopped mint

sea salt and freshly ground black pepper

¼ cup (35 g) plain flour

½ cup (50 g) dried breadcrumbs

1 tablespoon milk

vegetable oil, for deep-frying

✱ SPECIAL EQUIPMENT
   deep-fryer
   slotted spoon

1 Bring a small saucepan of water to the boil. Gently place the eggs in the pan, using a large spoon. Make sure the water covers the eggs completely. Use a timer to boil the eggs for 4 minutes. Turn off the heat and remove the eggs from the water with a slotted spoon, then place in a bowl of iced water.

2 Peel the eggs and set aside.

3 Place the minced lamb, mustard, rosemary and mint in a bowl, season with salt and pepper, then mix well.

4 Divide the mince mixture into quarters. Carefully mould one-quarter around each egg to cover it completely; don't press too hard as the yolk is still very soft and you don't want it to burst.

5 Place the flour and breadcrumbs on separate plates. Whisk the beaten egg with the milk in a shallow bowl. Roll the boiled eggs in the flour to lightly coat, then dip in the egg mixture to coat. Roll the eggs in the breadcrumbs to coat.

6 Preheat oil for deep-frying in a deep-fryer to 170°C (or in a heavy-based saucepan until a cube of bread browns in 35 seconds). Fry the eggs for 5 minutes or until golden. Carefully remove with a slotted spoon and drain on paper towel.

7 Cut the eggs in half and serve with extra mustard.

Crumbed calamari

This dish pays homage to my time cooking at the Mentone Hotel. I was sixteen years old when I was employed by a guy called Rabih Yanni, who is now a very close friend. My job on the weekends was to crumb kilos of calamari rings – I mean kilos of the stuff – then cook them to order. I am so humbled and thankful for my junior years. I learnt you have to give 100 per cent or not do it at all, whether you are running a pub or a fine-dining restaurant. Thanks Rab for the memories and our friendship. Love ya!

Serves 4

4 fresh calamari (about 15 cm long)

¼ cup (35 g) plain flour

1 egg

2 tablespoons milk

1½ cups (150 g) panko breadcrumbs (see page 203)

vegetable oil, for deep-frying

sea salt

lemon wedges and flat-leaf parsley sprigs (optional), to serve

* SPECIAL EQUIPMENT
kitchen scissors
deep-fryer
wire basket or slotted spoon

1 To clean the calamari, place in a sink filled with cold water. Pull the tentacles away from the body (the insides should come away with the tentacles). Use kitchen scissors to cut the tentacles just below the ink sac, which is purple. Open out the tentacles and you will see the 'beak'. Cut this away and discard along with the guts and the ink sac. Set the tentacles aside. Take the body and insert your fingers to remove the transparent cartilage and discard. Rinse inside the body well under cold running water. Gently pull off the purple membrane from the outside of the body and discard. Dry the body and the tentacles on paper towel.

2 Cut the calamari bodies into 5 mm-thick rings. Cut the tentacles in half.

3 Lightly dust each piece of calamari with flour. Whisk together the egg and milk in a wide shallow bowl. Place the breadcrumbs in a separate shallow bowl.

4 Dip the calamari in beaten egg and coat in breadcrumbs.

5 Preheat oil for deep-frying in a deep-fryer to 170°C (or in a deep heavy-based saucepan until a cube of bread browns in 35 seconds). Carefully deep-fry the calamari in batches for 30–60 seconds until golden and crisp. Remove with a wire basket or slotted spoon and drain on paper towel.

6 Season the calamari with salt and serve with lemon wedges, scattered with flat-leaf parsley, if you like.

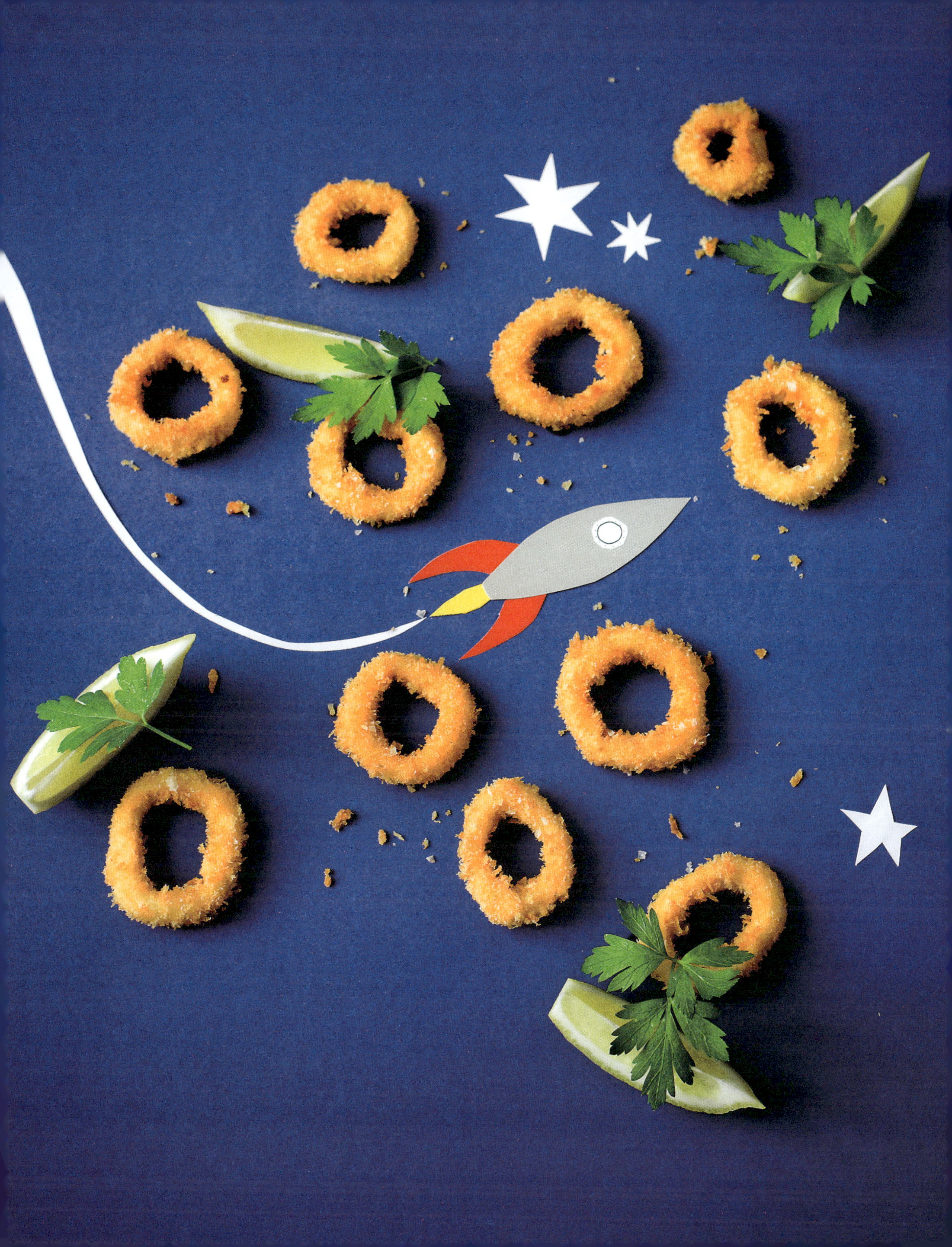

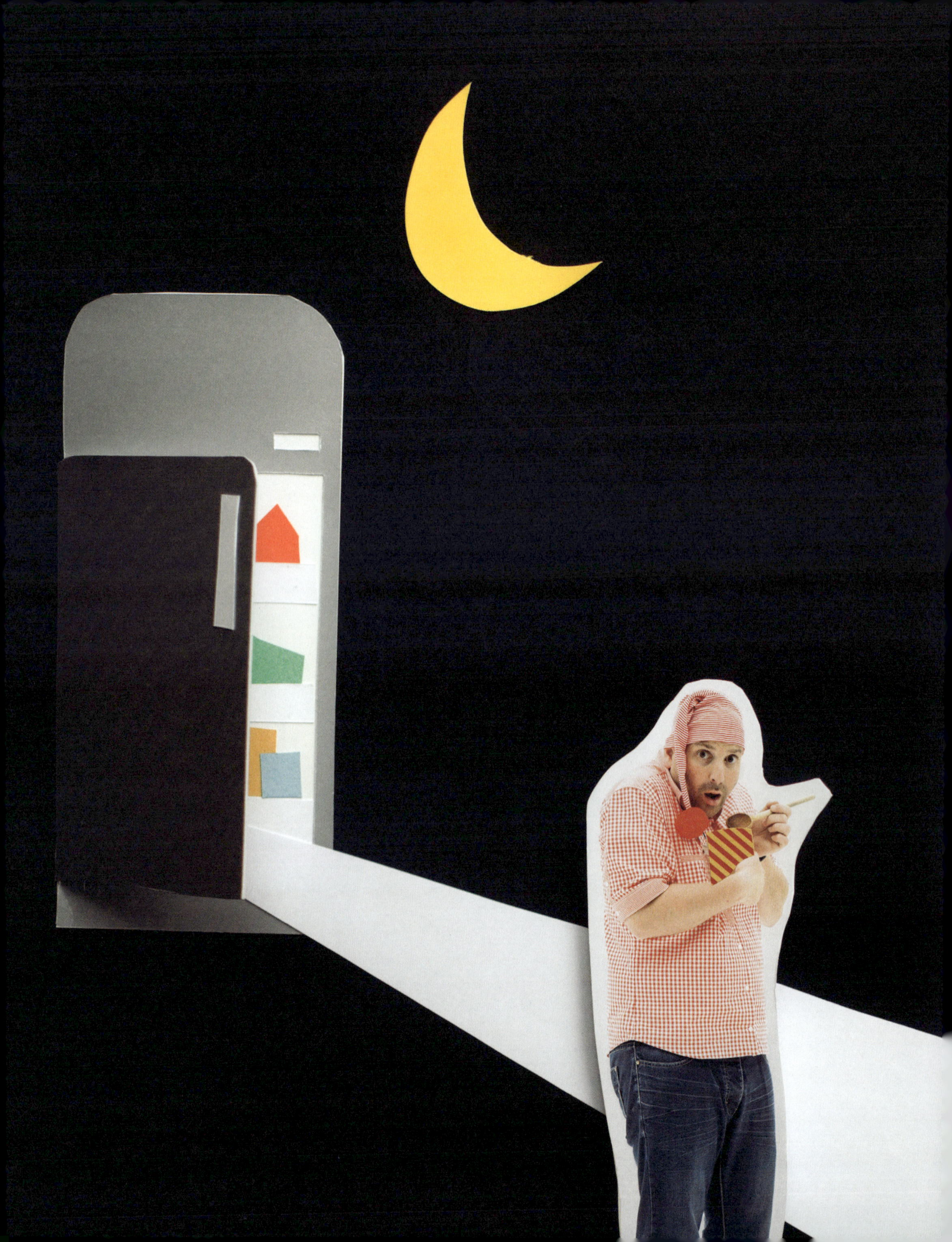

Pleasures

People seem to think chefs eat the same sort of fancy food every night that they prepare for customers in their restaurants. This isn't true. Staff meals are a quick pit-stop before food service starts, then something fast and simple at the end of the night. This is when many chefs indulge in guilty pleasures – food that's not necessarily healthy, and certainly not something you'd find on a restaurant menu.

I have included some of my guilty pleasure food here. I love the combination of big flavours, such as peanut butter with jam. Try making your own peanut butter (see page 55). It tastes yum!

Another great one is ham and pineapple pizza. Again, it's the flavour combination that makes it so good – the sweet and salty combination of pineapple and ham. Yes, it's a little bit daggy, but when you make it at home with your own dough (see page 52), you'll discover a dish that's a world away from the cheap takeaway version.

My fixation with condensed milk stems back to my childhood when I worked Saturdays in my parents' food store. The incredibly sweet flavour and smooth creamy texture of condensed milk was so moreish I'd eat it straight from the tube, then put the tube back on the shelf! Here I have used it to make an easy yet special dessert (see page 56).

Anything that's homemade is going to be better for you than nasty takeaway or processed supermarket food. So while the dishes that follow are a bit naughty, you can feel good about having made them yourself using the best and freshest ingredients.

Ham and pineapple pizza

People always laugh at me when I tell them I love ham and pineapple pizza. I love it! Sometimes I just crave the naff guilty pleasures in life. Life is too short to eat rubbish processed foods, so why not give making your own pizza a go – it tastes so much better. This is a more extravagant take on the regular version you'll find at your local pizza shop.

Makes 4

1 smoked ham hock

1 onion, halved

1 carrot, roughly chopped

1 stick celery, roughly chopped

1 tablespoon black peppercorns

4 litres water

1 quantity Pita Bread dough (see page 10)

sea salt

flat-leaf parsley leaves, chilli flakes (optional) and crumbled feta, to serve

PICKLED PINEAPPLE

1 small pineapple (about 800 g)

1 cup (250 ml) champagne vinegar

1 cup (220 g) white sugar

1 cup (360 g) honey

1 fresh long red chilli, thickly sliced

2 cloves garlic, sliced

2 cups (500 ml) water

✱ **SPECIAL EQUIPMENT**
pizza stone (optional)

1 Place the ham hock in a large stockpot or saucepan. Add the onion, carrot, celery and peppercorns and cover with approximately 4 litres cold water. Bring to the boil, then reduce the heat to low and simmer for 1½ hours or until the ham hock is tender and the meat is falling off the bone. Shred the meat into thick chunks and set aside. (Discard the skin and bones. Strain and keep the cooking liquid to use as ham stock for soup such as minestrone or pea and ham.)

2 While you wait, make the pickled pineapple. Peel and quarter the pineapple, then remove the core and cut the flesh into 5 mm-thick slices. Place the vinegar, sugar, honey, chilli, garlic and water in a saucepan and boil for 3 minutes. Add the pineapple and simmer over low heat for a further 20 minutes. Remove the pineapple, strain the liquid and reserve. (Any leftover pickled pineapple can be packed into hot sterilised jars [see page 203] with enough of the reserved cooking syrup to cover and stored in the cupboard for up to 2 weeks or fridge for up to 1 month.)

3 Preheat the oven to 230°C fan-forced (250°C conventional).

4 Divide the pita dough into 4, then place on a chopping board and roll out with a rolling pin until thin. Place the dough on a heavy-based baking tray lined with baking paper (or a pizza stone if you have one) and sprinkle with sea salt.

5 Bake the pita bases for 5 minutes or until golden and cooked, then remove from the oven. Place chunks of ham and pineapple all over the top, then scatter with parsley and chilli flakes (if using), crumble over a little feta and serve.

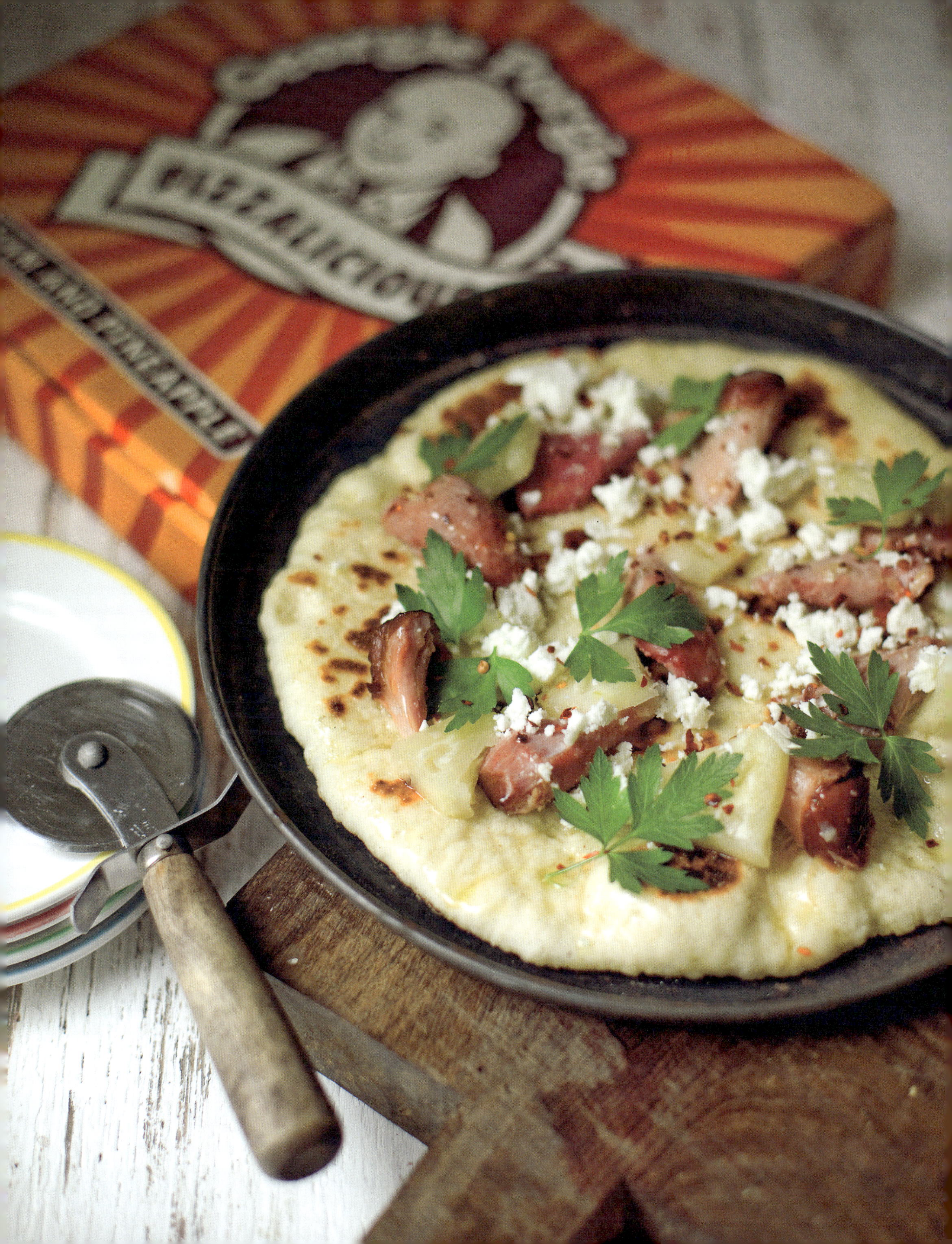

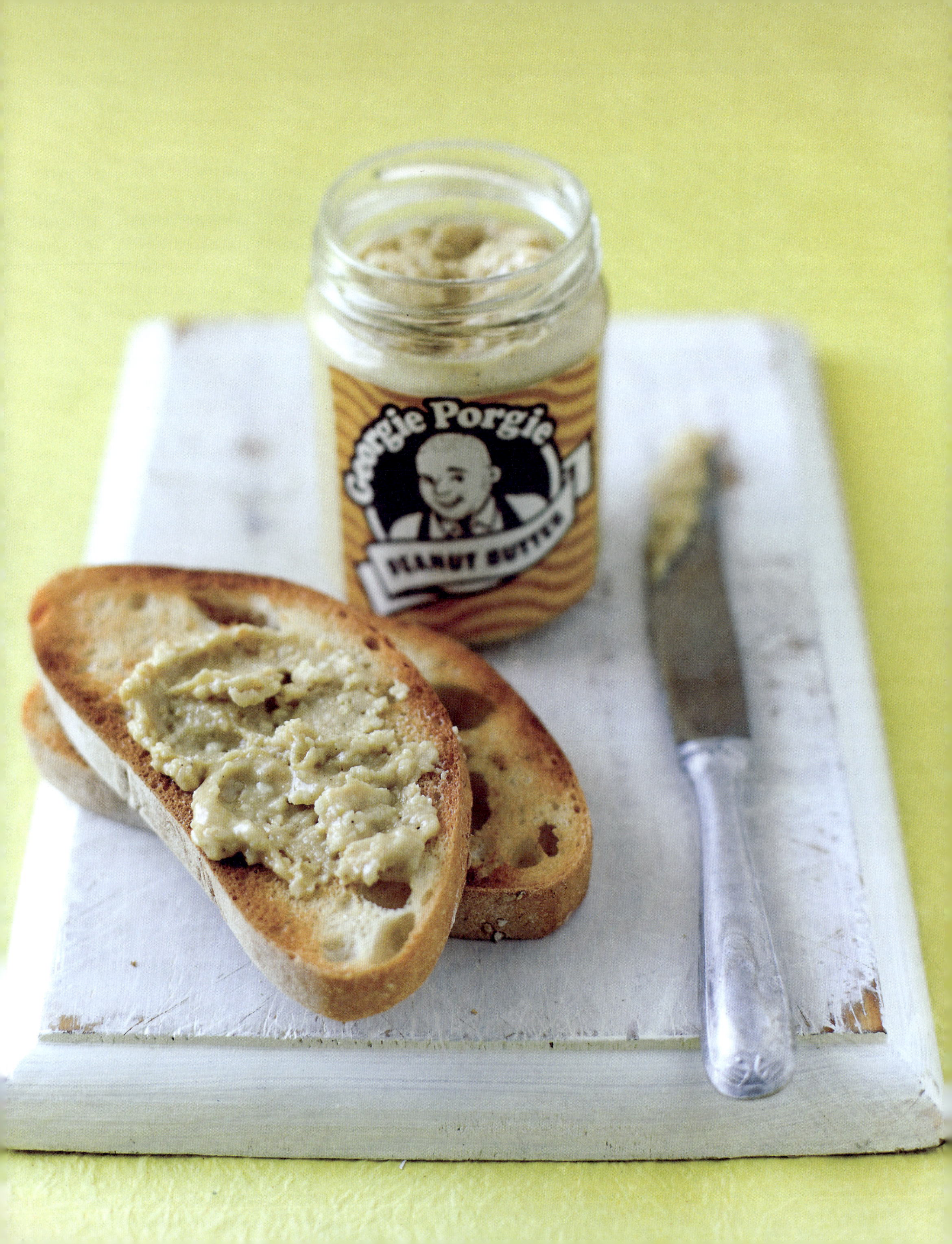
Georgie Porgie

Homemade peanut butter on toast

My all-time favourite breakfast is peanut butter on toast. I love the crunchy texture of the toast and the saltiness of the peanut butter. And I love it even more with jam on top. I guess I'm still a kid at heart!

Makes 375 ml

2 cups (300 g) roasted salted peanuts

2 tablespoons peanut oil or vegetable oil

1 teaspoon five spice powder (see page 202)

1 tablespoon honey (optional)

4 slices white sourdough

strawberry jam (optional), to serve

✱ SPECIAL EQUIPMENT
food processor

1 Place the peanuts and oil in a food processor and process for 5 minutes or until the mixture starts to form a chunky paste. Add the five spice and continue to blend. Add honey to taste, if desired. If you prefer a smoother peanut butter, keep processing until the mixture is quite smooth.

2 Spoon the peanut butter into an airtight container and store in the fridge for up to 2 weeks.

3 Toast the bread, spread with peanut butter and jam (if you like) and enjoy!

Condensed milk fool with lemon granita

This is a wonderful dessert. It tastes sweet, crunchy and creamy. It uses one of my favourite childhood ingredients – condensed milk.

Serves 8

1 × 395 g tin condensed milk

1 cup (250 ml) thickened cream

200 g clotted cream (see page 202)

LEMON GRANITA

finely grated zest and juice of 2 lemons

1 cup (220 g) caster sugar

3 cups (750 ml) water

* SPECIAL EQUIPMENT
fine-mesh sieve
deep stainless-steel tray
electric mixer

1 To make the lemon granita, strain the lemon juice through a fine-mesh sieve into a saucepan, then add the sugar and water. Bring to the boil over medium heat, stirring continuously. Reduce the heat to low and simmer for 3 minutes, stirring until the sugar has dissolved. Add the lemon zest, then set aside to cool completely.

2 Pour the lemon mixture into a deep stainless-steel tray and cover with foil. Freeze for 2 hours. Remove the mixture from the freezer and use a fork to break up the ice crystals.

3 Meanwhile, place the whole unopened tin of condensed milk in a saucepan and cover with cold water. Bring to the boil, cover with a lid and cook for 2 hours, topping up the water if necessary as it evaporates. Carefully remove the tin from saucepan and leave it to cool. Open the tin and pour the condensed milk into a shallow bowl – it will now be brown and caramel flavoured.

4 Whip the cream in the bowl of an electric mixer with a whisk attachment until stiff peaks form. Add the clotted cream and whisk again until the mixture is thick. Swirl through the condensed milk with a spoon. Spoon the mixture into serving glasses or dishes. Place in the fridge for 1 hour.

5 Remove the fool from the fridge and scoop the granita over the top. Serve immediately.

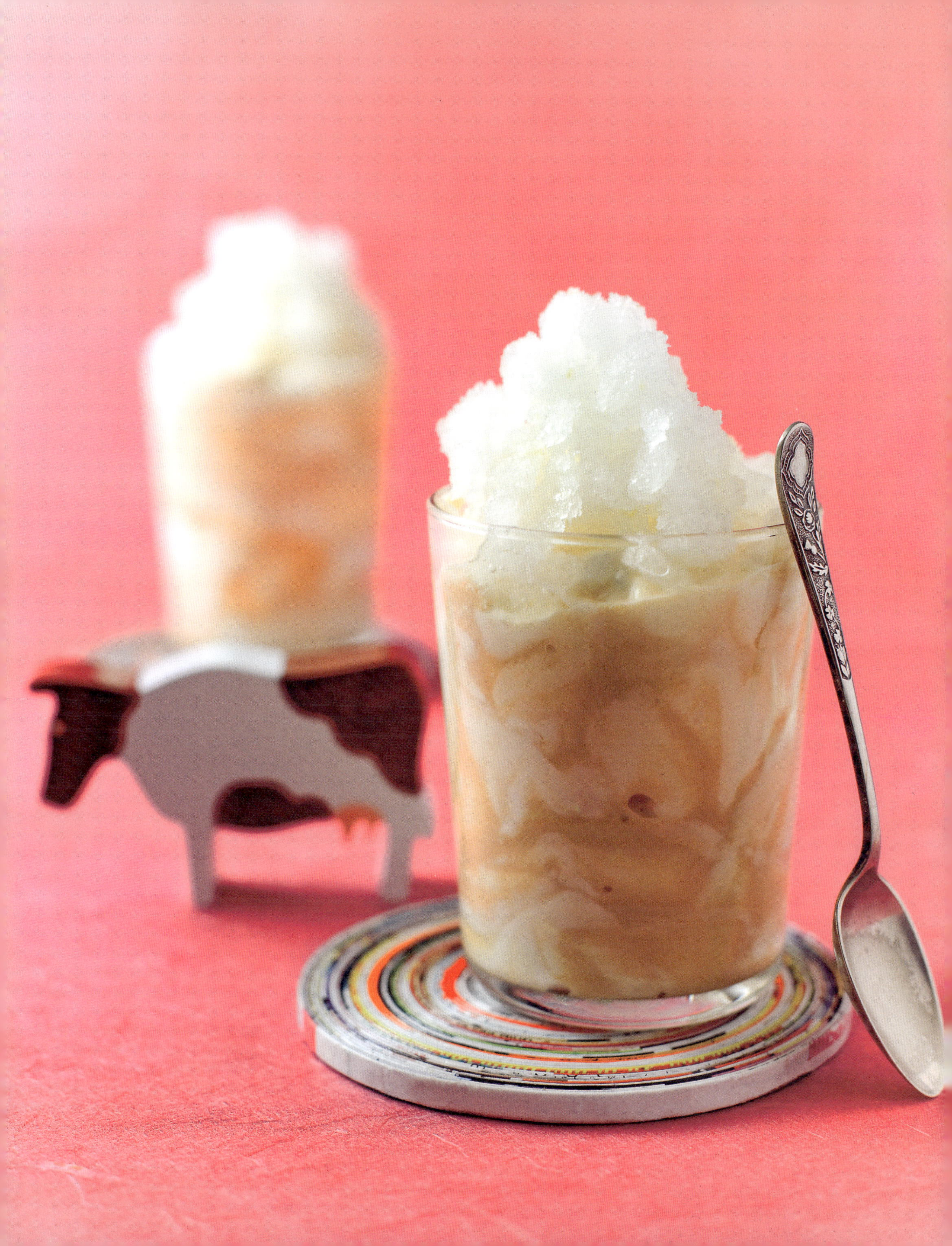

Did you know?

- For a vinaigrette, the ideal ratio of vinegar to oil is 1 part vinegar to 3 parts olive oil.
- Different flavoured vinegars include: white-wine vinegar, red-wine vinegar, balsamic, white balsamic condiment, rice, malt, cider, sherry and fruit vinegars.
- Different flavoured oils to use include: olive, avocado, sesame and varieties of nut and vegetable oils.

HEALTHY SALADS

There are so many delicious salads to try. Salads can be served cold, at room temperature, warm or hot. They can be part of a meal or meals in themselves. You can have salads for dessert (fruit salad – yum!). They can be made from an enormous range of ingredients, including lettuce, vegetables, herbs, pasta, noodles, rice, legumes, grains, seeds, nuts, eggs and fruit. Salads can include meat, poultry, seafood and cheese. Try experimenting with your favourite ingredients to create your own recipe.

Salads are often served with a dressing to add flavour and bind the ingredients together. Vinaigrettes are dressings made from a mixture of oil and an acidulant such as vinegar or citrus juice. Creamy dressings can be made from mayonnaise, yoghurt or sour cream.

Bread can be part of a salad, either soaked in the dressing to absorb and carry flavour, or added as crunchy croutons (such as in a classic Caesar salad) and crisp pita (used in the Lebanese salad fattoush) served on top.

Edible flowers make a pretty addition to a salad. Commonly used flowers are nasturtium, pansies, marigold, rose petals, violets and zucchini (courgette) flowers. Most herb flowers taste just like the leaves and add a pretty garnish to a salad. Just make sure any edible flowers you add to a salad have not been sprayed with pesticide.

Watermelon and feta salad

I loved school holidays down at the beach with all of my cousins. We had loads of fun. Life was so good and simple. We would go to the beach and have a massive day in the water, then come home in the afternoon and Mum would cut us up chilled watermelon, which we'd eat with juice running down our chins. We'd then back up the sweet flavour with a mouthful of salty, creamy feta. It was the best. This salad reminds me of those more relaxed times.

Serves 4

1.5 kg watermelon (about ¼ large)

200 g feta

a handful of mint leaves

1 lime

lime slices (optional), to serve

1 Remove the flesh of the watermelon from the rind and cut into bite-sized chunks. Place on a shallow serving platter or bowl and crumble the feta over the top. Scatter over the mint leaves, squeeze over some fresh lime juice and serve with lime slices to the side, if you like.

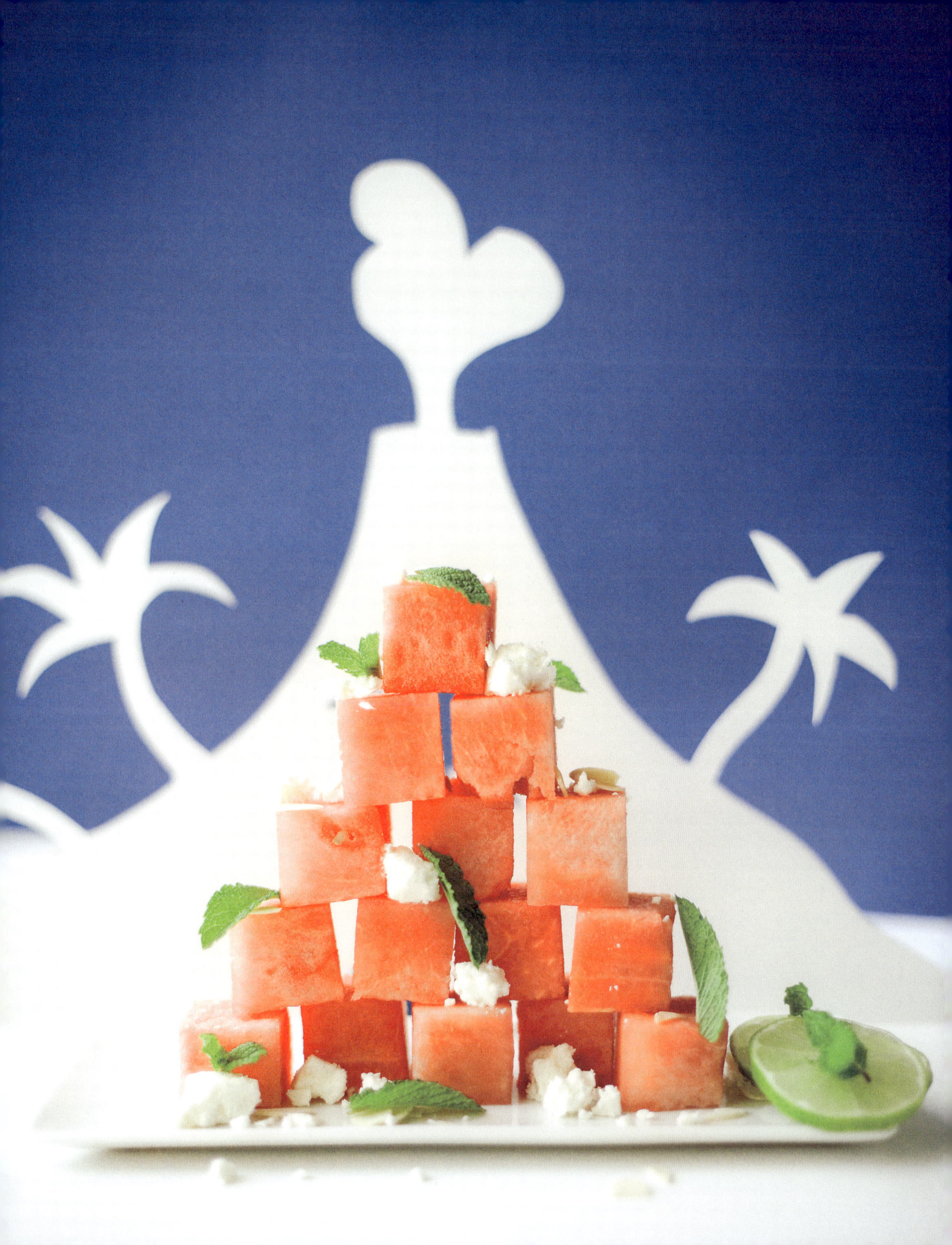

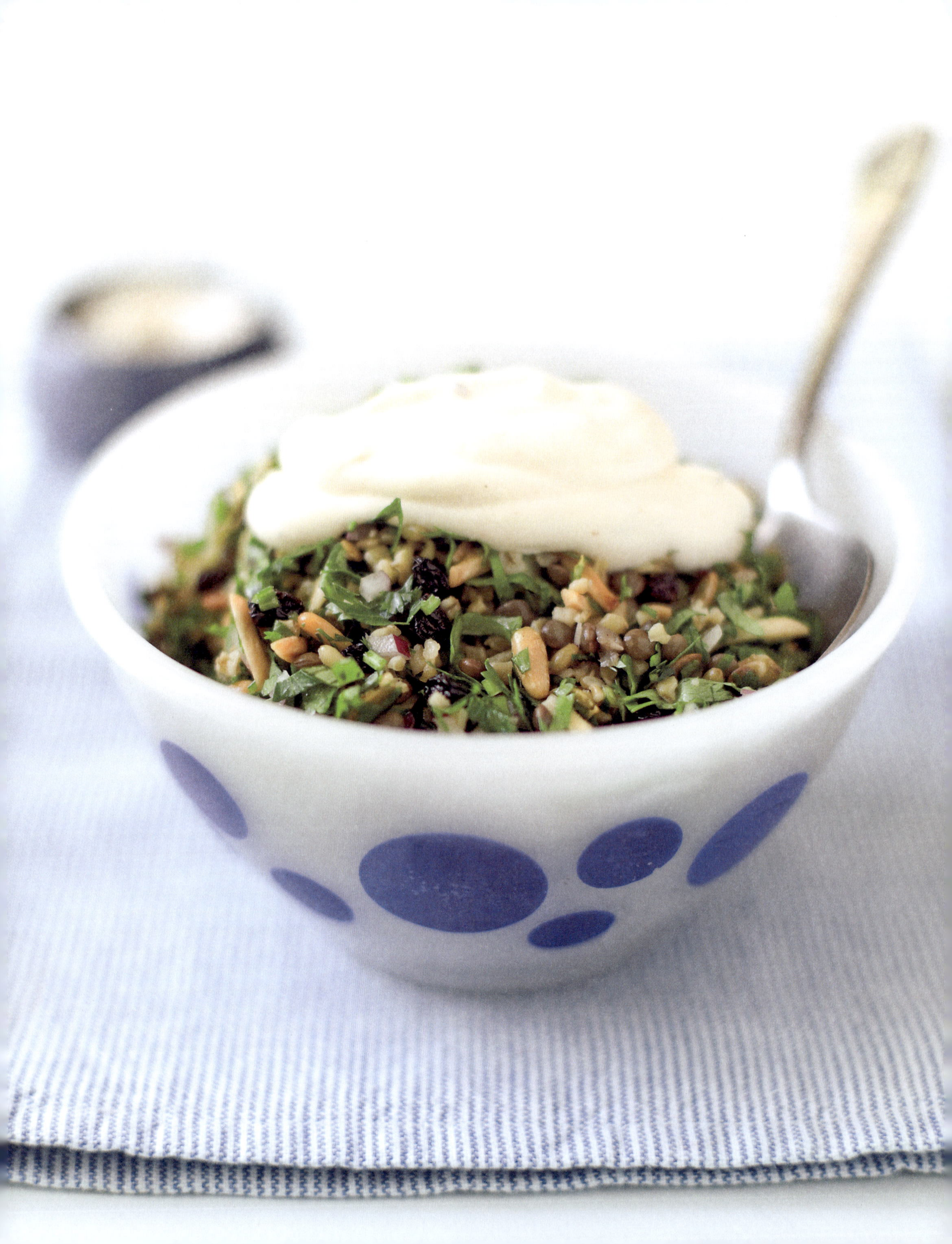

Cypriot grain salad

This recipe comes to you straight from the menu at my restaurant Hellenic Republic. Travis, my head chef, serves up hundreds of portions a night. We get inundated with requests for the recipe, so I thought it would be a good opportunity to share it here. It makes me cross when chefs won't share recipes. I think it's important to give and pass on.

Serves 8

1 cup (165 g) freekah (see page 202, or use burghul)

½ cup (100 g) green puy-style lentils

1 teaspoon cumin seeds

1 cup (280 g) natural Greek-style yoghurt

1 tablespoon honey

2 tablespoons pumpkin seeds

2 tablespoons slivered almonds

2 tablespoons pine nuts

1 cup (large handful) coriander leaves

1 cup (large handful) flat-leaf parsley leaves

½ red (Spanish) onion, finely chopped

2 tablespoons salted baby capers, rinsed

½ cup (75 g) currants

juice of 1 lemon

¼ cup (60 ml) extra virgin olive oil

sea salt and freshly ground black pepper

✱ **SPECIAL EQUIPMENT**
mortar and pestle
salad spinner

1 Bring two saucepans of water to the boil. Cook the freekah in one of the pans for 45 minutes or until just cooked. Drain well in a colander, rinse under cold running water and leave to cool. At the same time, cook the lentils in the second pan for 20 minutes or until just tender. Drain and rinse under cold running water, then set aside.

2 Meanwhile, place the cumin seeds in a small non-stick frying pan and cook over low heat for 1–2 minutes or until they smell fragrant and are lightly toasted. Remove the cumin seeds and grind with a mortar and pestle.

3 Mix the yoghurt, honey and cumin until combined. Cover with plastic film and set aside in the fridge.

4 Place the pumpkin seeds, almonds and pine nuts in a medium-sized non-stick frying pan and cook over low heat for 2 minutes or until they are lightly toasted. Remove from the pan and set aside.

5 Wash the coriander and parsley, then drain well and spin dry in a salad spinner. Roughly chop and set aside.

6 Place the pumpkin seeds, almonds, pine nuts, parsley, coriander, onion, capers, currants, lemon juice, olive oil, freekah and lentils in a bowl, then season to taste with salt and pepper and mix well. Place in a serving bowl and top with the cumin yoghurt.

7 Serve.

Roasted beetroot and yoghurt salad

I was fourteen years old when I first went to Greece. It was my first trip away from my mum and dad. They don't know this, but when I landed in Greece I was so scared and upset that I cried all night. I still don't know why – I guess I had to grow up. I still feel sad when I leave home, but there's always the thought of coming back, which makes me happy. During that initial trip to Greece, my Uncle Chris made this dish for me for the first time and I loved it. When I eat this now it reminds me of him. I love the fact that food not only feeds your body but nourishes your heart. I love my Uncle Chris and I know I'll see him again one day.

Serves 4

4 large beetroot (about 1 kg), leaves trimmed

1 tablespoon cumin seeds

2 tablespoons extra virgin olive oil

sea salt

1 cup (280 g) natural Greek-style yoghurt

freshly ground black pepper

* **SPECIAL EQUIPMENT**
  disposable kitchen gloves

1 Preheat the oven to 180°C fan-forced (200°C conventional).

2 Place each beetroot on a large piece of foil, then scatter with some of the cumin seeds, olive oil and salt. Wrap tightly to seal, then place on a baking tray and roast for 1½ hours or until tender when pierced with a skewer.

3 Leave the beetroot to cool slightly. Put on disposable kitchen gloves to protect your hands from staining, then gently rub off the skins; they should come away easily. Use a small, sharp knife to cut away the tops, then cut each beetroot into bite-sized pieces. Set aside to cool.

4 Place the yoghurt in a medium-sized bowl and gently fold the beetroot through. Season with salt and pepper and serve.

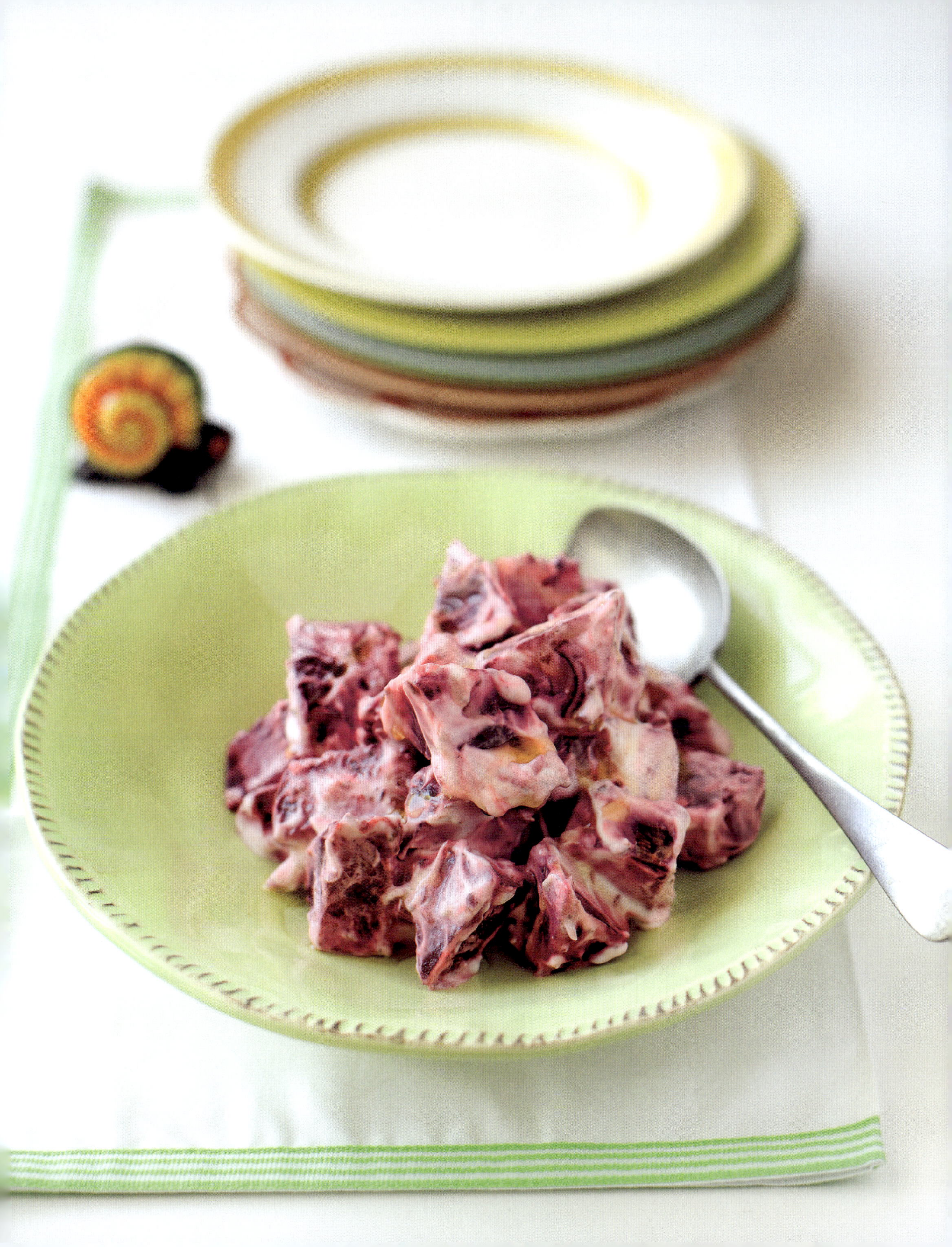

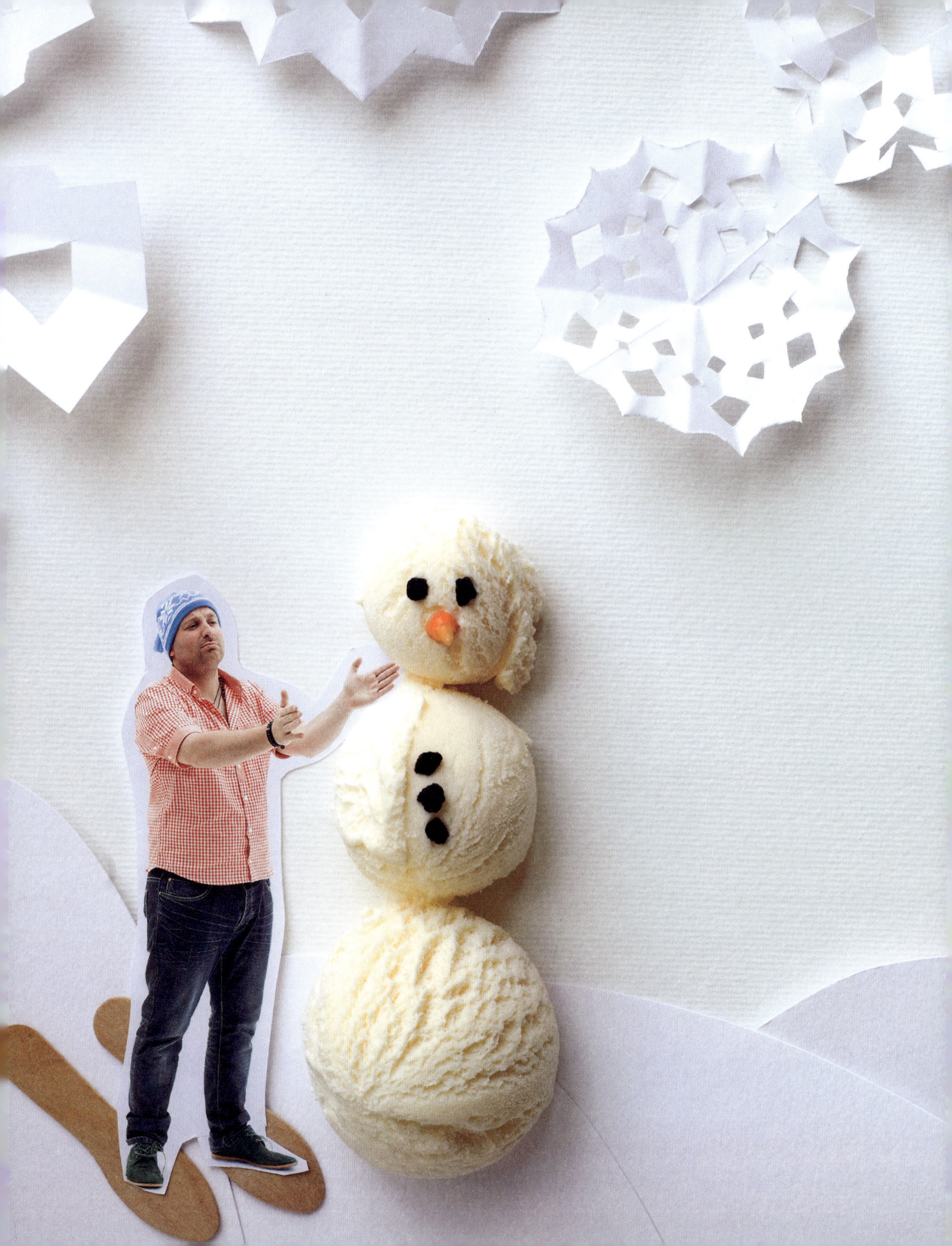

ICE CREAM

Before electric refrigeration, the first ice-cream churns used a mixture of salt and ice to freeze the custard base. Now, new ice-cream-making technology such as Pacojets can make ice creams and sorbets in a fraction of the time it takes using traditional methods. To make one serve takes just twenty seconds.

Ice cream is often made from a classic creme anglaise (custard) base, which is then churned in an ice-cream machine. When you make custard, you need to use a double boiler. This can simply be a heatproof bowl that sits on top of a saucepan of simmering water, or a double saucepan made especially for steaming. The custard cooks gently over the indirect heat provided by the simmering water underneath. It's important to make sure the bowl doesn't touch the water below or it will get too hot and the custard will curdle.

There are many types of ice cream. Semifreddo (meaning 'half cold' in Italian) is a semi-frozen dessert with a light mousse-like texture, made by adding whipped cream to a custard base. Gelato is the Italian version of ice cream. It has a lower fat content as it contains more milk than cream. Sorbet is similar to gelato, but doesn't contain any dairy products and is generally based on egg whites beaten with sugar. Turkish ice cream (called *dondurma*) is so hard and stretchy it needs to be eaten on a plate with a knife and fork! Indians make a form of ice cream called *kulfi*. It has a dense texture and takes longer to melt. Popular flavours include saffron, mango, rose, pistachio and cardamom.

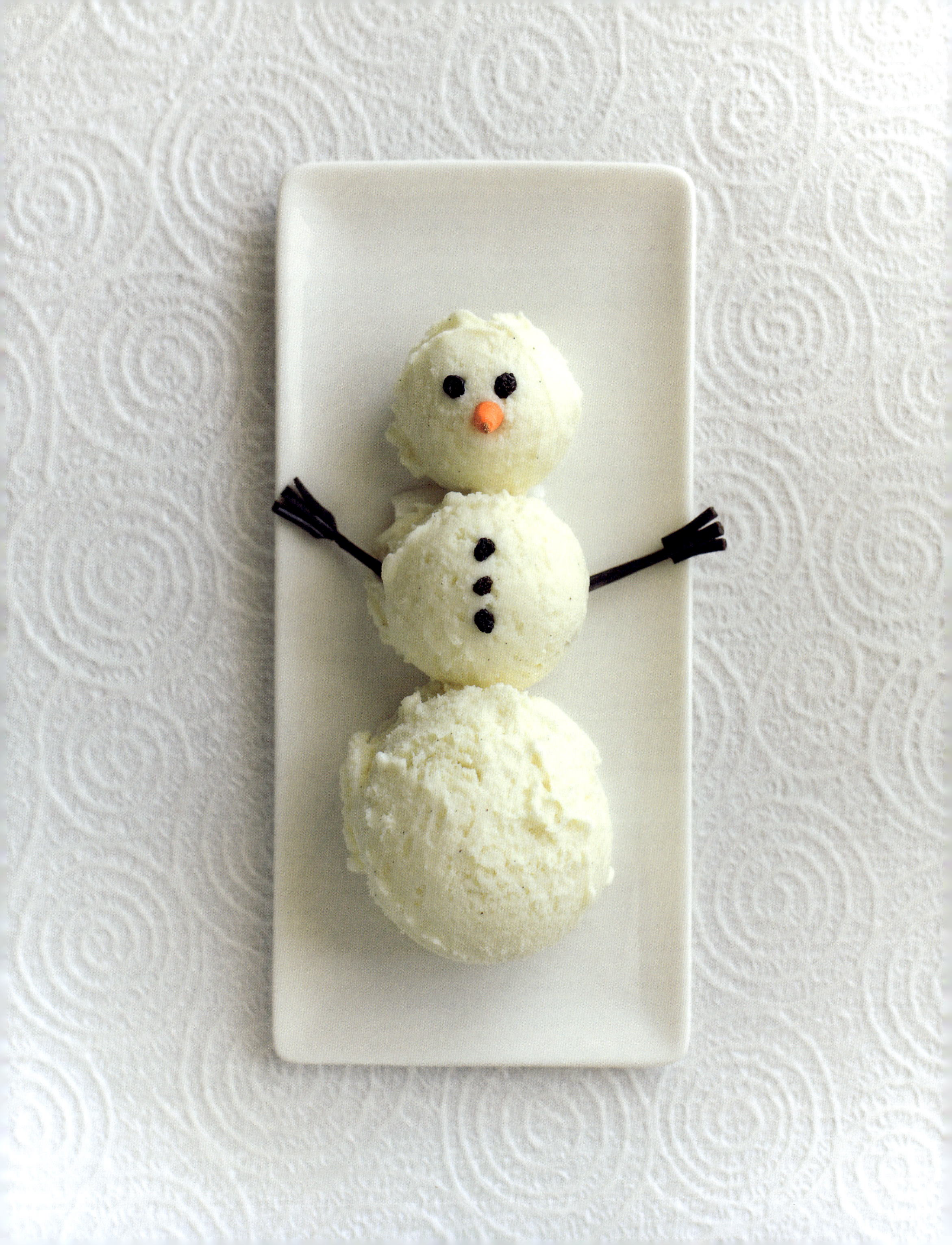

Vanilla-bean ice cream

There is nothing better than the flavour of real vanilla bean – you cannot compare it to the artificial stuff. As a kid I would put vanilla-bean ice cream in a bowl, let it go soft and then whip it up with a spoon to give it a soft-serve consistency. To make an ice-cream snowman (see opposite), you will need some currants for the eyes, the very end tip of a skinny carrot for the nose and liquorice straps for the arms.

Makes 1 litre

2 cups (500 ml) thickened cream

2 cups (500 ml) milk

150 g caster sugar

2 vanilla pods, split lengthways, seeds scraped

12 egg yolks

✱ SPECIAL EQUIPMENT
hand-held electric beaters
sugar thermometer (optional, see page 203)
fine-mesh sieve
ice-cream machine

1 Place the cream, milk, sugar and vanilla pods and scraped seeds in a heavy-based saucepan, then heat over medium heat until the mixture just starts to simmer. Remove the pan from the heat and set aside for 15 minutes to allow the flavour of the vanilla pods to infuse the mixture, then remove and discard the vanilla pods.

2 Use hand-held electric beaters to whisk the egg yolks in a heatproof bowl, then slowly whisk in the cream mixture.

3 Place the bowl over a saucepan of simmering water on medium–high heat (make sure that the bottom of the bowl does not come into contact with the water as this will scramble the egg yolks). Stir the mixture until it coats the back of a wooden spoon (or reaches 72°C on a sugar thermometer).

4 Remove the mixture from the heat, then strain it through a fine-mesh sieve into a bowl. Cover the surface closely with plastic film to stop a skin from forming on the surface, then cool in the fridge.

5 Churn the mixture in an ice-cream machine following the manufacturer's instructions.

6 Serve scoops of the ice cream in bowls. The ice cream will keep in an airtight container in the freezer for up to 1 month.

Pancake-and-maple-syrup-ripple ice cream

I love eating pancakes and maple syrup with ice cream, so I thought, 'Why not incorporate them into one dish?'. So I did. This pancake recipe makes thick pancakes. You can make them thinner if you prefer by adding a little more milk to the batter. For pancake lovers, you can always make another batch or two of the pancakes to serve with the ice cream, as I've done here (see opposite).

Makes 1.2 litres

1 quantity Vanilla-bean Ice Cream (see page 69)

½ cup (125 ml) maple syrup, plus extra for drizzling

PANCAKES

1 cup (150 g) plain flour

1 teaspoon baking powder

¼ teaspoon salt

2 tablespoons white sugar

2 eggs

½ cup (125 ml) milk

olive oil spray

* **SPECIAL EQUIPMENT**
  ice-cream machine

1 To make the pancakes, mix the flour, baking powder, salt, sugar, eggs and milk in a medium-sized bowl until combined. Set aside to rest for 1 hour.

2 Place a small non-stick frying pan over medium heat and spray lightly with cooking spray. Using a ¼ cup (60 ml-capacity) ladle, pour a little mixture into the pan to make a pancake about 10 cm in diameter. Cook the batter on one side for 2 minutes until bubbles start to form on the surface. Carefully and quickly flip the pancake over and cook on the other side for 1 minute or until golden brown.

3 Remove the pancake from the pan and continue with the remaining pancake batter. Set aside to cool (Makes 6.)

4 Cut the cooled pancakes into small dice.

5 Make the vanilla-bean ice cream following the instructions on page 69. Halfway through churning, fold the diced pancakes and maple syrup through the ice-cream mixture. Continue to churn, then freeze to set firm.

6 Serve scoops of the ice cream drizzled with extra maple syrup, with extra pancakes alongside, if desired. (The ice cream will keep in an airtight container in the freezer for up to 1 month.)

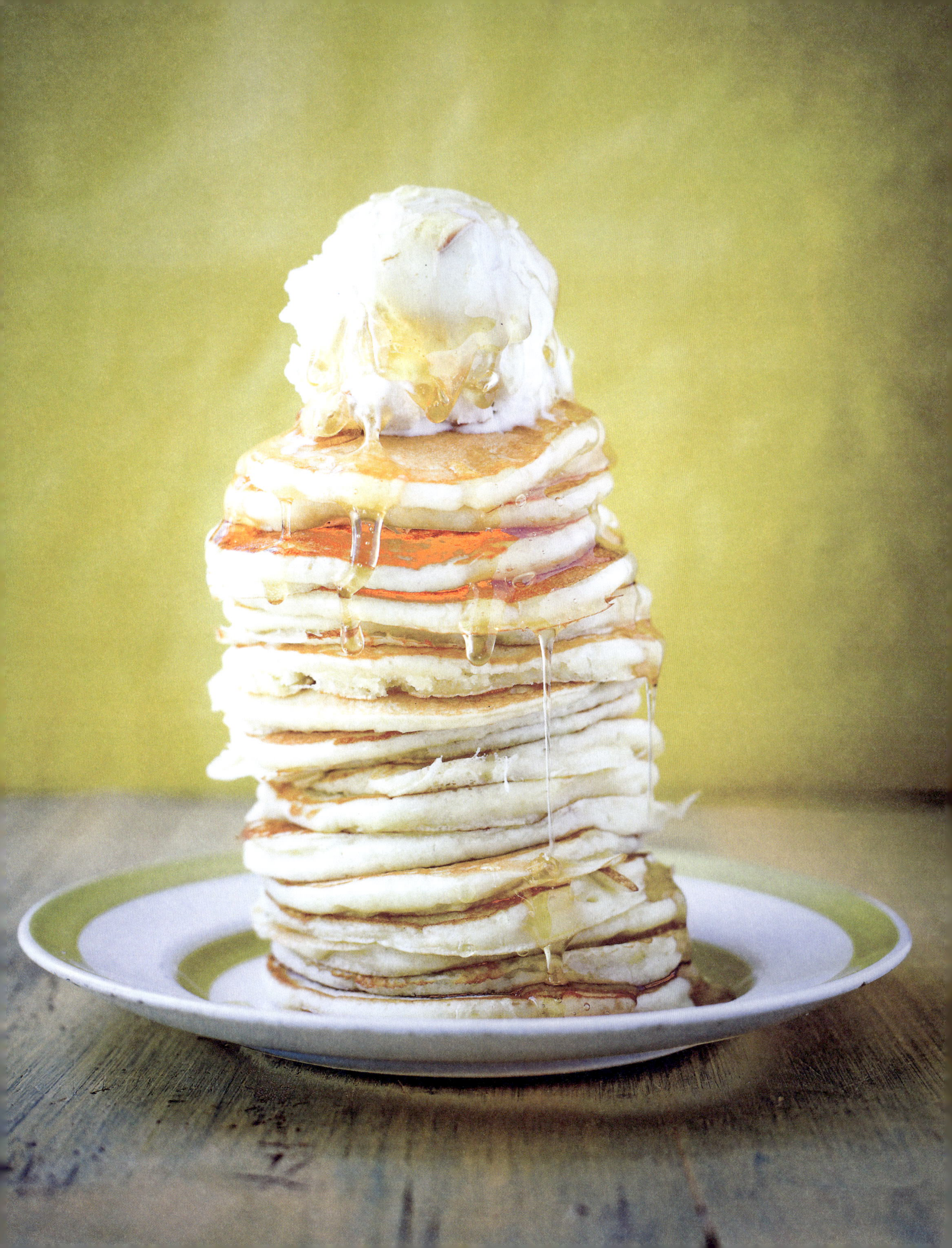

Raspberry ice cream

This recipe was given to me by Caroline Velik, who I believe is one of Australia's best food stylists. She made it for me, and I thought it was so yummy I had to include it in this book. It's easy to make because you don't need an ice-cream machine. Caroline also tested all my recipes in this book. Thanks Caroline – you're a legend! This is more like a sorbet than a traditional ice cream, because it does not have a custard base, but the end result still has a great ice-cream-like texture. Some people don't like the texture of raspberry seeds in sorbet. To get rid of the seeds, use double the amount of raspberries (500 g), puree them in a blender, then press the puree through a fine-mesh sieve and discard the seeds.

Makes 1 litre

250 g raspberries

½ cup (110 g) caster sugar

1 egg white

* **SPECIAL EQUIPMENT**
  electric mixer

1 Place the raspberries, sugar and egg white in the bowl of an electric mixer with a whisk attachment and whisk on high speed for 5 minutes or until the mixture more than doubles in volume.

2 Transfer the mixture to a 1 litre-capacity container and freeze for 4 hours (or overnight if possible).

3 Serve scoops of the ice cream in bowls or cups. (The ice cream will keep in an airtight container in the freezer for up to 1 month.)

Did you know?

- In ancient times, snow was mixed with fruit juice and enjoyed as a cool treat.

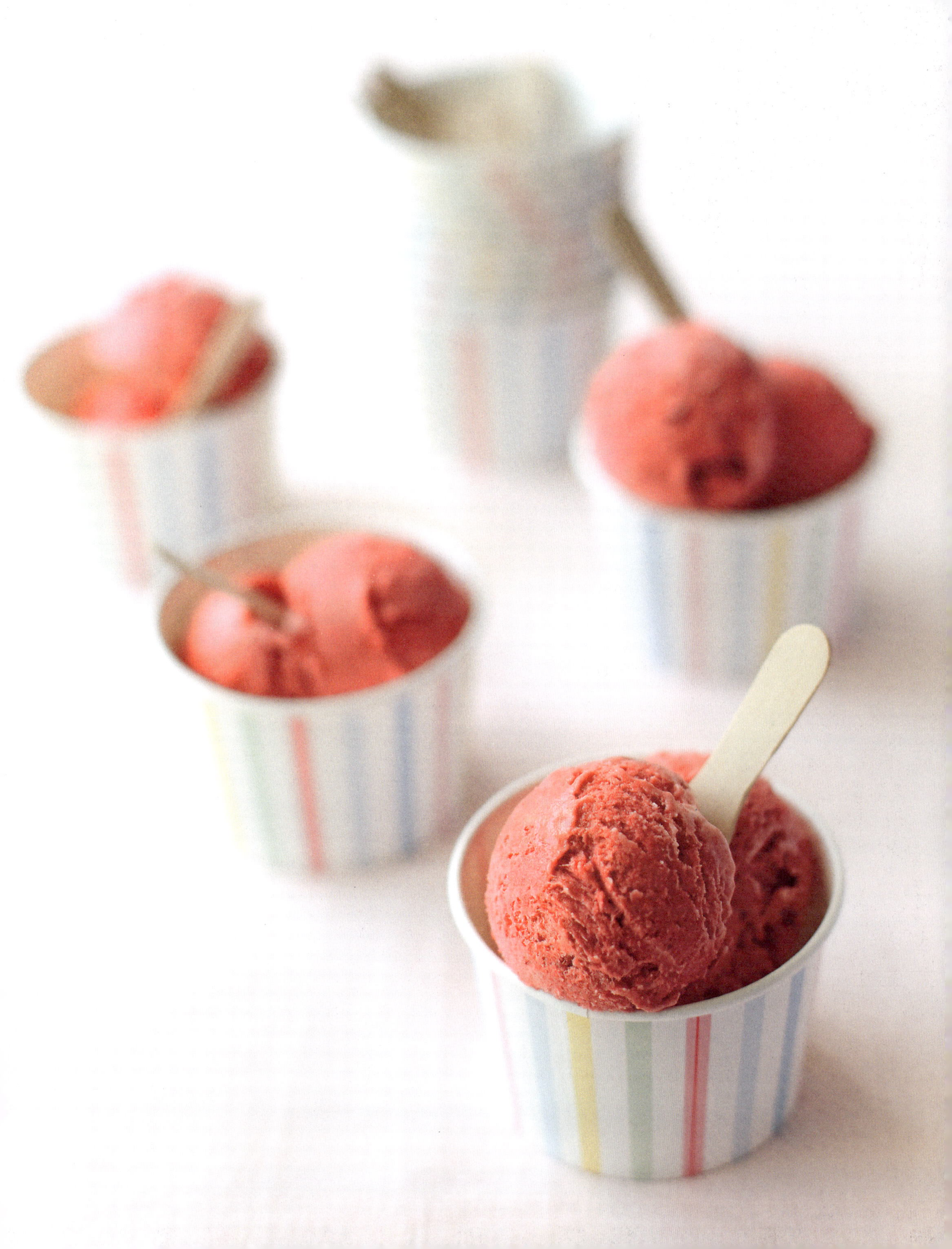

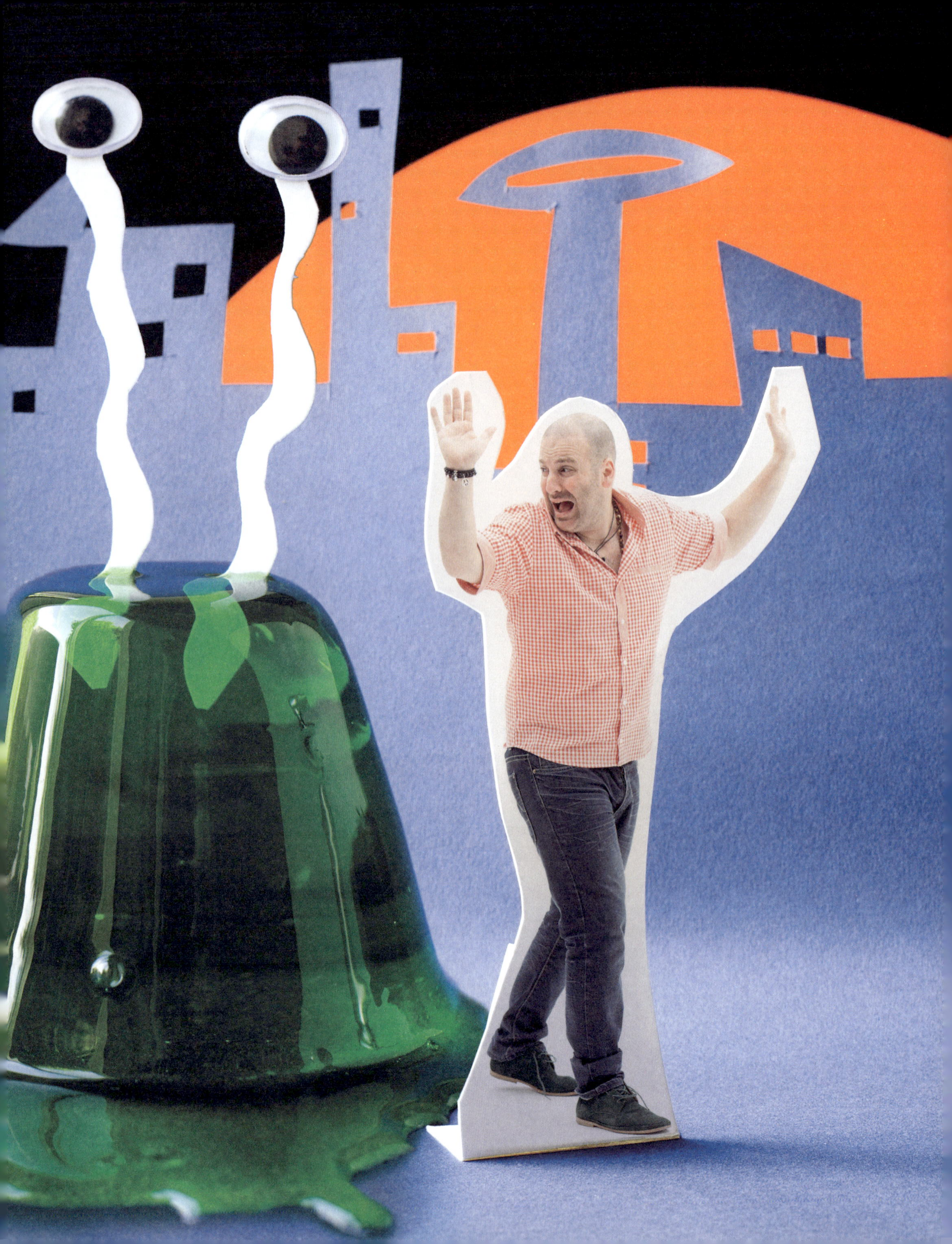

Jelly

Jelly was first made by the ancient Egyptians. Savoury jellies were once just as popular as sweet jellies. Jelly is soft and wobbly. It is made by setting a liquid with gelatine. Gelatine is made from collagen, a protein derived from animals. It acts as a thickener. Dried or powdered gelatine is most commonly used to make jelly, as it's readily available from supermarkets. However, you can also buy leaf gelatine, used by professionals to create jellies with a smooth, clearer consistency. Leaf gelatine is usually not available from supermarkets, but can be found in specialist cooking shops. Gelatine is also used to make foods such as marshmallows, panna cotta and ice cream.

There are many ways to create interesting-looking jellies, such as using decorative moulds, creating multicoloured layers (see page 79) or suspending other ingredients in the jelly, such as marshmallows or fruit (grapes work especially well). Adding more gelatine will increase the stability of the jelly.

Some fruit cannot be used to make jelly. For example, the enzymes in paw paw, pineapple and kiwi fruit prevent jelly from setting.

The world's biggest jelly was made at Blackpool Zoo in the United Kingdom in 1997. The jelly was almost one metre tall by seven metres wide, and took about twelve hours to set with a blast chiller.

Milk jelly with fudgy chocolate brownies

Milk and chocolate – is there any better combination? The key to this dish is making sure the brownies are soft and gooey and the milk jelly is just set. This recipe takes yummy childhood flavours and turns them into a sophisticated yet achievable dessert. My jelly monster mother and babies (see opposite) have wobbly eyes from the craft shop, just for fun. If you want to make jelly monsters like I have, please remember not to eat the eyes!

Serves 6

700 ml milk

90 g caster sugar

1 vanilla pod, split lengthways, seeds scraped

6½ leaves gelatine (gold strength, see page 202)

FUDGY CHOCOLATE BROWNIES

250 g unsalted butter, chopped

500 g caster sugar

90 g dutch-process cocoa powder (see page 202), plus extra for dusting

5 eggs

1 cup (150 g) plain flour

½ teaspoon baking powder

175 g dark couverture chocolate buttons (see page 202)

125 g macadamias (optional), roughly chopped

✱ SPECIAL EQUIPMENT
6 × 125 ml-capacity jelly or dariole moulds (see page 202)
slice tin (26 cm × 18 cm)

1 Heat the milk, sugar and vanilla pod and scraped seeds in a small saucepan over medium heat. Remove the vanilla pod and discard. Transfer the milk mixture to a heatproof jug.

2 Soak the gelatine leaves in cold water for a few minutes to soften. Squeeze to remove excess water. Add the softened gelatine to the milk mixture and stir to dissolve.

3 Pour the milk and gelatine mixture into six 125 ml-capacity jelly or dariole moulds. Refrigerate overnight or until set.

4 Meanwhile, to make the chocolate brownies, preheat the oven to 160°C fan-forced (180° conventional). Grease and line a 26 cm × 18 cm slice tin with baking paper.

5 Melt the butter in a medium-sized saucepan over medium heat. As soon as the butter has melted, remove the pan from the heat and add the sugar and cocoa. Mix well with a wooden spoon. Add the eggs, one at a time, and beat well after adding each one.

6 Sift the flour and baking powder and add to the butter mixture. Fold in the chocolate and macadamias (if using).

7 Pour the brownie batter into the prepared tin and bake for 35 minutes; the brownie will be just set and still a little gooey in the middle. Leave to cool in the tin. Dust with extra cocoa, then cut into pieces.

8 To unmould the jellies, briefly and carefully dip each mould into a bowl of hot water, then turn upside down onto a small serving plate and shake gently to release the jelly. Serve each jelly with a piece of brownie.

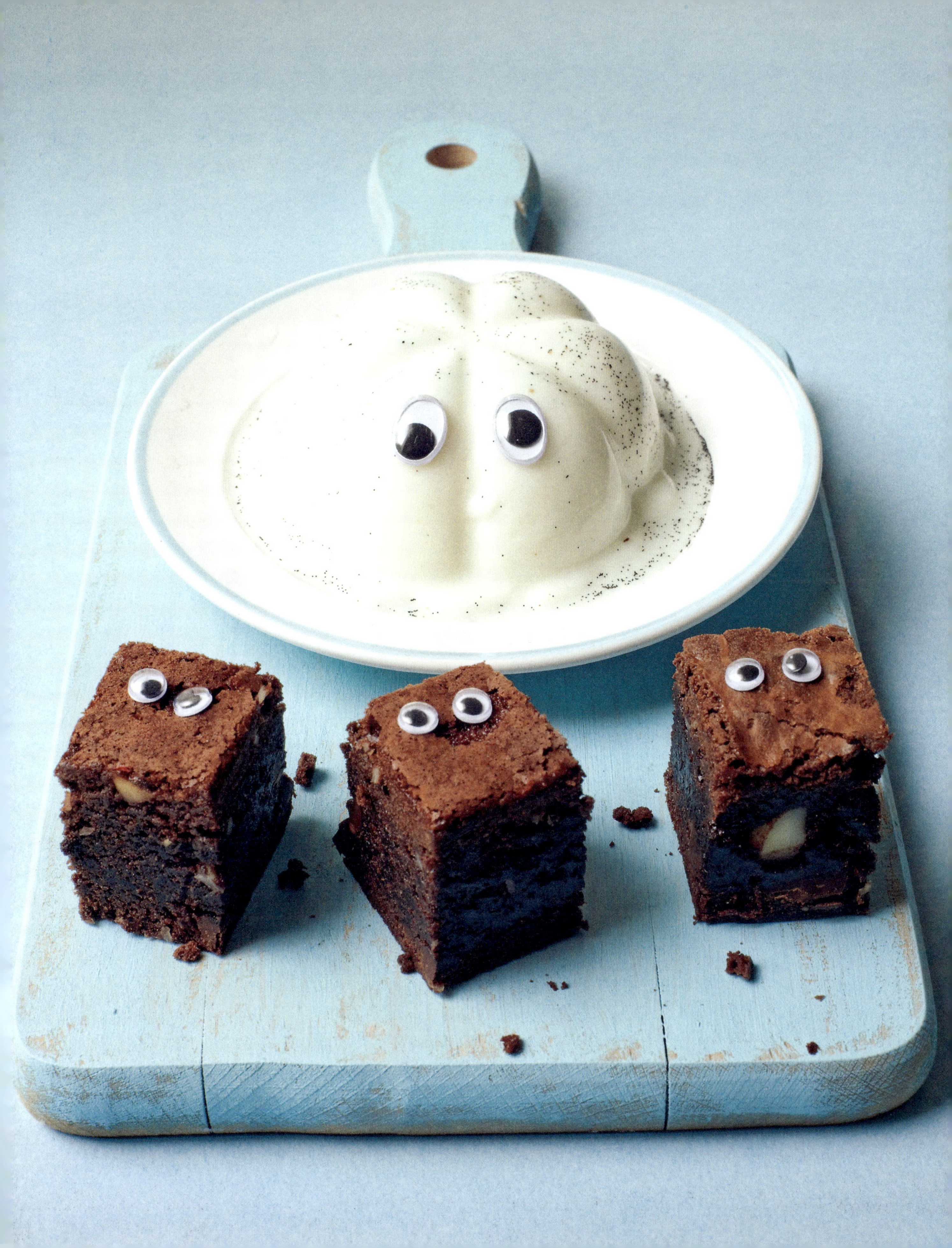

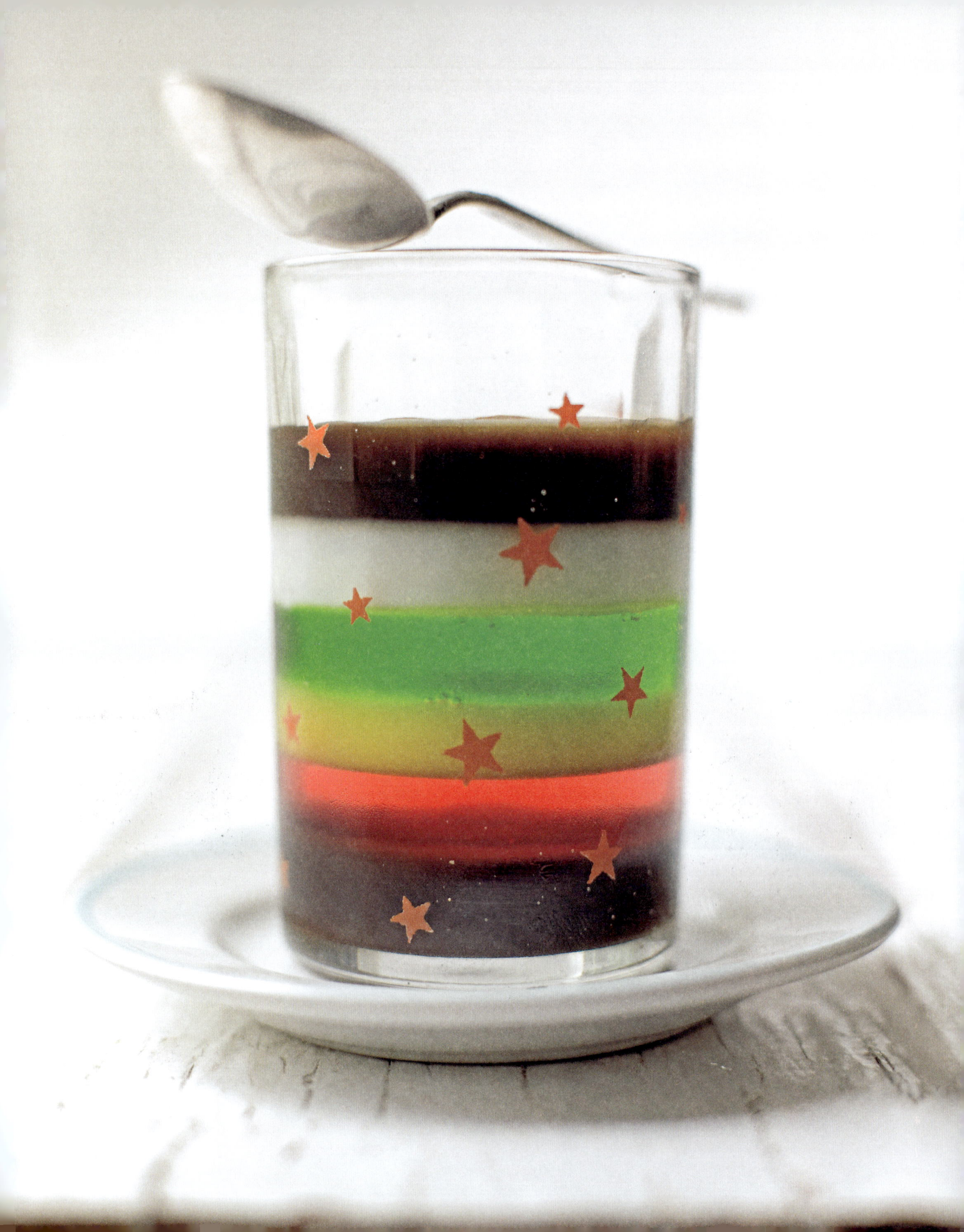

Liquorice allsorts jelly

I was around ten years old when my dad got cancer. I remember quite vividly that he loved to eat liquorice during his chemotherapy, and I loved to eat it with him. It's funny how food reminds you of so many good times but also the tough times. I hated to see my dad suffering, but that's what happens sometimes in life. Experiences like this remind us what's important.

Serves 6

1 cup (250 ml) strawberry jelly (use ½ packet jelly crystals and make up mixture according to packet directions)

1 cup (250 ml) lime jelly (use ½ packet jelly crystals and make up mixture according to packet directions)

1 cup (250 ml) Passionfruit Jelly (see page 80)

1 cup (250 ml) Milk Jelly (see page 76)

LIQUORICE JELLY

8 pieces (100 g) soft black liquorice, cut into small pieces

2 cups (500 ml) water

⅓ cup (75 g) white sugar

2 teaspoons vanilla extract

a few drops of black food colouring (optional)

6 gelatine leaves (gold strength, see page 202)

✱ SPECIAL EQUIPMENT
  fine-mesh sieve
  6 × 250-ml capacity tall glasses

1 To make the liquorice jelly, place the liquorice and water in a small saucepan over low heat and cook for 10 minutes, pressing down on the liquorice with a wooden spoon to extract the flavour. Remove the pan from the heat and strain the liquid through a fine-mesh sieve over a bowl to remove and discard any remaining solids. Mix the sugar, vanilla and food colouring (if using) into the liquid.

2 Soak the gelatine leaves in a bowl of cold water for a few minutes to soften. Squeeze to remove excess water. Add the softened gelatine to the liquorice mixture and stir to dissolve.

3 Make the strawberry and lime jelly following the instructions on the packet.

4 To assemble, carefully pour 2 tablespoons of the warmed liquorice jelly into 6 tall glasses to form a 1–2 cm-deep layer (depending on the size of your glass). Leave to set in the fridge for 1 hour. When set, add 2 tablespoons of the warmed strawberry jelly mixture to each glass to make the next layer. Set in fridge again for 1 hour. For the next layer, add 2 tablespoons of the warmed passionfruit jelly. Set in the fridge for 1 hour. Next add 2 tablespoons of the warmed lime jelly to each glass to form the green layer and set in the fridge for 2 hours. Add 2 tablespoons of the warmed milk jelly to form the white layer, then set in the fridge for 2 hours. When this is set, add a final layer of warmed liquorice jelly.

5 Refrigerate the liquorice allsorts jellies for at least 2 hours to set the final layer.

6 Serve.

Passionfruit jelly

I especially love the tartness and sweetness of homemade passionfruit jelly. It might sound strange, but place some of this jelly on top of a freshly shucked oyster and you'll discover a perfectly delicious combination of flavours and textures. Passionfruit skin is quite tough and can be difficult to cut, so I suggest you carefully use a serrated knife to cut the passionfruit in half. Push the juice through a fine-mesh sieve with the back of a large metal spoon to remove the seeds. Alternatively, use two 170 g tins passionfruit pulp and strain to yield 200 ml juice.

Serves 4

3 teaspoons gelatine powder

½ cup (125 ml) boiling water

200 ml strained passionfruit pulp (from about 14 passionfruit)

1 cup (250 ml) strained fresh orange juice

⅓ cup (75 g) caster sugar, plus extra if needed

raspberries (optional), to serve

✱ SPECIAL EQUIPMENT
4 × 140 ml-capacity jelly moulds

1 Whisk the gelatine and water until the gelatine has dissolved. Place the passionfruit pulp and orange juice in a small saucepan over low heat and warm, then add the sugar and gelatine mixture and stir to combine. Taste the mixture and check if you need to sweeten it with extra sugar. Remove the pan from the heat and pour the mixture into a heatproof jug.

2 Divide the jelly mixture among four 140 ml-capacity jelly moulds and refrigerate for 3 hours or until set.

3 To unmould the jellies, briefly and carefully dip the moulds into a bowl of hot water, then turn upside down onto small serving plates and shake gently to release the jelly. Serve with raspberries, if you like.

Did you know?

- Jelly does not wobble under water.

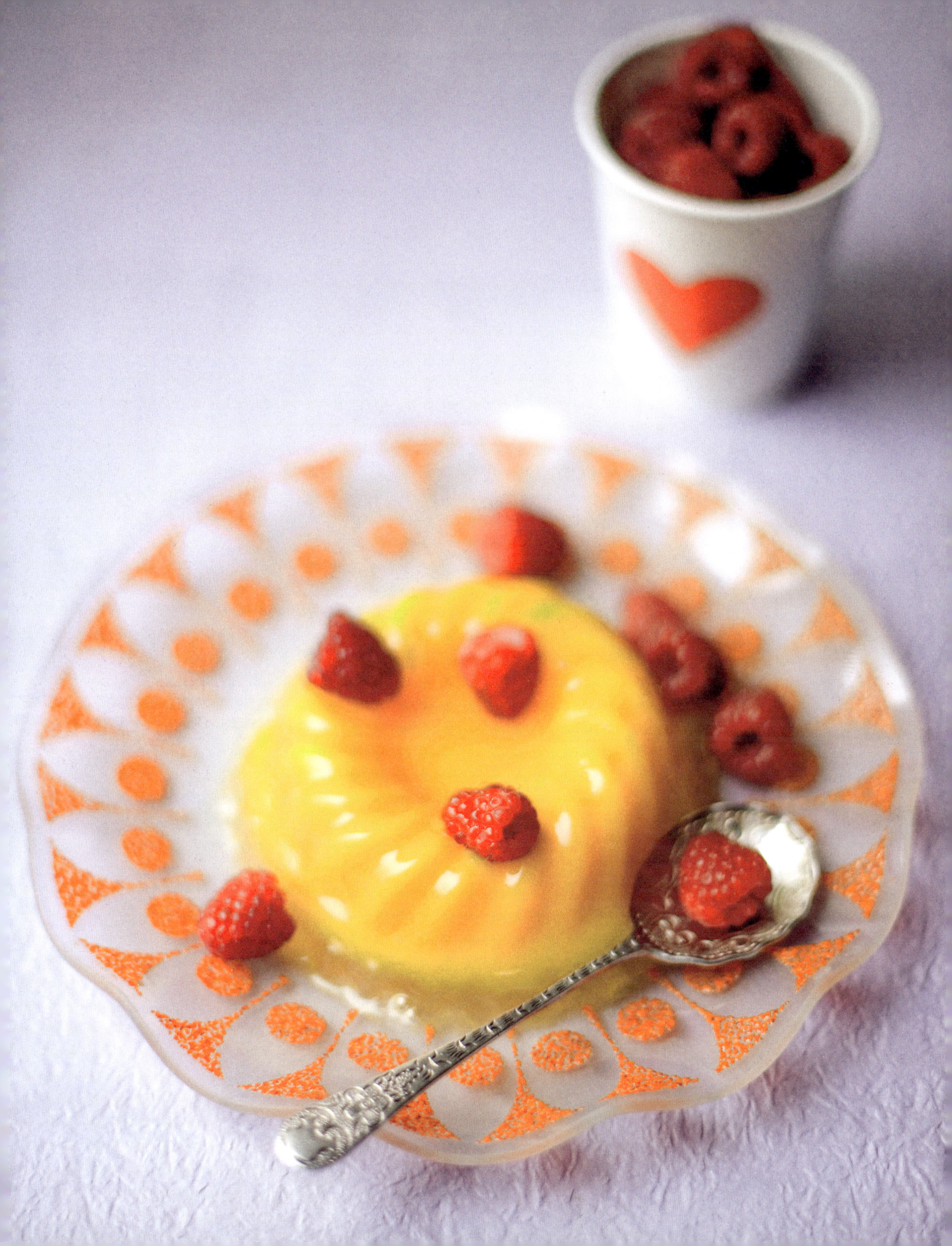

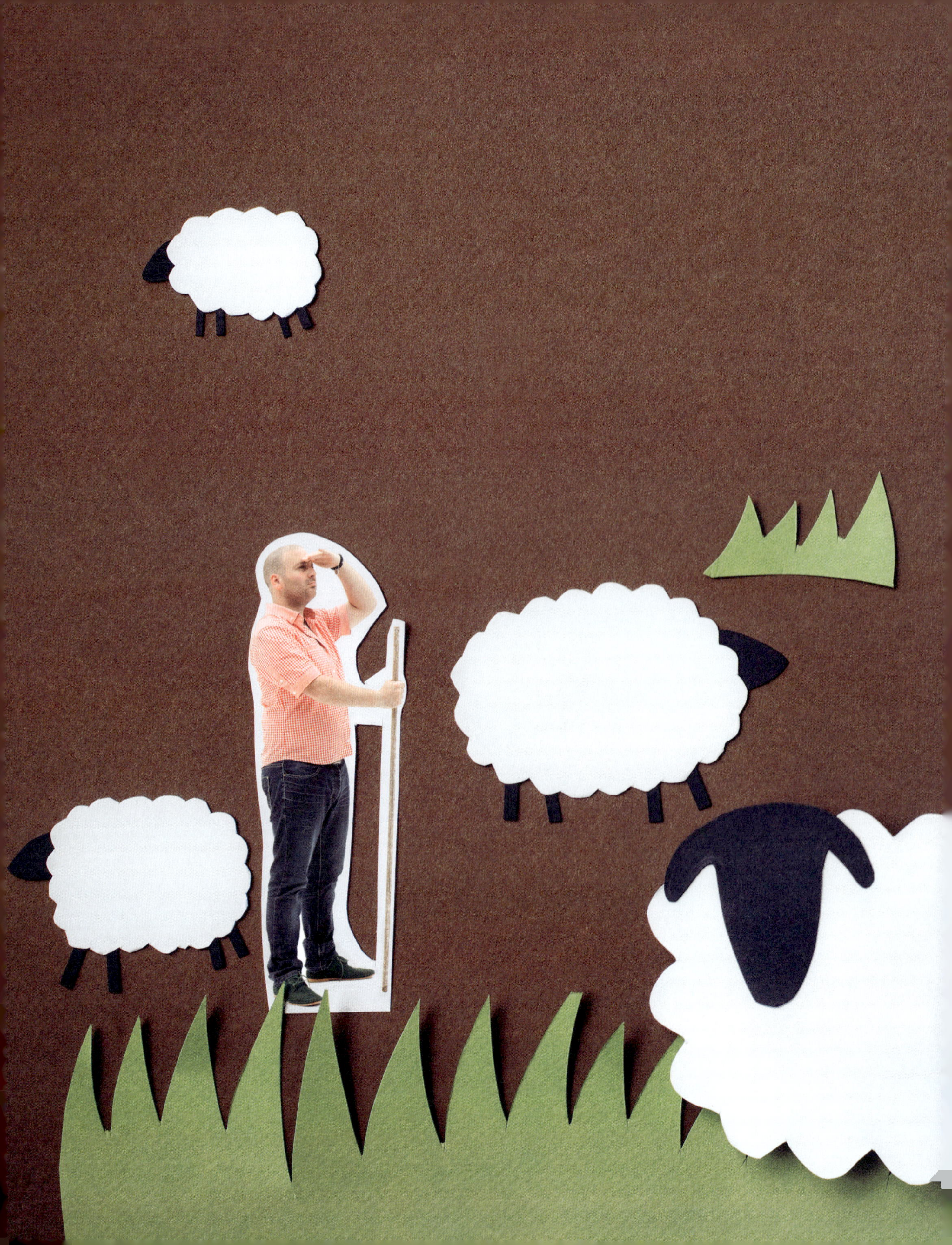

LAMB

Sheep were among the first animals to be domesticated. Lamb is the name for meat from a sheep that is less than one year old and mutton is the name used for a sheep that is more than two years old. Two-tooth is the name for sheep between one and two years of age. Saltbush lambs have been allowed to graze on saltbush. The meat from these sheep has a particularly delicious flavour. Different breeds of sheep are used for meat than those used for wool.

Lamb is sorted into three main cuts: forequarter (neck, shoulder, front leg, upper ribs), hindquarter (rear legs and hip) and loin (which includes the ribs in between). Lamb contains the lowest amount of cholesterol of all red meats. There are many different ways to cook lamb. Grill the most tender cuts from the loin, including backstraps, fillets, loin chops and cutlets. Roast a leg of lamb and serve it from rare to well done, depending on your preference. Butterflied legs of lamb (legs that have had the bone removed and been opened out for stuffing and rolling) are quicker to roast because they have no bone and can also be grilled or barbecued. Racks of lamb are quick and impressive to roast, too (see page 88) and are very easy to carve into same-sized portions.

Forequarter cuts can be a bit tougher so are best cooked slowly by braising, stewing or slow roasting. Lamb shanks, which are cut from the upper part of the legs, are also best when cooked slowly as this makes the meat seriously tender. Lamb can also be minced and made into meatballs and burger patties.

Did you know?

- Sheep have a natural tendency to follow the leader, which makes them easy to herd.
- They are ruminants, which means their stomachs are divided into four parts.
- Sheep can recognise individual human voices and remember them for years.

Lamb doner kebabs

Eating with your fingers is such a great way to enjoy food. This dish is easy, cheap and quick to make. When I was at high school, I'd eat leftover kebabs for lunch. I can remember me and my mates hanging around the south lounge at Mazenod College, and most of us would be eating something multicultural and flavoursome. I guess that's why food is so great – it represents different nationalities, religions and histories. Regardless of where we come from, we all have to eat.

Serves 4–6

1 onion, peeled

1 clove garlic, peeled

1 fresh long red chilli, chopped

olive oil, for cooking

2 tablespoons tomato paste

1 teaspoon ground cumin

1 teaspoon sweet paprika

1 teaspoon ground allspice

500 g minced lamb

2 tablespoons chopped flat-leaf parsley

1 cup (70 g) dried breadcrumbs

finely grated zest of 2 lemons

1 tablespoon Dijon mustard

1 egg, beaten

sea salt

Pita Bread (see page 10 or use purchased), Hummus (see page 31) and Cypriot Grain Salad (optional, see page 63), to serve

* **SPECIAL EQUIPMENT**
  food processor

1 Place the onion, garlic and chilli in a food processor and blend until finely chopped.

2 Heat a large frying pan over medium heat, then add a splash of olive oil and cook until the onion mixture is soft. Add the tomato paste, cumin, paprika and allspice and cook for 1 minute. Remove the mixture from the heat and set aside to cool.

3 Place the minced lamb, parsley, breadcrumbs, lemon zest, mustard, egg and 2 teaspoons salt in a large mixing bowl. Mix well. Add the cooled onion mixture and mix well to combine.

4 Form ¼ cup (3 tablespoonfuls) of the mixture into 5 cm-long ovals and set aside.

5 Heat a large non-stick frying pan (or barbecue grill plate) over high heat until hot. Brush the meatballs with a little olive oil and grill for 5–6 minutes on each side or until cooked through.

6 Serve with pita bread, hummus and Cypriot grain salad (if using).

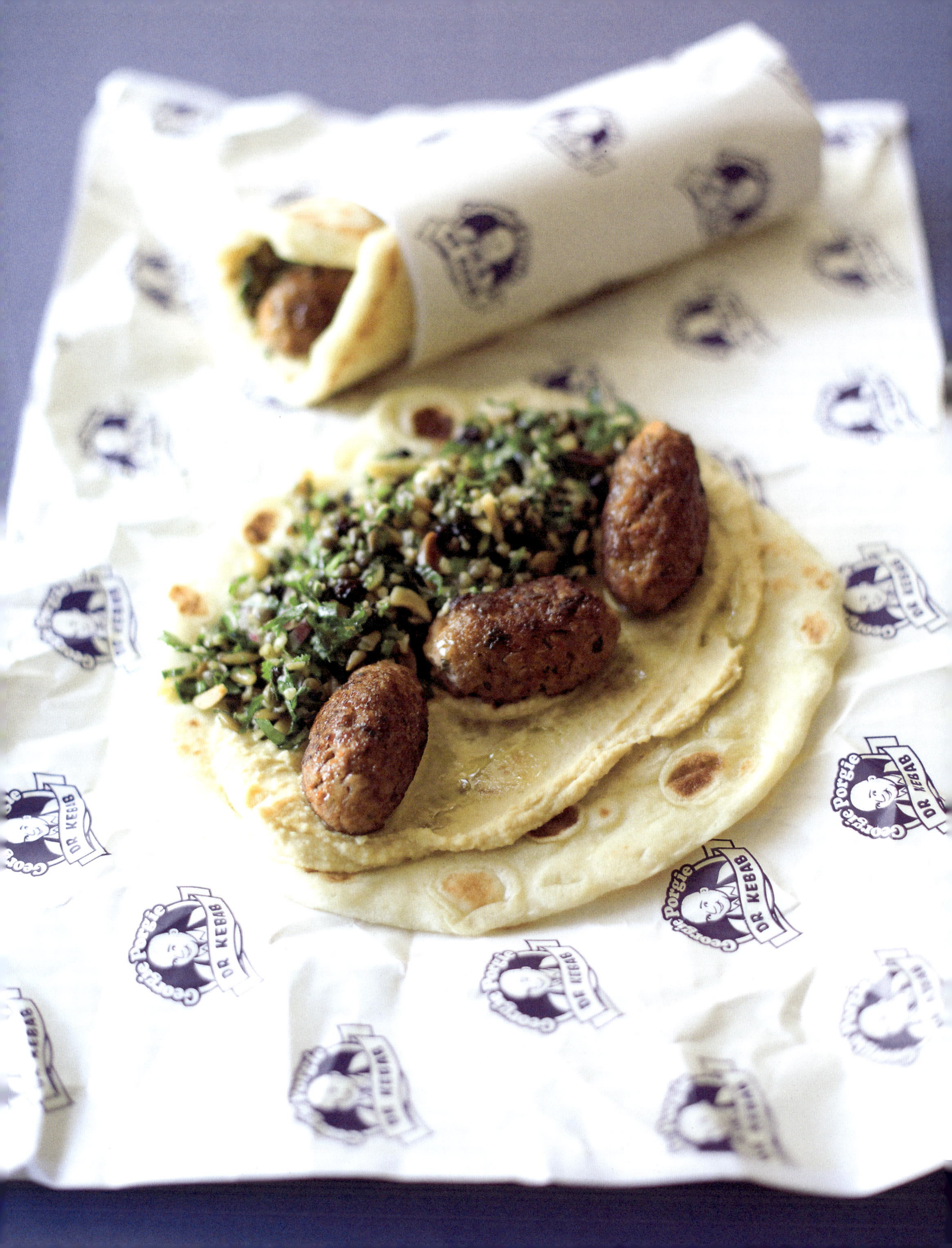
Georgie Porgie
DR KEBAB

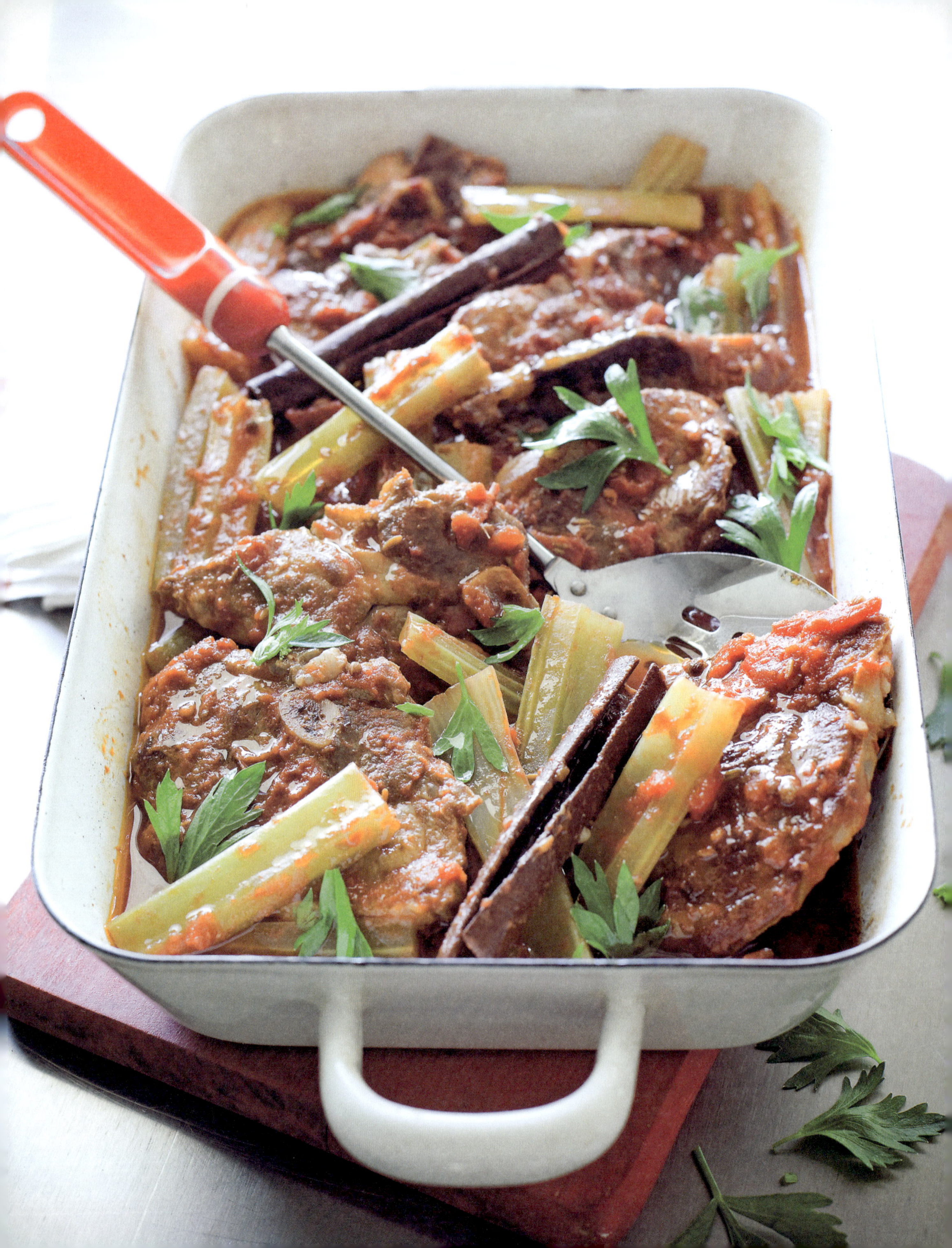

Mum's slow-cooked lamb with celery

Kids: don't take your parents' food for granted. As a kid I would sometimes complain about my mum's cooking but now I can't get enough of it. This dish is so good and the leftovers taste even better the next day.

Serves 4

- ¼ cup (60 ml) olive oil
- 8 large outer sticks celery, cut into 5 cm lengths
- 8 lamb chump chops
- 1 tablespoon coriander seeds
- 1 tablespoon cumin seeds
- 2 sticks cinnamon
- 1 × 400 g tin crushed tomato
- 2 cups (500 ml) water
- sea salt and freshly ground white pepper
- flat-leaf parsley, to serve

1 Preheat the oven to 140°C fan-forced (160°C conventional).

2 Drizzle half of the olive oil over the base of a large roasting pan or baking dish. Place the celery and lamb chops in the dish. Scatter over the coriander, cumin, cinnamon, tomato and water. Season with salt and pepper and cover tightly with foil.

3 Bake the lamb for 3 hours or until tender. Remove the foil and bake for a further 20 minutes to brown the top of the lamb. Remove the pan from the oven, drizzle with the remaining olive oil and scatter with parsley.

4 Serve.

Mint-crusted lamb racks

This dish epitomises the kind of home-cooking I love – classic flavours, cooked simply. Make sure you rest the lamb before you carve it so it stays nice and juicy. Resting meat simply means leaving it to stand for five or ten minutes once it comes out of the oven. To make the clarified butter, melt the butter in a heavy-based saucepan. The milk fats will separate out and sink to the bottom. Some will float to the surface and should be skimmed off. The clarified butter can then be poured into a container to use later. Ghee is a form of clarified butter commonly used in Indian cooking and can be found in the refrigerator section of supermarkets.

Serves 4

4 × 4-cutlet lamb racks

sea salt and freshly ground black pepper

olive oil, for drizzling

Potato Fondants (optional, see page 119), to serve

mint leaves and thyme sprigs (optional), to serve

MINT-CRUMB CRUST

2 cups (140 g) fresh breadcrumbs

3 cloves garlic, crushed

12 mint leaves

½ cup (large handful) flat-leaf parsley leaves

½ cup (125 ml) clarified butter (see page 201), at room temperature

✱ SPECIAL EQUIPMENT
food processor

1 Preheat the oven to 180°C fan-forced (200°C conventional).

2 To make the mint-crumb crust, place the breadcrumbs, garlic, mint and parsley in a food processor and blend to combine. Add the clarified butter and process to form a paste. Remove and place between 2 layers of baking paper. Roll out thinly with a rolling pin and set aside; you should be able to cut 4 strips of the crust to cover the tops of the lamb racks.

3 Place the lamb racks on a baking tray, season with salt and pepper and drizzle with a little olive oil. Roast the lamb racks for 10–12 minutes, then remove from the oven and leave to rest for 5 minutes. Top the racks with a strip of the mint-crumb crust.

4 Preheat the griller until hot, then grill the lamb racks until the crumb coating is cooked. Serve with potato fondants topped with extra mint leaves and thyme sprigs, if you like.

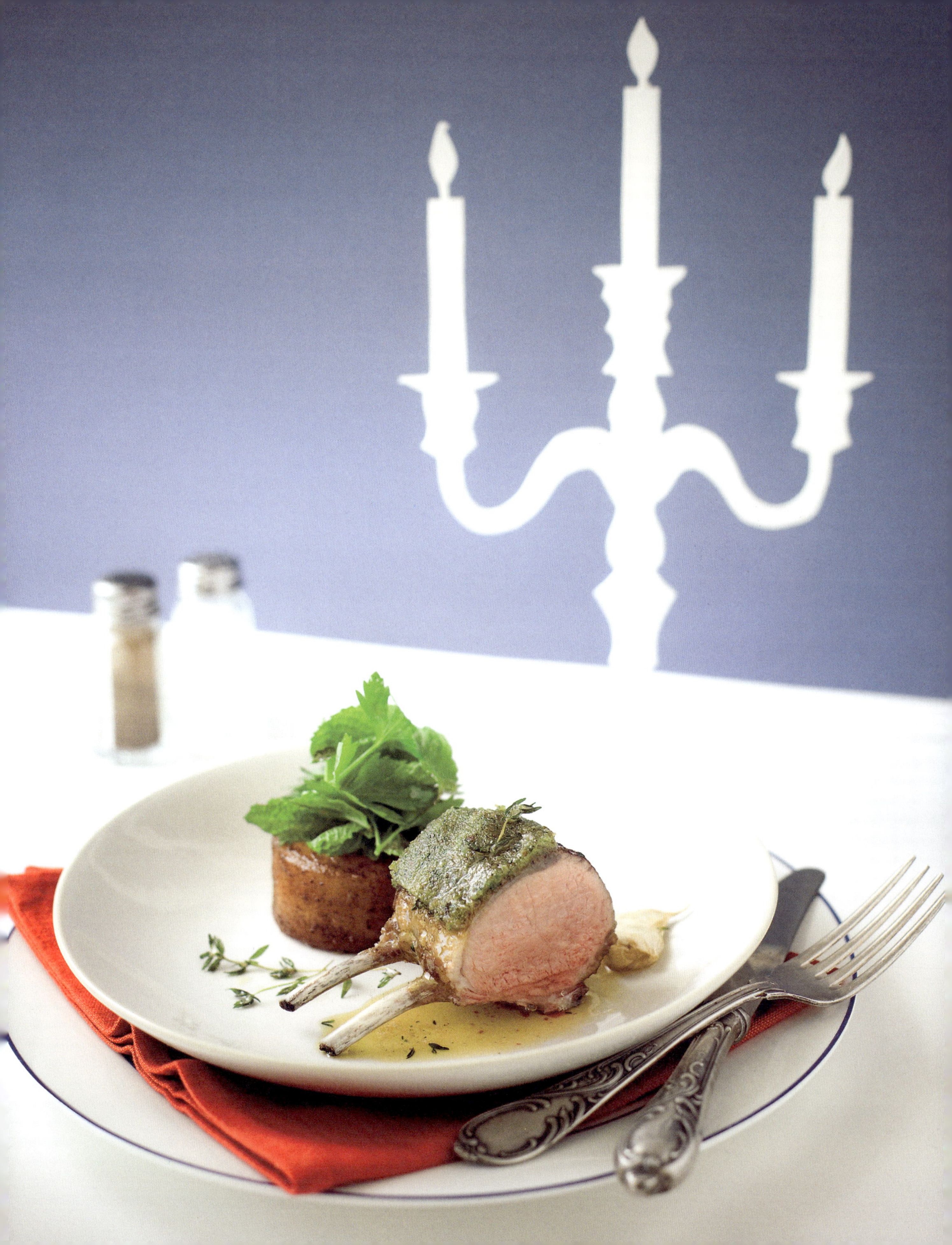

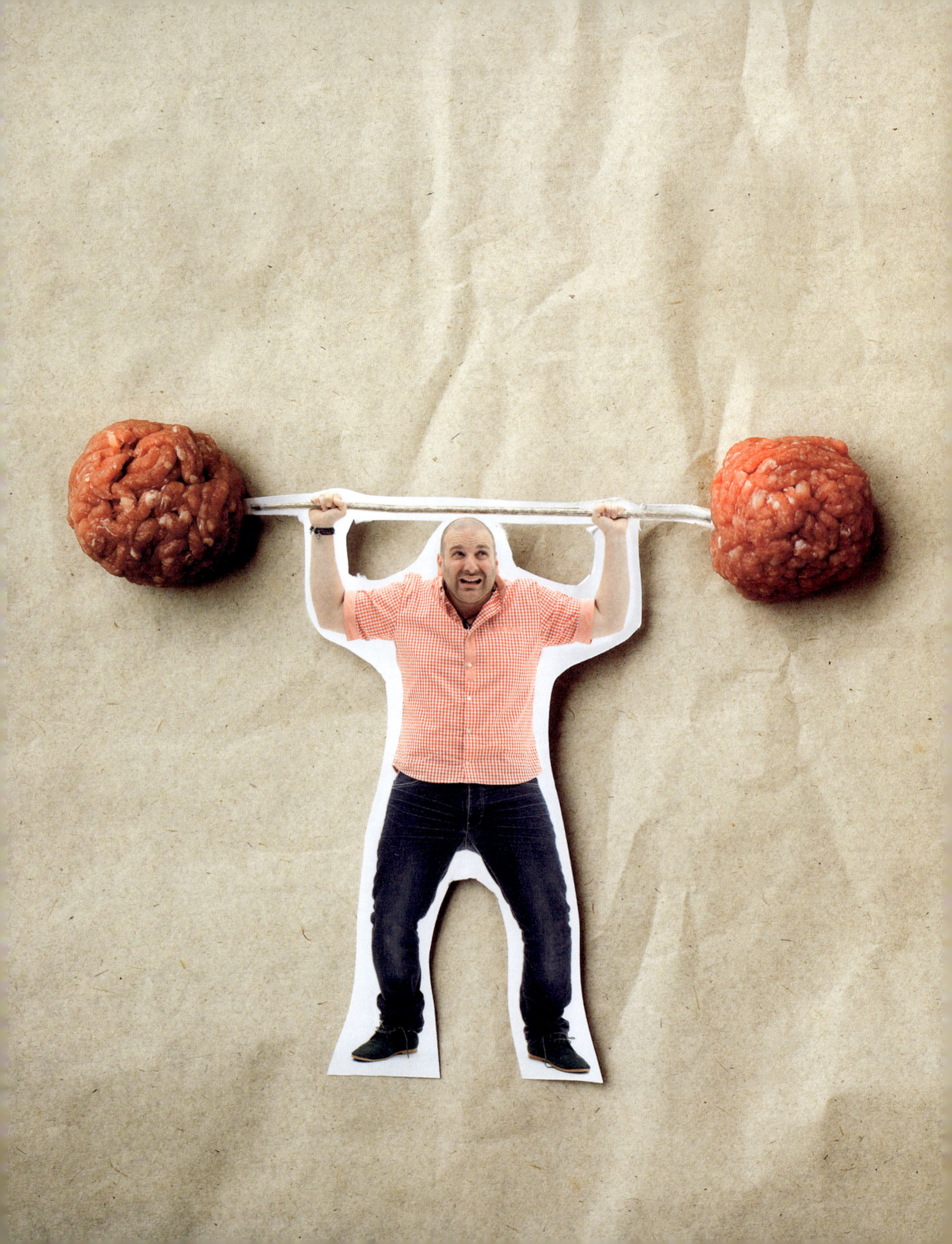

MINCE

All types of boneless meat, including beef, lamb, pork, veal and chicken, can be minced. Fish and seafood can also be minced.

Mince is usually made by putting meat through a meat grinder or mincer. You can also mince small quantities of meat by hand, using a very sharp knife. There are many grades of mince available. Your choice will be based on health considerations, your budget and what you want to use the mince for.

Lean grades of mince are the best choice for health. A slightly higher fat content will give a better result in some recipes, especially where the mince needs to be bound together. Coarser minces contain more fat. They are best used when making burgers, meatballs and keftedes as the extra fat helps to keep them moist.

You can use lots of different ingredients to flavour mince, including onion, garlic, fresh herbs, and spices such as cumin, allspice and paprika. Adding soaked torn bread lightens the mince mixture, while adding beaten eggs helps to bind it together.

Mince is so versatile. Use it in bolognese sauce (see page 92), lasagne or pastitsio (see page 112), meatballs or keftedes (see page 95), hamburgers (see page 96), shepherd's pie, Scotch eggs (see page 47), meat loaf and doner kebabs (see page 84).

Best-ever spaghetti bolognese

This has to be one of the most frequently eaten dishes at the Australian dinner table. Make sure the boiling water for the pasta is as salty as the sea, and be careful not to overcook the spaghetti – it should still have some bite and texture. My version of this famous sauce has seventeen ingredients. Cinnamon and nutmeg are the (now not so) secret ingredients.

Serves 4–6

¼ cup (60 ml) olive oil

2 onions, finely chopped

2 carrots, finely chopped

2 sticks celery, finely chopped

3 cloves garlic, crushed

4 bay leaves

1 teaspoon cloves

300 g minced beef

300 g minced pork

300 g minced veal

2 cups (500 ml) dry white wine

1 teaspoon ground nutmeg

1 teaspoon ground cinnamon

1 × 425 g tin crushed tomato

200 g tomato paste

sea salt and freshly ground white pepper

400 g spaghetti

shaved parmesan and oregano sprigs (optional), to serve

1 Heat the olive oil in a large deep saucepan over medium–high heat and cook the onion, carrot and celery for 5 minutes or until softened and coloured. Add the garlic, bay leaves and cloves and continue to cook for another 1–2 minutes, stirring with a wooden spoon. Add the mince and use the spoon to break up any large pieces. Cook for 6 minutes or until browned. Add the wine, nutmeg, cinnamon, tomato and tomato paste and bring to the boil.

2 Reduce the heat to low and simmer for 30 minutes uncovered; the sauce should be reduced and rich. Season to taste with salt and pepper. Remove the cloves.

3 Cook the spaghetti in a large saucepan of salted boiling water following packet instructions until al dente. Drain, then serve with the bolognese sauce, topped with shaved parmesan and scattered with oregano, if you like.

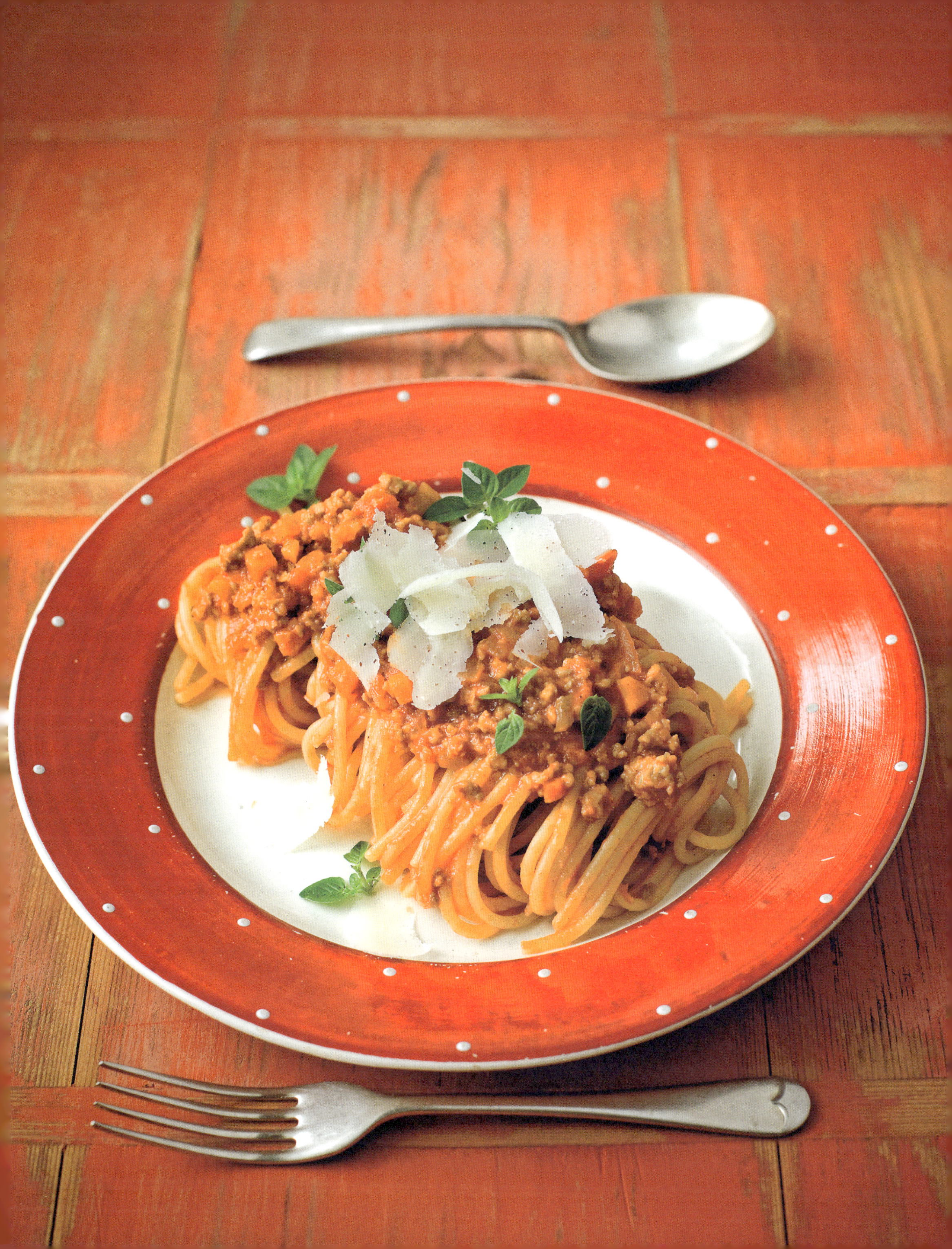

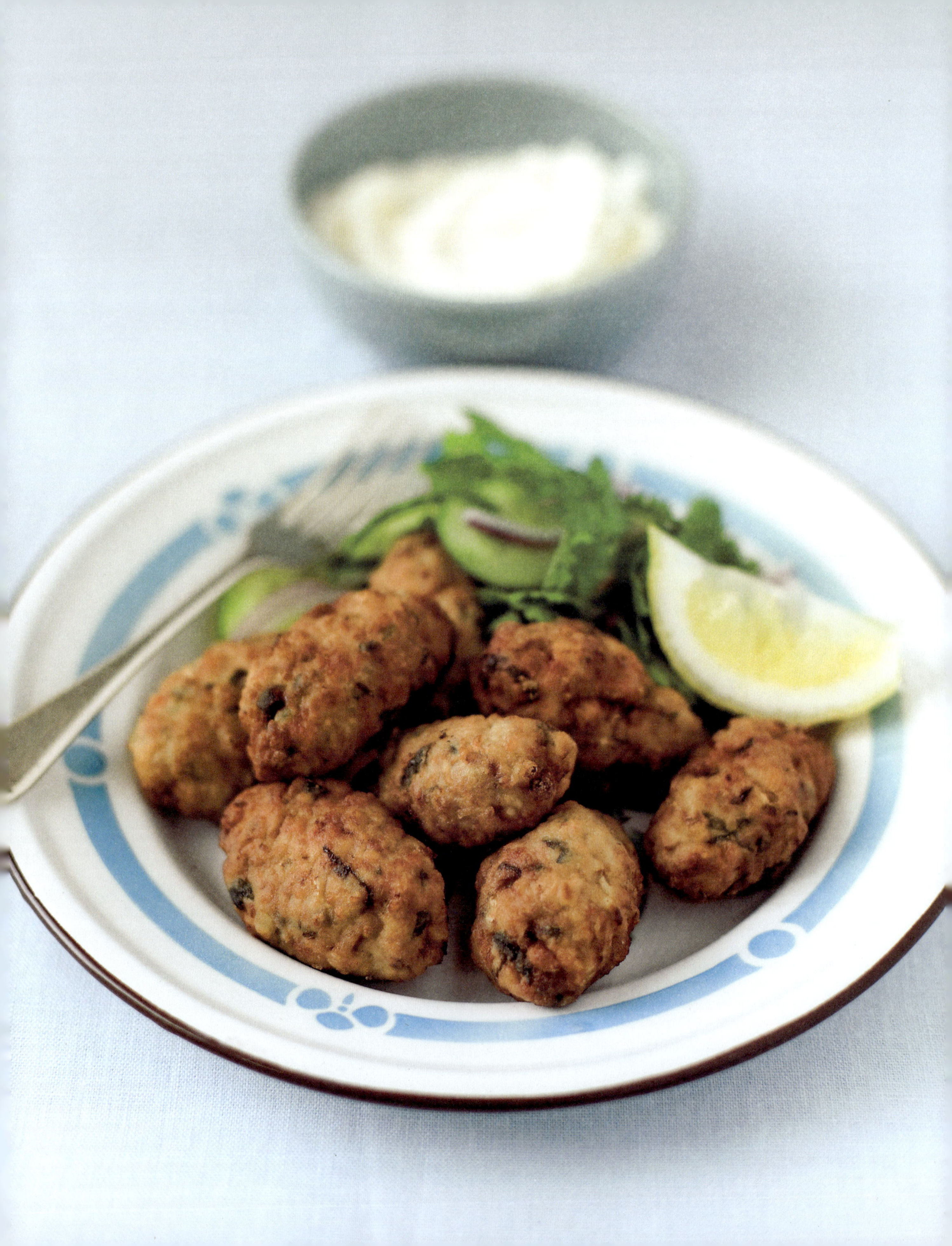

Keftedes

Keftedes are the Greek version of meatballs. I love eating them, even when they are cold. They taste especially good slipped into a white bread sandwich along with some pickles.

Serves 4

- 3 slices stale white bread with crusts (75 g), torn
- 1 cup (250 ml) milk
- 500 g minced lamb
- 1 onion, finely chopped
- 2 cloves garlic, finely chopped
- 1 tablespoon chopped oregano
- 1 tablespoon chopped mint
- ¼ cup (3 tablespoons) chopped flat-leaf parsley
- 2 teaspoons white-wine vinegar
- 1 egg, beaten
- ¼ teaspoon freshly grated nutmeg
- sea salt
- ⅓ cup (50 g) plain flour, for coating
- olive oil, for frying
- natural Greek-style yoghurt and lemon wedges, to serve
- cucumber, coriander, onion and mint salad (optional), to serve

1 Soak the bread in the milk for 5 minutes, then squeeze out excess milk and place the bread in a large bowl. Discard the leftover milk.

2 Add the minced lamb, onion, garlic, oregano, mint, parsley, vinegar, egg, nutmeg and salt to the bowl and mix well with your hands, squeezing the mixture well to combine all the ingredients. Cover with plastic film and place in the fridge for 30 minutes to allow the flavours to develop.

3 Remove the mince mixture from the fridge, then roll into long meatballs; you should have about 24. Roll in flour to coat.

4 Pour enough olive oil for shallow-frying into a frying pan until it covers the base. Heat over medium heat, then cook the meatballs in batches for 3 minutes on each side or until cooked and browned.

5 Remove the meatballs from the pan and leave to drain on paper towel.

6 Serve the keftedes on a plate with lemon wedges and a bowl of yoghurt with salad to the side, if desired.

Did you know?

- If you are mixing herbs, onion or spices through mince, make sure the flavouring ingredients are spread evenly by placing all the ingredients in a large ziplock bag, then seal and massage.

Hamburger with haloumi

There is no excuse for buying fast-food hamburgers when they are so easy to make at home. I always have a lot of fun making them with my nieces and nephews. It is rewarding too, as there is a certain pleasure in holding a homemade burger in your hands. Feel free to make a big mess of your shirt. I always do.

Serves 6

2 slices stale white bread (50 g)

½ cup (125 ml) milk

500 g minced beef

½ onion, finely chopped

2 cloves garlic, finely chopped

1 tablespoon chopped oregano

1 tablespoon chopped mint

2 tablespoons chopped flat-leaf parsley

1 egg, lightly beaten

¼ teaspoon freshly grated nutmeg

1 teaspoon ground cumin

sea salt and freshly ground black pepper

1 tablespoon olive oil

6 thick slices haloumi (see page 202)

6 small bread rolls, sliced in half widthways

6 lettuce leaves

shredded pickled beetroot, to serve (optional, see page 203)

Hot Chips (optional, see page 116), to serve

✱ **SPECIAL EQUIPMENT**
food processor

1 Soak the bread in the milk for 5 minutes, then squeeze out any excess milk and place the bread in a large bowl. Discard the milk. Add the minced beef.

2 Place the onion, garlic, oregano, mint and parsley in a food processor and process until finely chopped. Add the onion mixture, egg, nutmeg and cumin to the mince, then season with salt and pepper and mix well. Form the mince mixture into 6 round patties and place on a baking tray, cover with plastic film and refrigerate for 30 minutes to firm.

3 Heat a large non-stick frying pan over medium–high heat and cook the hamburgers for 4 minutes on each side or until cooked through. Remove the hamburgers from the pan and set aside.

4 Heat another frying pan over high heat. Add the olive oil and cook the haloumi for 2 minutes on each side or until golden. Remove and place on top of each burger patty.

5 Place some lettuce on the base of each bun, then top with the burger, haloumi and beetroot (if using). Add the top of the burger bun, then serve immediately with chips to the side, if you like.

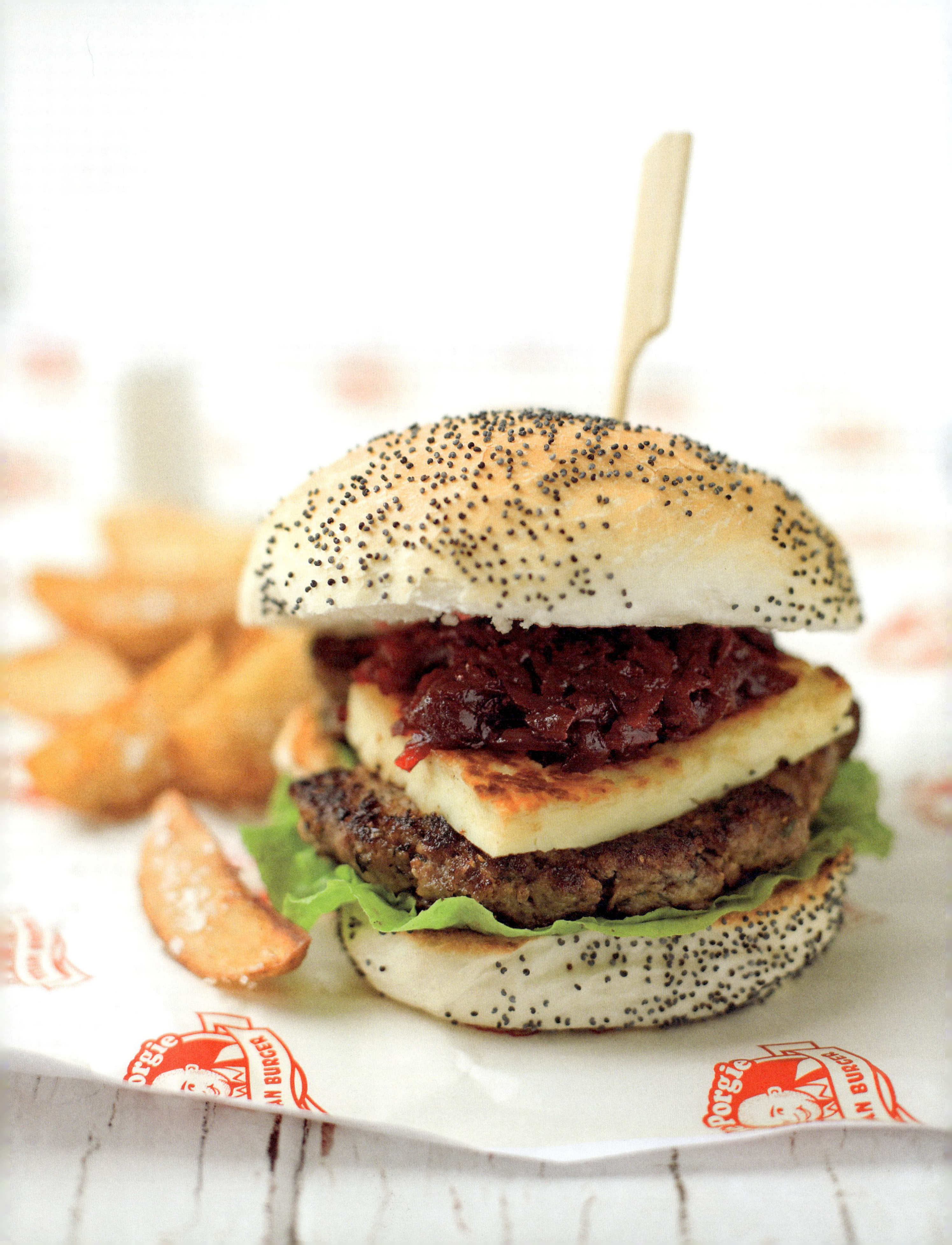
Porgie

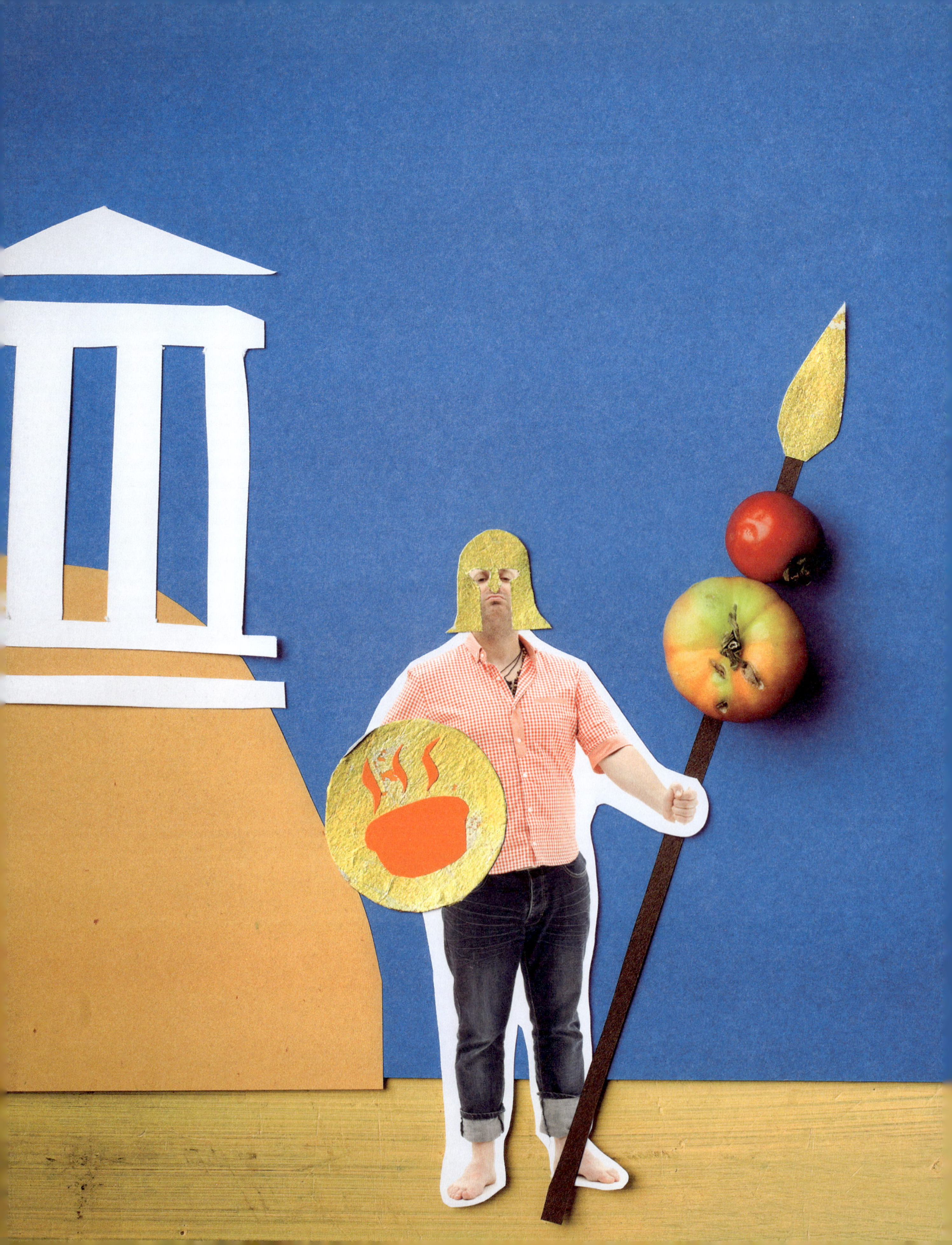

ON A STICK

People have cooked and eaten food on skewers for many centuries. In ancient times, soldiers cooked meat over an open fire, then skewered it with their swords and ate it straight from the blade. These days, lots of street food around the world is served on skewers. It is very convenient as you don't need to use cutlery or even sit down. In Greece, they have kalamaki, while in Japan they have yakatori, and in Central Asia they have shasliks. Then there are kebabs in India and Iran, and satays in Malaysia.

The skewers themselves are made from bamboo, wood or metal. Soak bamboo or wooden skewers in water for thirty minutes before use to prevent them from burning. Skewers can be thin or flat, long or short, simple or decorated. A rotisserie in a barbecue or oven is essentially a large skewer used to rotate large pieces of meat during cooking. It is best to cook skewered food over medium or low–medium heat, with the bottom or handle of the skewer away from the heat source. Use the handle to turn the skewers.

You can cook all sorts of meat and seafood on skewers, including beef, lamb, chicken, pork, fish, prawns and scallops. Vegetables such as button mushrooms, onion wedges, cherry tomatoes and pieces of spring onion, capsicum (pepper), eggplant (aubergine) and zucchini (courgette) work well too, and fruit skewers (see page 104) make an easy dessert. Just be sure to cut all the ingredients to the same size so that they cook evenly.

Prawns wrapped in kataifi

Kataifi pastry is a special type of shredded pastry. It is traditionally used to make a nut-filled dessert that has nothing to do with prawns. That's why my mum gets so annoyed when I make this dish – but I can't resist. I love the contrast between the crunch of the crispy pastry and sweet juiciness of the prawn. You can buy kataifi pastry from Middle Eastern food stores.

Serves 4

12 large raw prawns

½ cup (125 ml) clarified butter (see page 201), melted

50 g kataifi pastry (see above)

vegetable oil, for shallow-frying

lemon wedges (optional), to serve

TARTARE SAUCE

1 egg, straight from the fridge

1 cup (250 ml) Mayonnaise (see page 203)

1 teaspoon salted capers, rinsed and drained

2 cornichons (see page 202), finely chopped

2 tablespoons chopped dill

1 tablespoon lemon juice

sea salt and freshly ground black pepper

✱ SPECIAL EQUIPMENT
  fine-mesh sieve
  12 small bamboo skewers, soaked in water for 30 minutes

1 To make the tartare sauce, hard-boil the egg in a pan of simmering water for 9 minutes, then plunge into cold water. Peel, then push through a fine-mesh sieve into a bowl and set aside. Mix the mayonnaise, capers, cornichons, dill, lemon juice and egg, then season to taste with salt and pepper. Cover closely with plastic film and set aside in the fridge. (Makes about 280 ml.)

2 Peel the prawns, removing the heads and shells, leaving on the tail. Make a small slit along the back to remove the intestinal tract. Rinse the prawns under cold running water and set aside to dry on paper towel.

3 Thread each prawn onto a skewer, then brush the prawns with clarified butter and wrap in kataifi pastry.

4 Pour a 2 cm layer of oil into a frying pan and heat over medium heat until hot. Cook the pastry-wrapped prawns for 3 minutes on each side or until golden and cooked through, then remove and drain on paper towel.

5 Serve the prawns with a bowl of tartare sauce and lemon wedges to the side, if desired.

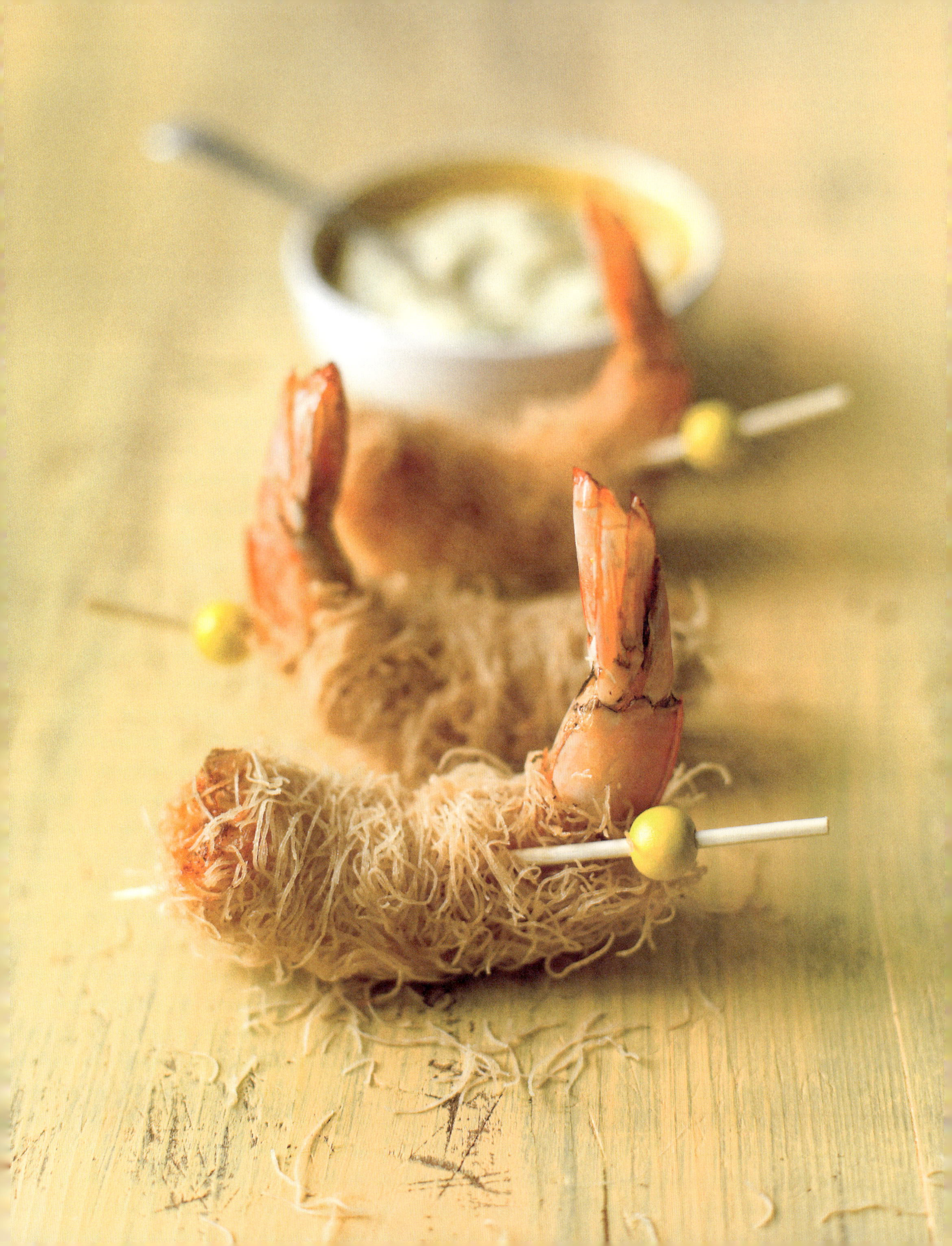

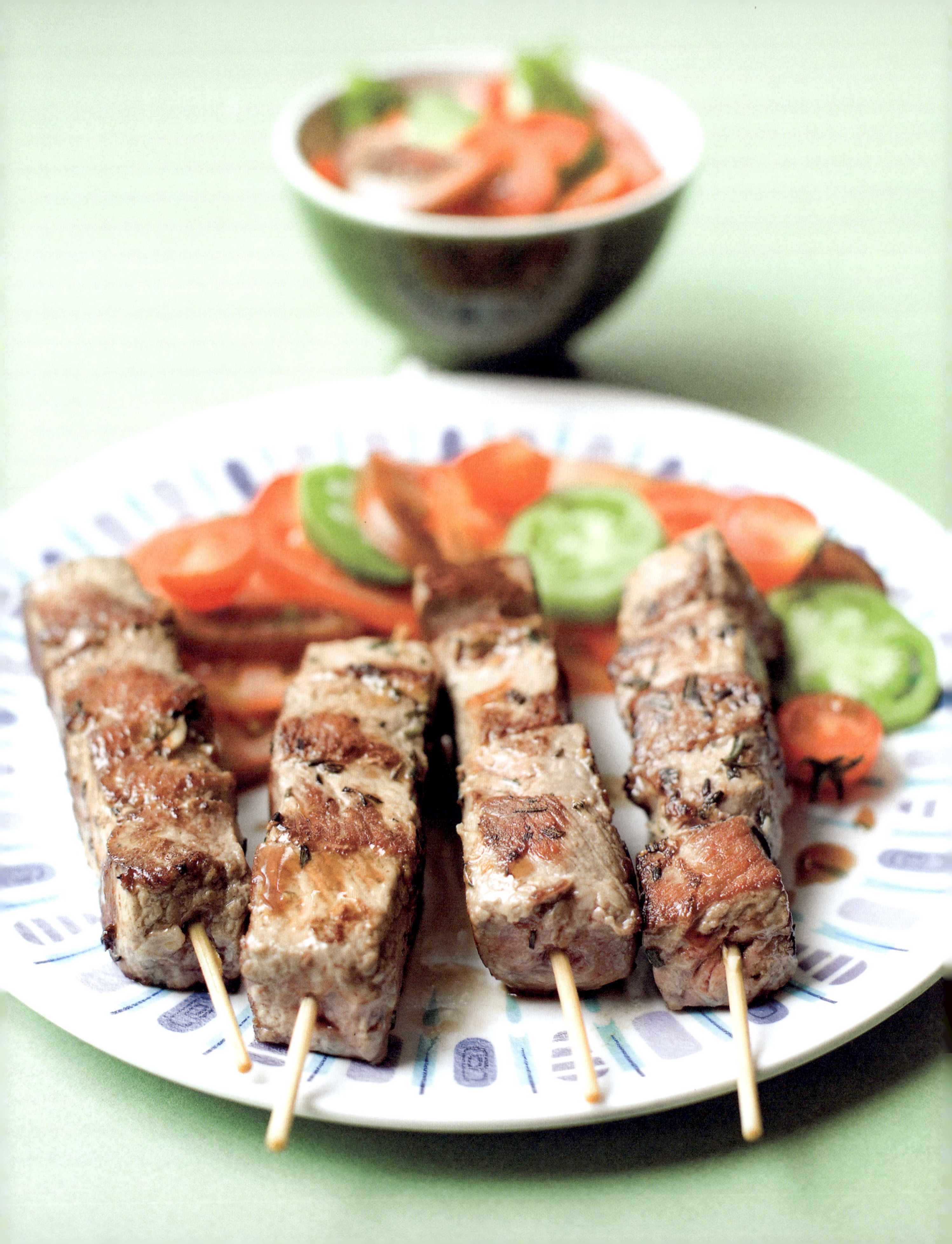

Lamb kebabs with tomato salad

I love street food. Every time I eat this dish, I remember walking through Athens in winter and watching Greek guys grilling lamb kebabs (kalamaki) on the street. Marinating the meat makes it more tender, as well as giving it more flavour. For the tomato salad, make sure that the tomatoes are at room temperature. They will taste so much better.

Serves 4

¼ cup (60 ml) olive oil

finely grated zest of 1 lemon

1 tablespoon chopped rosemary

2 cloves garlic, finely chopped

2 lamb backstraps (about 400 g), cut into 2.5 cm pieces

sea salt and freshly ground black pepper

TOMATO SALAD

400 g mixed tomatoes, thickly sliced widthways

¼ cup (60 ml) extra virgin olive oil

1 tablespoon red-wine vinegar

sea salt and freshly ground black pepper

✱ **SPECIAL EQUIPMENT**
4 long bamboo skewers, soaked in water for 30 minutes

1 Mix the olive oil, lemon zest, rosemary and garlic in a medium-sized bowl. Add the lamb, then season with salt and pepper, cover with plastic film and marinate in the fridge for 30 minutes.

2 Meanwhile, make the tomato salad. Put the tomato into a medium-sized bowl. Add the olive oil and red-wine vinegar and season to taste with salt and pepper.

3 Remove the lamb from the fridge and thread onto the soaked bamboo skewers.

4 Heat a chargrill pan or barbecue grill or flat plate until hot. Cook the lamb skewers for 3 minutes on each side for medium–rare or until cooked to your liking. Rest on a plate for 5 minutes, loosely covered with foil.

5 Serve the lamb skewers with the tomato salad.

Fruit skewers with fairy floss

Parents keep telling me that they can't get their kids to eat fruit. My response? Well, first always buy ripe fresh fruit that is in season. It tastes so much better. Secondly, make it exciting so that the kids actually want to eat it. What do you reckon about these fruity skewers, kids? If you have a fairy floss machine stashed away in the back of a kitchen cupboard, you can make your own fairy floss.

Makes 8

325 g (about ¼) honeydew melon, seeded

325 g (about ¼) rockmelon (cantaloupe), seeded

400 g (about ¼) small watermelon

100 g Persian fairy floss (available from specialty food stores)

* SPECIAL EQUIPMENT
melon baller
8 bamboo skewers

1 Press the melon baller into the honeydew and rotate to make as many balls as you can. Repeat with the rockmelon and watermelon.

2 Thread the melon balls onto skewers.

3 Twist a small amount of the fairy floss around the melon sticks and serve immediately, or else the fairy floss will start to stick and dissolve.

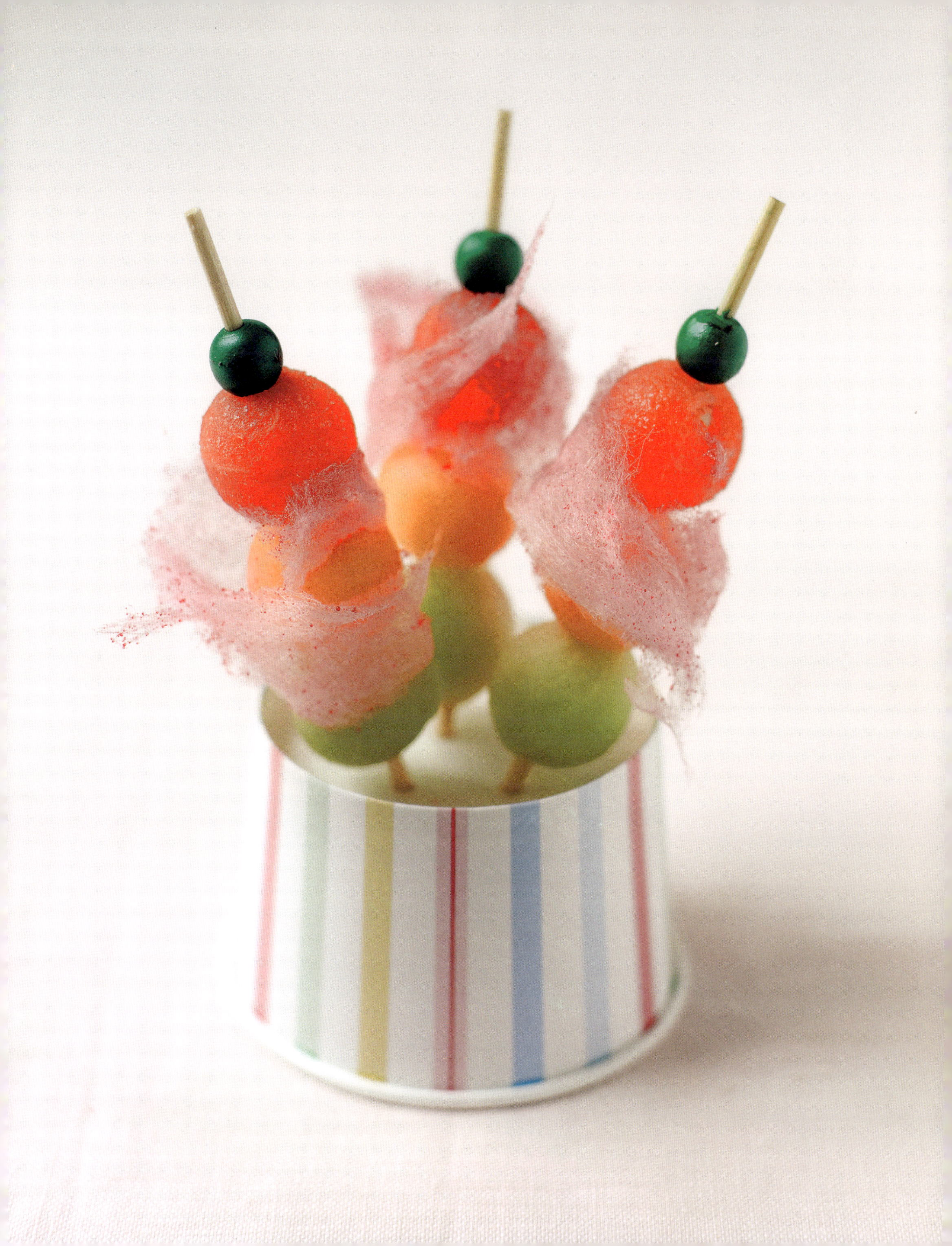

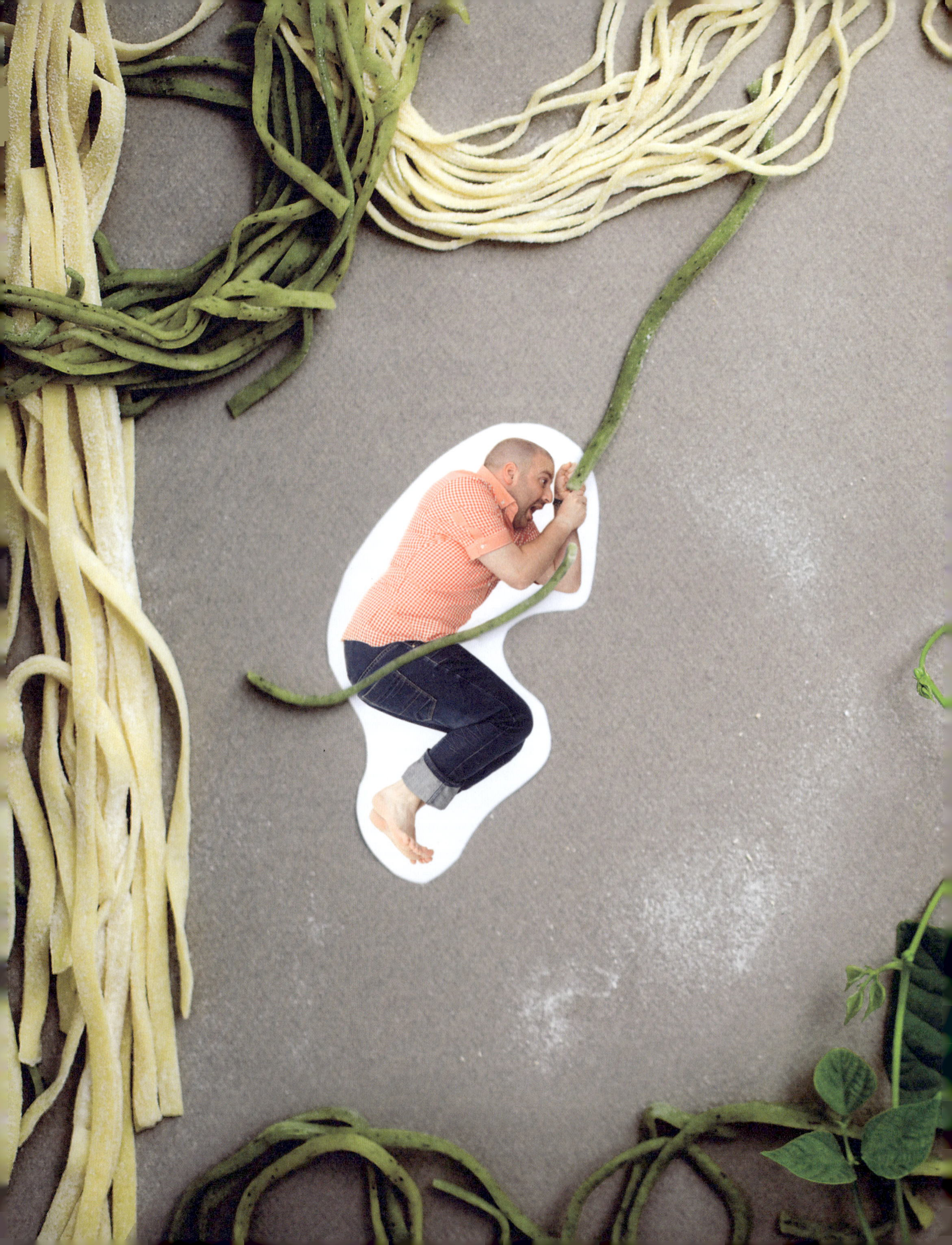

PASTA

The word pasta comes from the Italian word *paste*, which is what the pasta mixture of flour, water, salt (and sometimes eggs) looks like before it is kneaded, cut into various shapes and cooked. Pasta is categorised into two basic types, dried and fresh. Dried pasta is made without eggs and can be stored for up to two years under ideal conditions, while fresh pasta will keep for a few days in the fridge.

Pasta is generally served with some type of sauce. Flat pastas such as fettuccine and pappardelle are typically served with cream sauces, whereas tomato-based sauces cling better to tubular pasta shapes such as rigatoni or penne.

To cook perfect pasta, first boil enough water in a pan large enough to easily accommodate the quantity of pasta you intend to cook, then add salt (do not add oil). Add the pasta, then stir and return the water to the boil. Stir the pasta occasionally during cooking. The best way to determine whether your pasta is cooked is to taste it. Perfectly cooked pasta should be al dente, or firm-to-the-bite, yet cooked through. Drain the pasta immediately, add your sauce and then serve promptly.

Nonna Nicoletta's spaghetti with fresh ricotta and parmesan

When I was growing up, I was lucky to have one amazing grandmother who cooked me fantastic Cypriot–Greek food and another wonderful grandmother who fed me beautiful southern Italian food. This dish comes from my dad's mother, Nonna Nicoletta, and is as easy as it is good. For a quick meal you could always use dried spaghetti instead.

Serves 4

salt

200 g firm fresh ricotta, well drained

sea salt and freshly ground black pepper

1 × 100 g piece parmesan, grated

WHOLE-EGG PASTA DOUGH

4 × 55 g eggs

400 g strong '00' plain flour (see page 203), plus extra for dusting

1 tablespoon olive oil

✶ SPECIAL EQUIPMENT
   food processor
   pasta machine

1 To make the pasta, blend the eggs, flour and oil in a food processor. Transfer the dough to a lightly floured bench and knead for 5 minutes or until smooth. Wrap the dough in plastic film and set aside to rest for 30 minutes.

2 Divide the dough in half and press out with your hands until it is flat enough to pass through a pasta machine on the thickest setting. Roll out one half of the pasta through the machine, dusting with extra flour to prevent it from sticking. Continue to roll the pasta through the settings, reducing the notch each time, until you reach the second thinnest setting; as the pasta gets longer, you can cut it into 2 or 3 lengths to help make it easier to roll through the machine. Repeat with the second piece of pasta.

3 Feed the dough through the spaghetti attachment. Lay the spaghetti flat and loosely cover with a tea towel until required.

4 Cook the spaghetti in a large saucepan of boiling salted water for 3 minutes or until al dente (cooked through, but firm-to-the-bite). Reserve 1 cup (250 ml) of the cooking liquid and set aside.

5 Drain the pasta and return it to the pan. Add the ricotta and a little of the cooking liquid and stir to combine. Season to taste with salt and pepper.

6 Divide the spaghetti among serving bowls and top with grated parmesan, then season to taste with salt and pepper.

7 Serve.

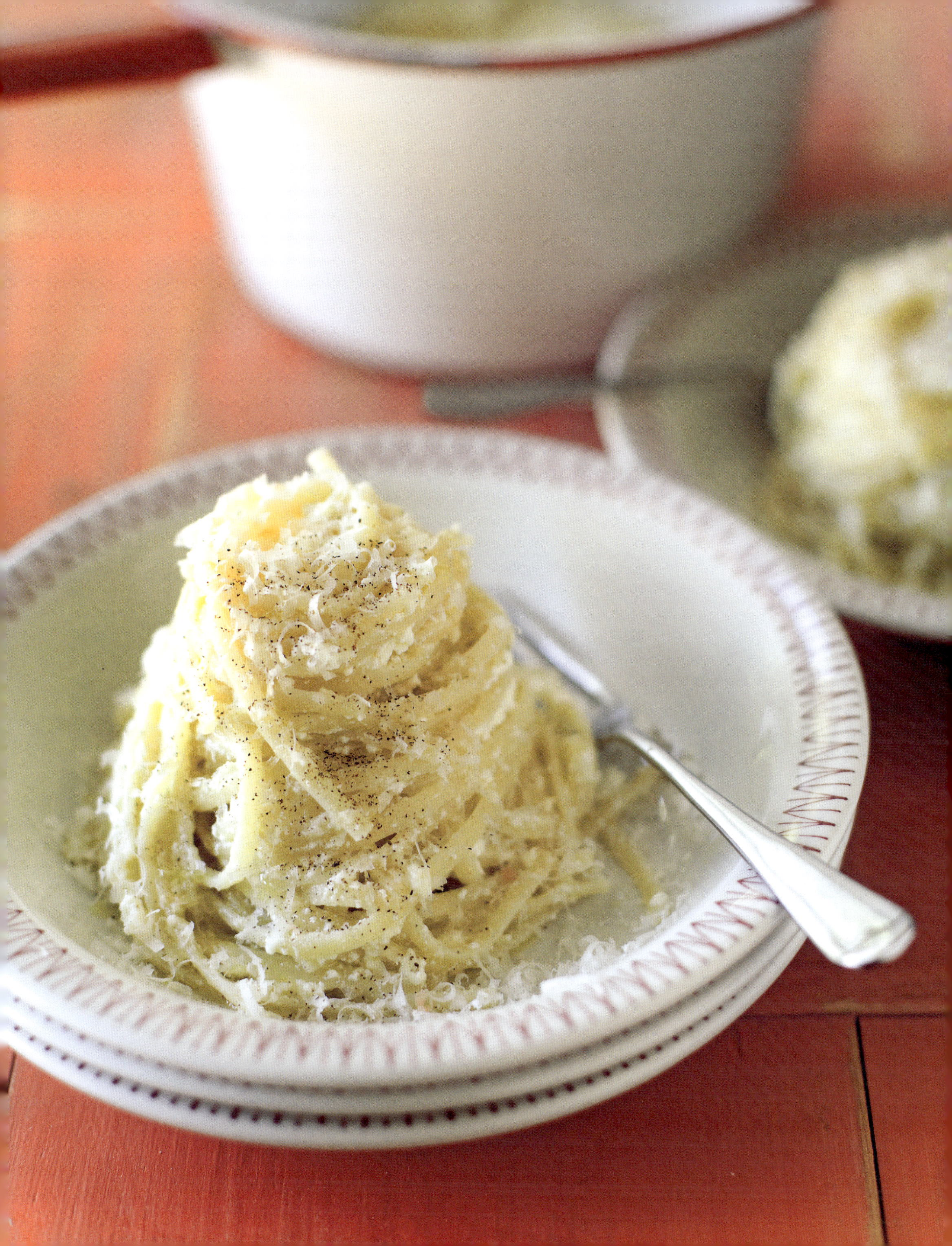

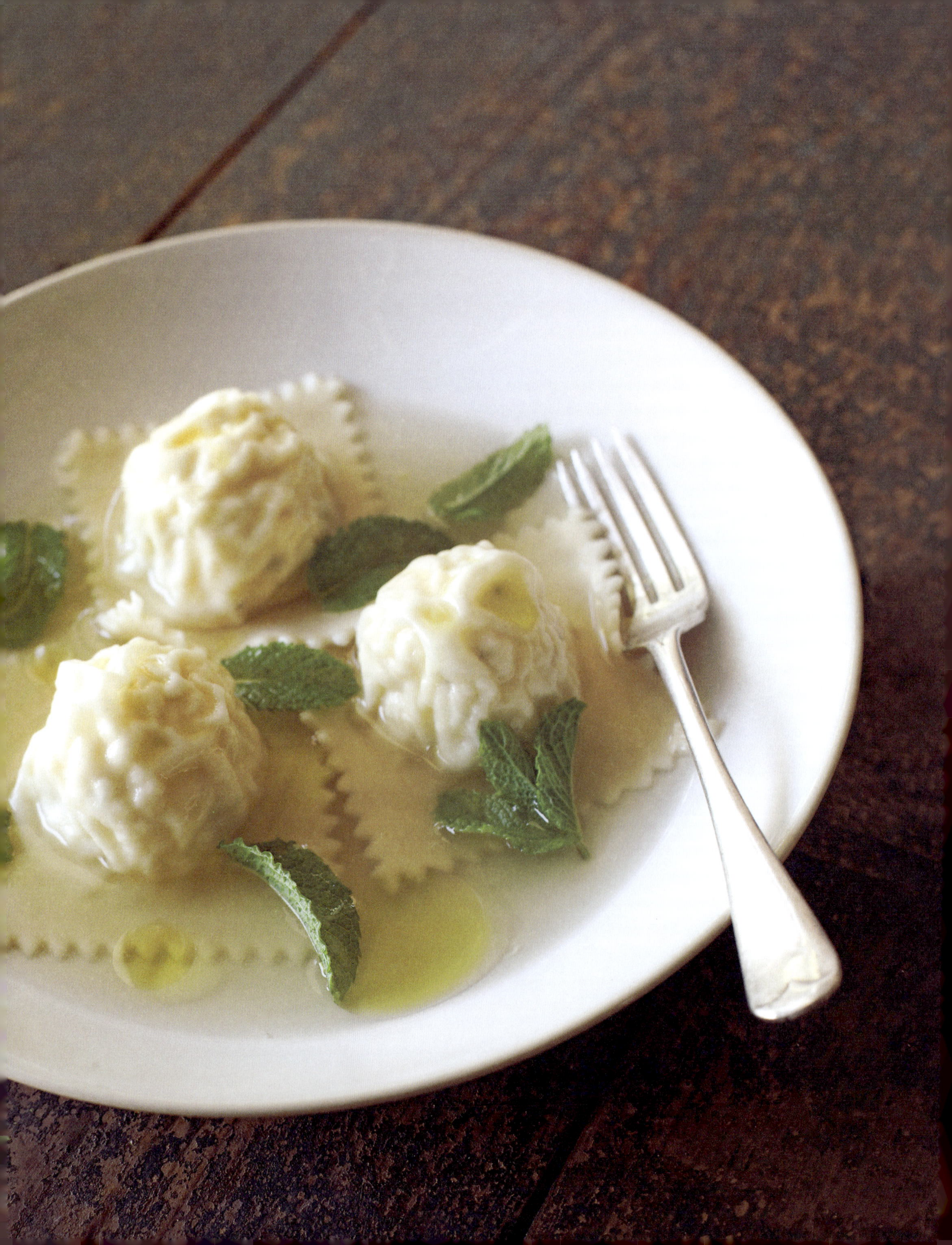

My Yia Yia's Cypriot ravioli

God bless my mum's mother, Yia Yia Kaili. She played a major part in my food life and every time I make or eat this dish I remember her. Good food really gratifies your heart and soul. You could always buy fresh lasagne sheets or even wonton wrappers instead of making your own pasta. If you don't have a ravioli cutter, use a small sharp knife to cut squares of dough or a small cup to cut out rounds.

Serves 4

200 g haloumi (see page 202), grated

200 g firm fresh ricotta, well drained

1 tablespoon dried mint

2 eggs

sea salt and freshly ground black pepper

1 litre Chicken Stock (see page 201)

mint leaves and extra virgin olive oil, to serve

CYPRIOT EGGLESS RAVIOLI DOUGH

2½ (375 g) cups unbleached plain flour, plus extra for dusting

1 cup (250 ml) cold water

2 teaspoons olive oil

salt

* **SPECIAL EQUIPMENT**
    pasta machine
    ravioli wheel or
      8 cm ravioli cutter
    pastry brush
    slotted spoon

1 To make the pasta, place the flour on a clean bench and make a well in the centre. Place the water, oil and a pinch of salt in the well, then use your hands to incorporate the flour gradually into the wet ingredients. Once the mixture has come together, knead it until you have a smooth ball. Wrap the dough in plastic film, then chill in the fridge for 1 hour.

2 Mix the haloumi, ricotta, mint and 1 egg to combine. Season to taste with salt and pepper. Set aside.

3 Divide the dough in half and press out with your hands until it is flat enough to pass through a pasta machine on the thickest setting. Roll out one half of the pasta through the machine, dusting with extra flour to prevent it from sticking. Continue to roll the pasta through the settings, reducing the notch each time, until you reach the second thinnest setting; as the pasta gets longer, you can cut it into 2 or 3 lengths. Repeat with the second piece of pasta.

4 Cut the dough into 8 cm squares with a ravioli cutter. Place tablespoonful-sized mounds of filling in the centre of half of the pieces of dough. Beat the remaining egg in a small bowl. Use a pastry brush to lightly brush the egg around the edges of the filling. Place a second piece of dough on top and press around the filling to remove any air bubbles and seal well. Repeat with the remaining dough, filling and beaten egg.

5 Bring the stock to a gentle simmer in a saucepan, then cook the ravioli in batches for 4 minutes or until they float to the surface. Transfer to serving bowls with a slotted spoon. Ladle over the stock, scatter with mint, drizzle with a little olive oil and serve.

Pastitsio

My Italian friends and I often argue about what's better, lasagne or pastitsio. I have come to the conclusion that I love them both. Pastitsio is such a comforting dish that is fun to make and yummy to eat. Pastitsio means 'mess' in Greek, so now's your chance to be as messy as you want.

Serves 4–6

250 g dried Greek macaroni (available from Greek delicatessens or use penne)

salt

olive oil, for drizzling

MEAT SAUCE

olive oil, for cooking

1 onion, finely chopped

2 cloves garlic, sliced

1 tablespoon chopped thyme

300 g minced lamb

100 g minced veal

100 g minced pork

2 tablespoons tomato paste

1 × 400 g tin crushed tomato

1 stick cinnamon

sea salt

BECHAMEL SAUCE

100 g unsalted butter, chopped

100 g plain flour

400 ml milk

400 ml thickened cream

200 g parmesan, grated

3 eggs, beaten

sea salt and freshly ground white pepper

1 To make the meat sauce, heat 1 tablespoon olive oil in a frying pan over medium heat. Cook the onion, garlic and thyme for 3 minutes or until soft, then add the minced lamb, veal and pork and cook for 5 minutes or until browned, using a wooden spoon to break up any lumps. Add the tomato paste, tomato and cinnamon, then reduce the heat to low, cover with a lid and simmer for 30 minutes. Season to taste with salt and set aside.

2 To make the bechamel sauce, melt the butter in a medium-sized saucepan over low heat. Add the flour, then stir for 2 minutes or until you have a smooth paste. Slowly add the milk and cream, continuing to stir until the sauce is smooth and thick; this can take up to 15 minutes. Remove the pan from the heat and cover with a lid. Leave to cool for 10 minutes. Stir in half of the grated parmesan and the beaten eggs. Season to taste with salt and pepper.

3 While you wait, cook the pasta in a saucepan of boiling salted water following packet instructions until al dente, then drain and toss with a splash of olive oil. Leave to cool on a flat tray.

4 Preheat the oven to 180°C fan-forced (200°C conventional).

5 Lightly oil a 30 cm × 20 cm baking dish. Arrange the pasta on the base of the dish, then scatter over the remaining parmesan. Cover with a little of the bechamel, then top with the meat sauce and finish with a thick layer of bechamel.

6 Bake the pastitsio for 30–40 minutes or until the top is golden brown. Leave it to sit for 20 minutes before cutting and serving.

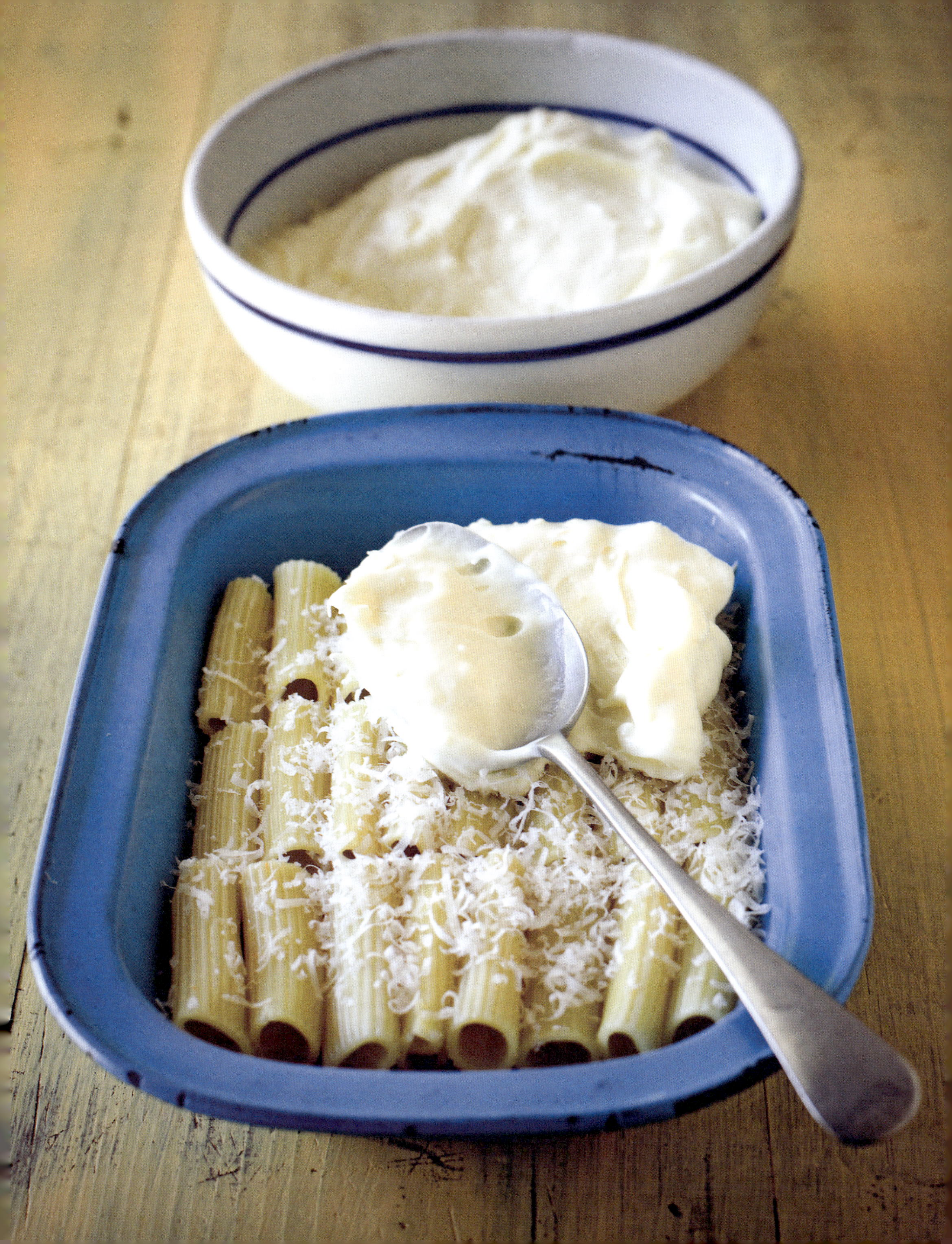

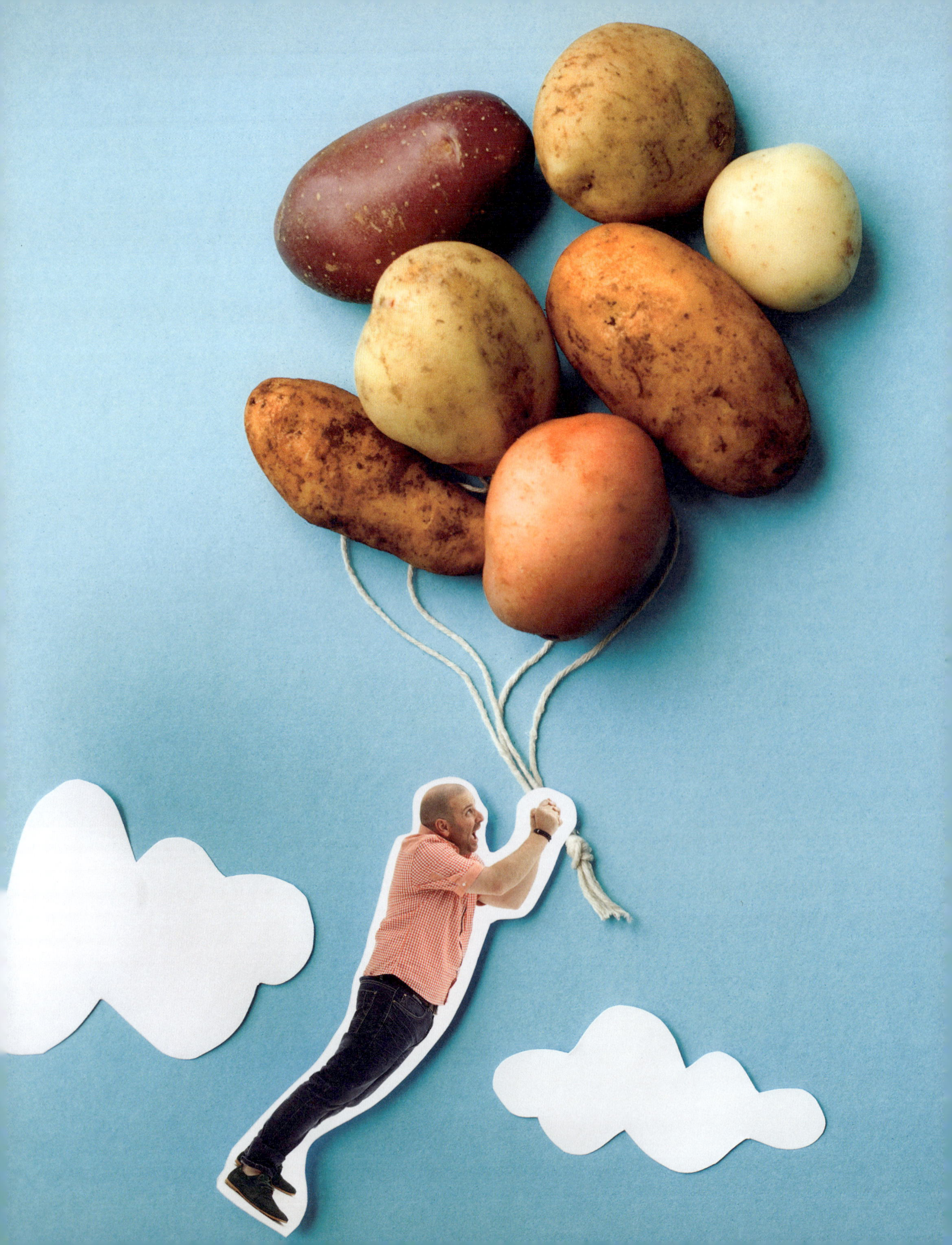

POTATO

Potatoes, sometimes called spuds, are a very popular and versatile vegetable. They vary in size and shape, from round or oval to long and thin. Their skin can be creamy-to-white, yellow, red or even purple. Potatoes have small buds, or 'eyes', from which a new plant can grow.

Potatoes originated in South America and were not known in Europe until the 1500s, when Spanish explorers brought them back. In 1995, the potato became the first food grown in space, when plants were taken aboard the space shuttle Columbia.

There are about five thousand potato varieties worldwide. They are divided into two main groups, floury and waxy. Floury potatoes contain more starch and are better for baking. Waxy potatoes are better for boiling, as they hold their shape better. Varieties of floury potatoes include Sebago, Pontiac and Coliban. Waxy potatoes include Kipfler, Nicola, Dutch Cream and Pink Eye. Desirees are regarded as all-purpose potatoes, while Russet Burbanks are the potato of choice for making chips or French fries.

Potatoes are sold by variety, size and whether or not they have been washed. Choose potatoes that have firm, dry skin. Store them in a cool, dry, dark and well-ventilated place and use them within seven days. Unwashed new-season potatoes will keep for weeks.

To prepare potatoes, scrub them with a brush to remove any dirt. Peeling the skin is optional, depending on the recipe. Be sure to remove any eyes. Do not use green potatoes – they can make you ill, so if in doubt, throw it out.

Hot chips with taramosalata

Crunchy, golden hot chips with salty, creamy taramosalata are so good. I love this snack and could happily eat it every day. The most important thing is to make the chips properly. Leaving them in the fridge for 1–2 hours before deep-frying helps them become fluffy on the inside and crisp on the outside, rather than soggy.

Serves 4

10 Russet Burbank potatoes, washed well and dried

sea salt

olive oil, for deep-frying

1 cup (250 ml) Taramosalata (see page 28)

✱ SPECIAL EQUIPMENT
deep-fryer

1 Cut the potatoes into chips the thickness of your index finger, leaving on the peel.

2 Place the potato in a saucepan of salted cold water over high heat and bring to the simmer, then simmer for 4 minutes; the potato should be tender but hold its shape. Drain the potato, then place in one layer on a paper towel-lined baking tray and leave in the fridge for 1–2 hours.

3 Heat enough olive oil for deep-frying in a deep-fryer until it reaches 130°C (or heat the oil in a large heavy-based saucepan until a cube of bread browns in 40 seconds). Cook the chips for 1–2 minutes, then remove and place on a baking tray lined with a clean tea towel or paper towel in the fridge to dry out for at least 1 hour or for up to 1 day.

4 Reheat the olive oil to 180°C and fry the chips for 2–3 minutes or until golden and crisp.

5 Drain the chips on paper towel, then sprinkle with a little salt and serve with a bowl of taramosalata to the side.

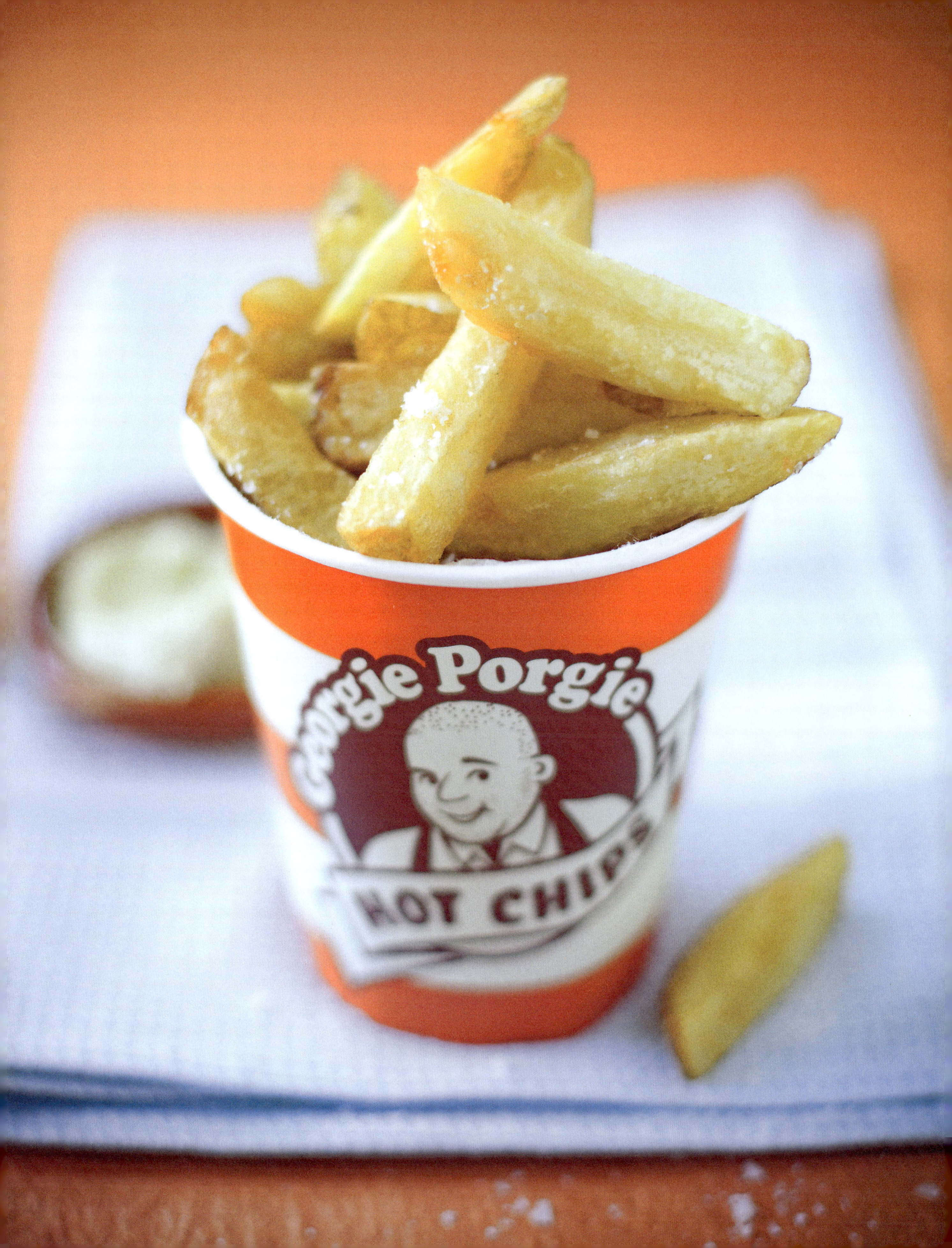
Georgie Porgie
HOT CHIPS

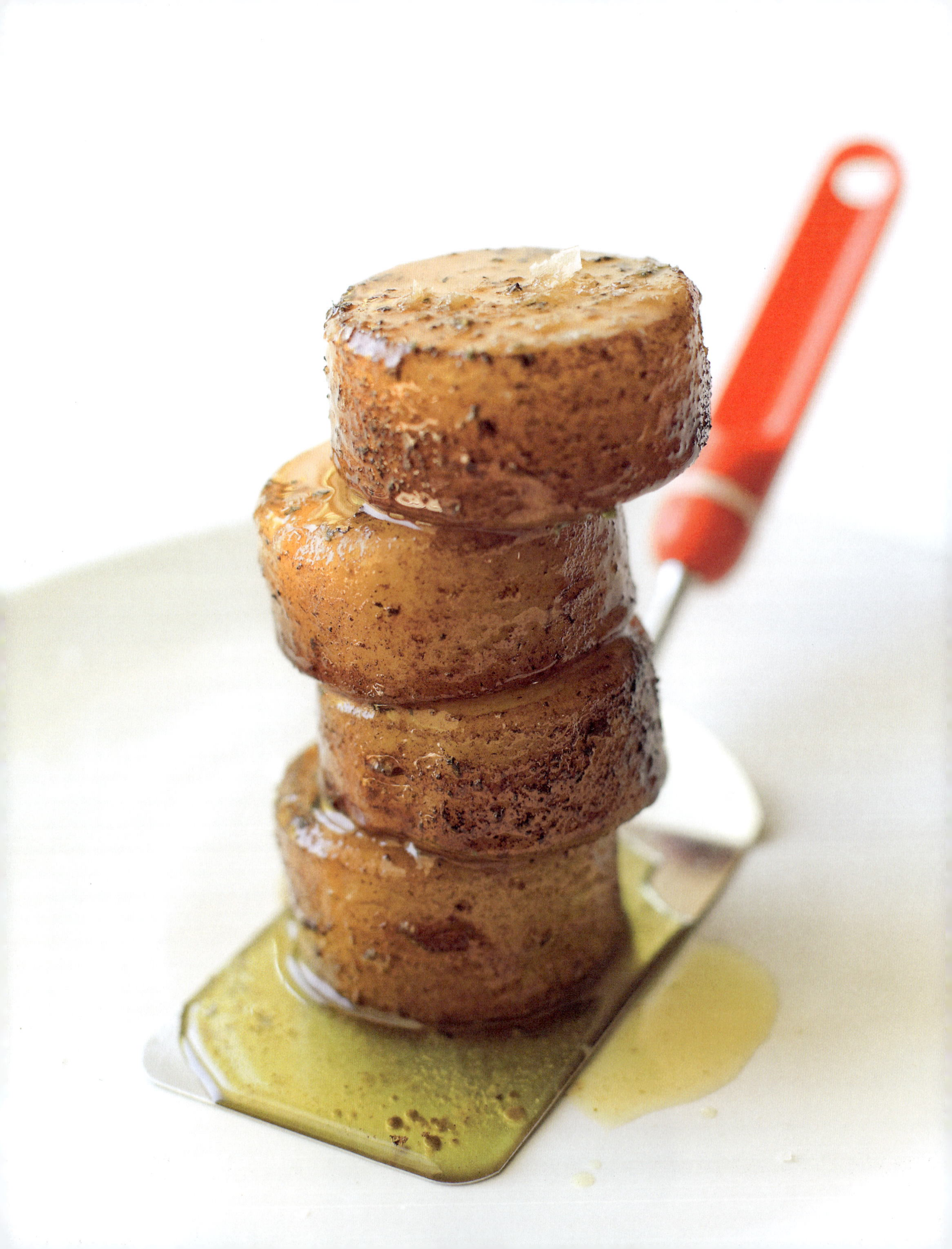

Potato fondants

When I think about my apprenticeship, potato fondants are the first thing to come to mind. Every day I had to prepare and cook around fifty of these yummy, buttery potato shapes. The skill in making them is all about controlling the temperature so the butter doesn't burn. If this happens, quickly add some cold butter to the pan to cool it down. The potatoes are delicious with roasted or barbecued beef, lamb, pork or chicken.

Serves 4

4 large desiree potatoes

170 g unsalted butter, cut into 5 mm-thick slices

100 ml Chicken Stock (see page 201)

1 clove garlic, sliced

4 sprigs thyme

sea salt

✱ SPECIAL EQUIPMENT
  6 cm round cutter
  20 cm ovenproof frying pan

1 Preheat the oven to 160°C fan-forced (180°C conventional).

2 Cut a thin slice from the potatoes on their widest sides, so they sit flat on a chopping board. Use a 6 cm round cutter to cut a circle into each potato; it should be about 2 cm high. Use a vegetable peeler to cut around the top edge; this will smooth (bevel) it so it is not at a sharp angle (see opposite).

3 Place a layer of sliced butter (about 120 g) in a cold 20 cm ovenproof frying pan, then place the potato rounds on top. Cook the potato over medium heat for 5 minutes or until the butter starts to bubble and turn nut-brown. Reduce the heat to low–medium and add the remaining butter, then turn the potatoes over and continue to cook for another 5 minutes or until they are brown on both sides.

4 Deglaze the pan with chicken stock, then add the garlic and thyme. Transfer the pan to the oven and cook the potatoes for 20 minutes or until tender. Season with salt.

5 Serve.

Potato gnocchi

The secret to this dish lies in making sure the gnocchi are soft and pillowy in texture. If they are like rubber bullets, you have overworked the potato and added too much flour. So make sure you are gentle when you handle the dough.

Serves 4

500 g rock salt

1 kg floury potatoes (see page 115) such as Sebago, well scrubbed

300 g strong '00' plain flour (see page 203), plus extra if needed

sea salt

1 × 60 g egg, beaten

½ cup (40 g) flaked almonds

100 g unsalted butter, chopped

a handful of sage leaves

1 tablespoon salted capers, rinsed and drained

shaved parmesan, to serve

✻ SPECIAL EQUIPMENT
disposable kitchen gloves
potato ricer or drum sieve
slotted spoon

1 Preheat the oven to 160°C fan-forced (180°C conventional).

2 Place a layer of rock salt and the potatoes on a baking tray lined with foil. Bake for 35 minutes or until cooked through. Carefully peel the hot potatoes (use disposable kitchen gloves to protect your hands). Discard the rock salt.

3 Use a potato ricer or drum sieve to mash the potatoes into a large bowl. Place the flour in another large bowl, then sprinkle with 1 teaspoon sea salt and mix well. Add half of the flour and the egg to the potato. Knead, gradually adding more flour, until the mixture is soft, smooth and slightly sticky. (You might need a little more flour.)

4 Divide the dough into 4, then shape each quarter into a 2.5 cm-diameter roll. Cut the dough into 2 cm pieces.

5 Bring 5 litres water to the boil in a large saucepan; do not add salt as this tends to make the gnocchi stick together.

6 Preheat the oven to 130°C fan-forced (150°C conventional). Toast the almonds on a baking tray for 5 minutes or until lightly browned. Set aside. Melt 80 g of the butter in a baking dish in the oven. Add the sage and capers.

7 Cook the gnocchi in the boiling water, about 20 at a time. After the gnocchi rise to the surface, cook for a further 20 seconds, then remove with a slotted spoon. Drain on paper towel, then add to the baking dish and toss lightly in the sage butter.

8 Melt the remaining butter in a frying pan over medium heat, then fry the gnocchi in batches until light golden. Add the butter and sage mixture and toss to coat the gnocchi.

9 Divide the gnocchi mixture among serving bowls, then scatter with flaked almonds and shaved parmesan and serve.

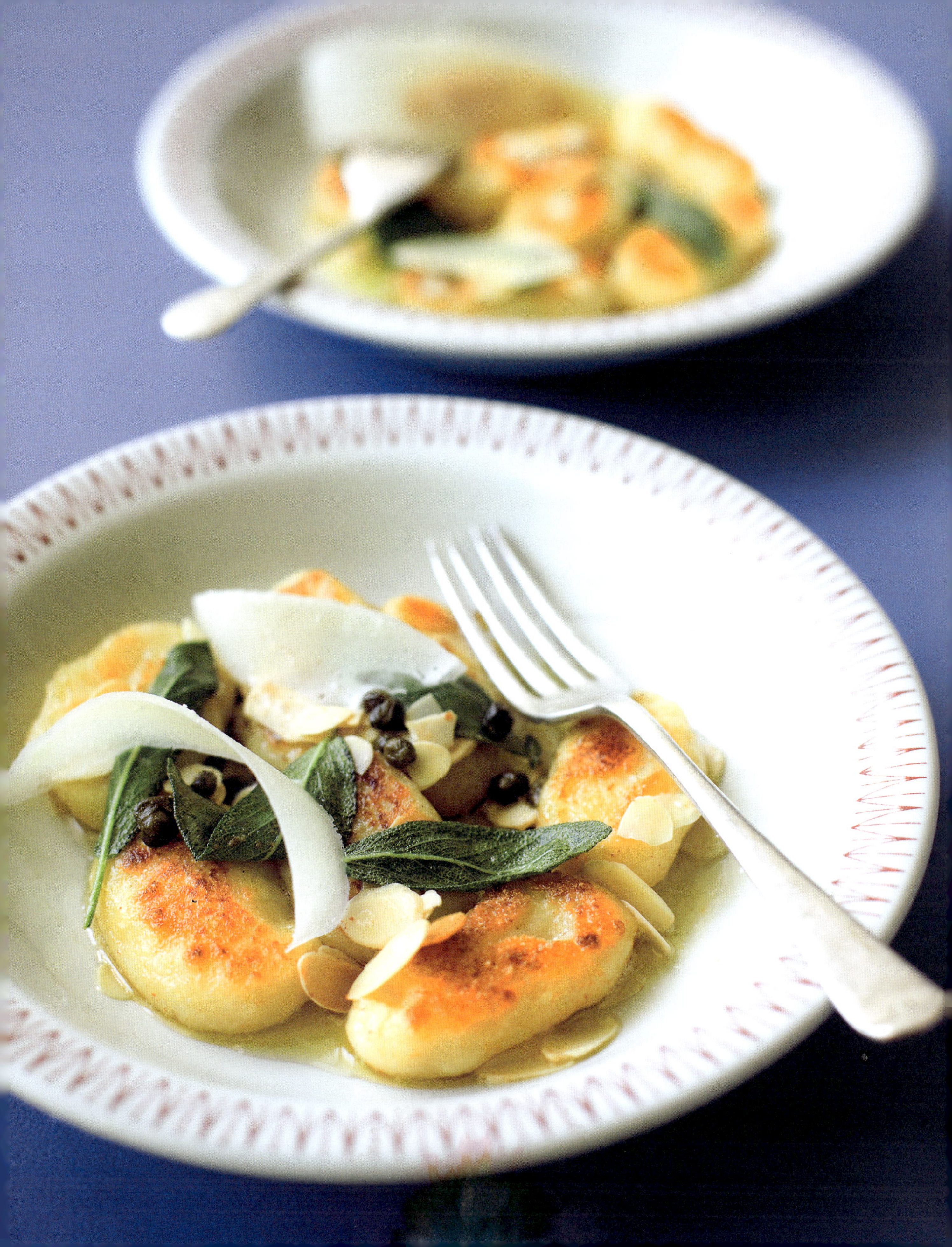

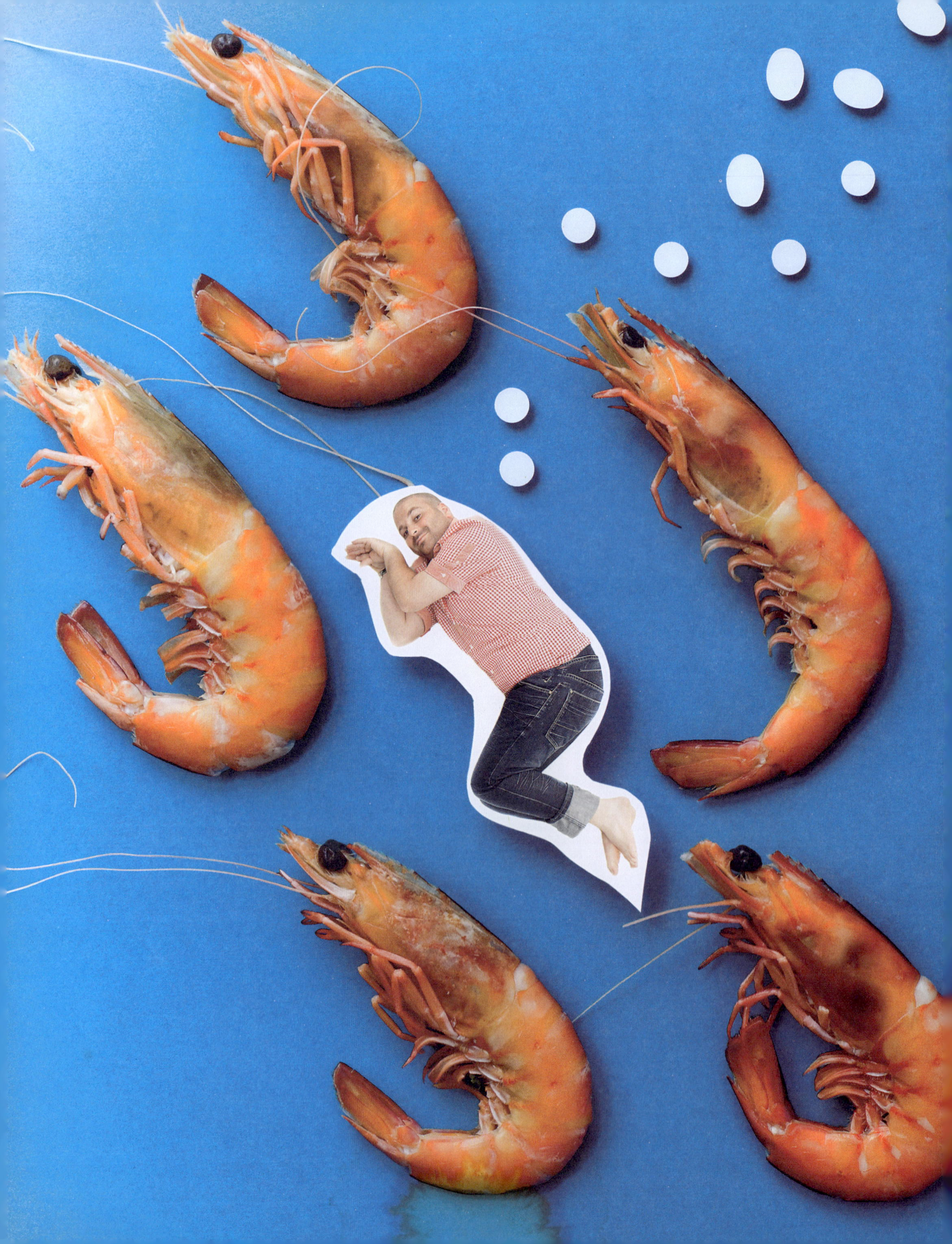

PRAWNS

Prawns are crustaceans that are found in calm, warm waters. They nest in water plants and lay eggs. As invertebrates, prawns do not have a backbone; they have an exoskeleton (the hard shell surrounding the flesh). They are omnivores, meaning that they eat both plants and animals. Prawns have five pairs of walking legs (pereopods) and five pairs of swimming legs (pleopods), and they can swim backwards really quickly.

More than twenty-five species of prawn are found in Australian waters, including school prawns, king prawns and tiger prawns. While large prawns may look impressive, they are slightly tougher to eat. School prawns are small, smooth-shelled prawns that taste very sweet and can be eaten shell and all. King prawns are the largest and best-known prawn. They come in different sizes, from medium to extra large. Tiger prawns have stripes, hence their name.

To prepare prawns for cooking, first peel and clean them. Pull off the head, then peel away the shell from the thick end, working down to the tail. The prawn legs should come off with the shell. The tail can be left on, but if you want to remove it, simply squeeze the prawn and pull out the meat. Remove the intestinal vein along the outer curve using a small knife or thin skewer. Do not throw the shells out – use them to make prawn stock for risotto (see page 128). To butterfly a prawn, use a small knife to cut into the flesh of the back (but not all the way through), then press apart. The sides should be the same thickness, forming a butterfly shape when flattened.

Prawns can be barbecued, poached, steamed and fried. They go really well with basil, chilli, chives, coriander, cumin, fish sauce, garlic, ginger, lemons, limes, mayo, mint, noodles, olive oil, onions, rice, soy sauce, spring onions, tomatoes and Worcestershire sauce.

Golden thread prawns with cocktail sauce

This great party snack is a real crowd-pleaser. When you make it, please think of me. In my early days as a chef, I would make a thousand of these prawns a week, but hey, that's my job and I love it. No matter how old you are, I bet you will enjoy threading the potato strips around the prawns. Use an Asian spiral vegetable cutter (see page 201) to make the strips.

Serves 4

12 large raw prawns

1 large Coliban potato

½ cup (60 g) custard powder

vegetable oil, for deep-frying

lime wedges (optional), to serve

COCKTAIL SAUCE

1 cup (250 ml) Mayonnaise (see page 203)

½ cup (125 ml) tomato sauce (ketchup)

1 tablespoon Worcestershire sauce

a few drops of Tabasco sauce (optional)

juice of 1 lemon

✻ SPECIAL EQUIPMENT
Asian spiral vegetable cutter
deep-fryer (optional)

1 Peel the prawns, removing the heads and shells and leaving on the tails. Make a small cut along the back to remove the intestinal tract. Rinse the prawns under cold running water and set aside to dry on paper towel.

2 Peel the potato and place in a bowl of water to prevent it from turning brown. Use an Asian spiral vegetable cutter to make spiral strips from the potato.

3 Mix the custard powder with a little water to make a thin paste. Dip the potato strips in the custard mixture and roll around the prawns. Set aside.

4 Meanwhile, to make the cocktail sauce, mix the mayonnaise, tomato sauce, Worcestershire sauce, Tabasco (if using) and lemon juice in a small bowl. Adjust the flavours to taste by adding more tomato sauce, Worcestershire sauce, Tabasco and lemon juice, if necessary. Set aside. (Makes about 375 ml.)

5 Preheat oil for deep-frying in a deep-fryer to 180°C (or in a heavy-based saucepan until a cube of bread browns in 30 seconds).

6 Deep-fry the potato-wrapped prawns for 4 minutes or until golden brown and crisp. Drain on paper towel, then serve with cocktail sauce for dipping, with lime wedges to the side, if you like.

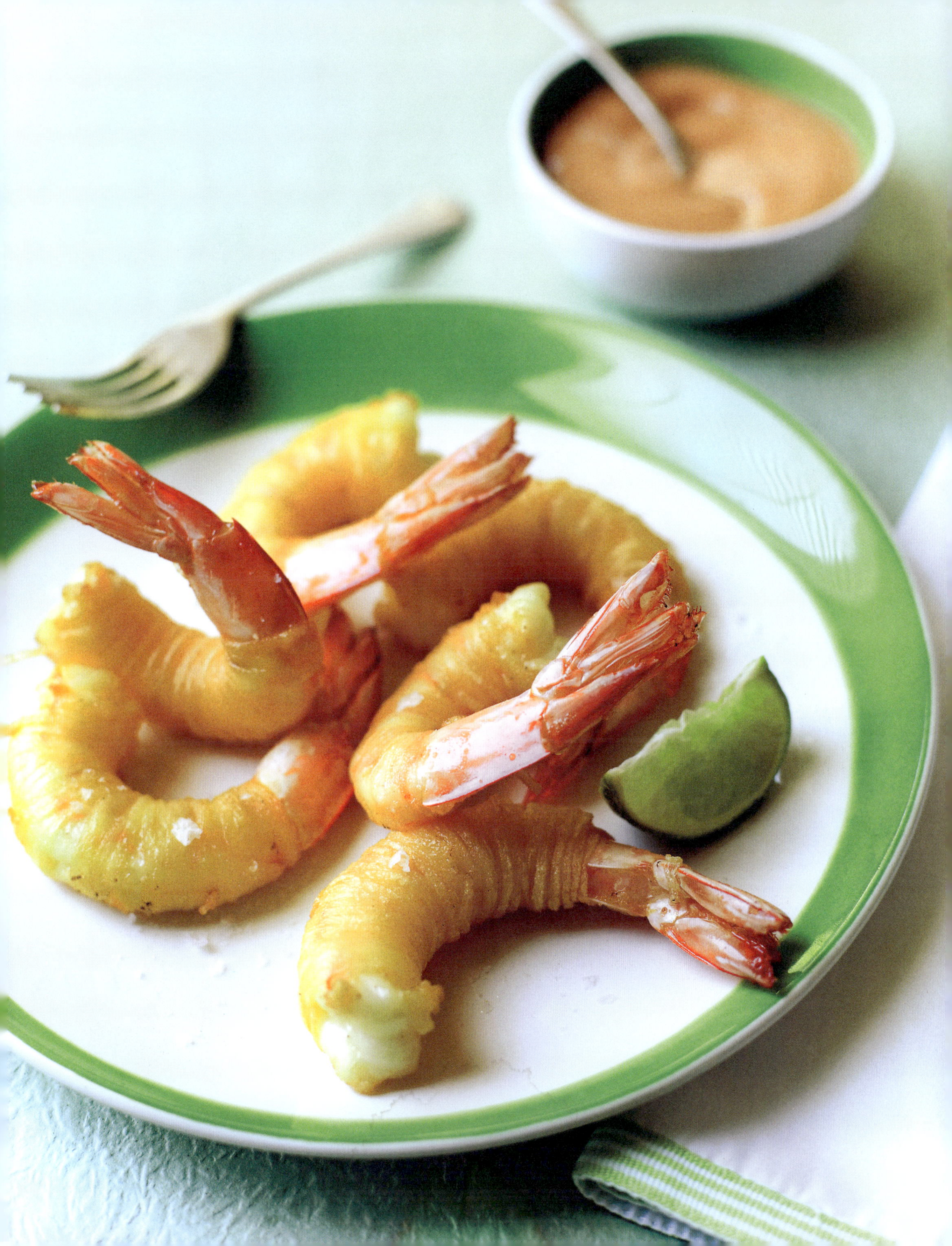

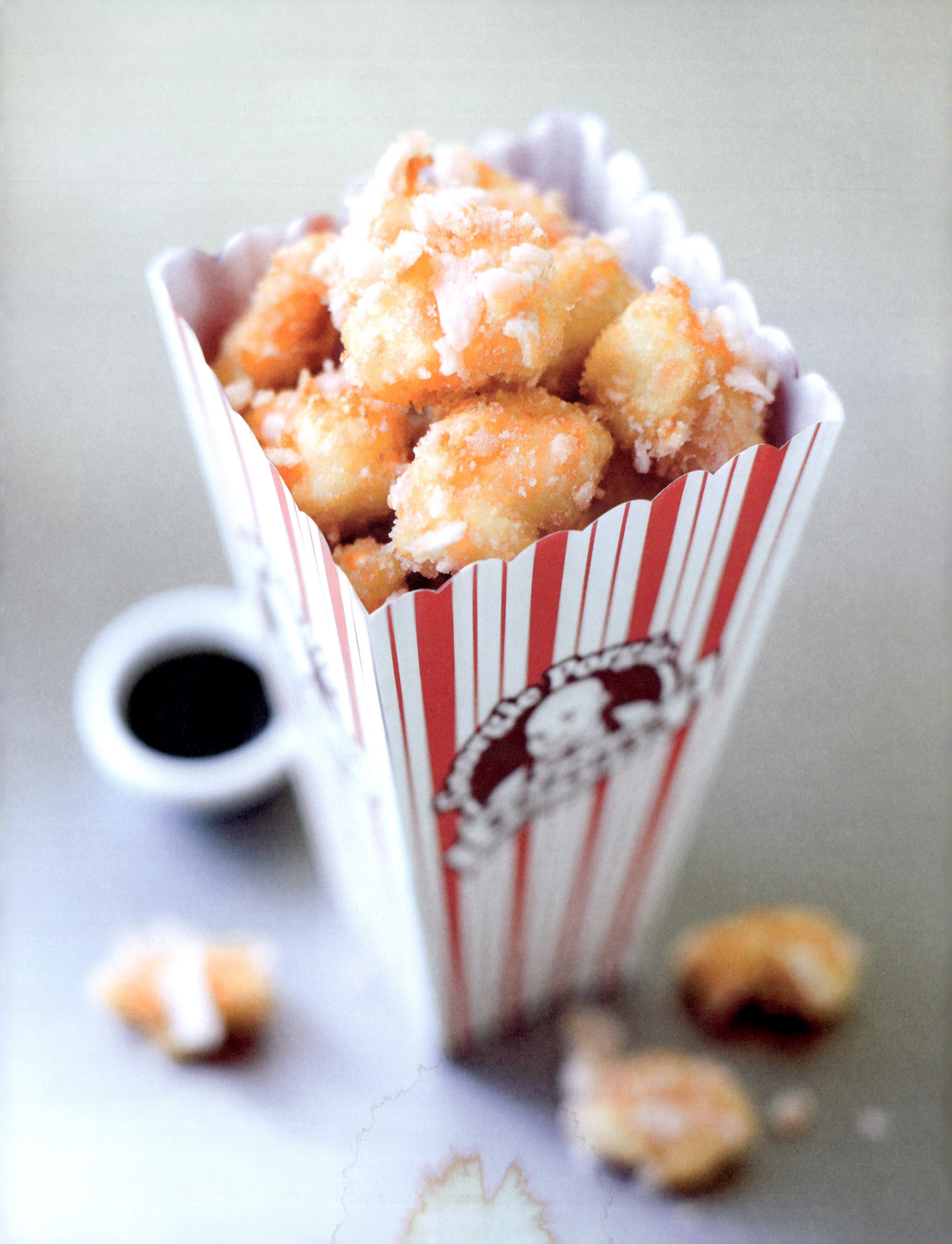

Popcorn prawns with salt-and-vinegar dipping sauce

Crispy, crunchy, salty – what more can I say? I love this dish, and it's so much better than that fast food stuff! Asian prawn crackers are the light and crunchy ones you buy from Asian takeaway shops (the ones that stick to your tongue). You can also buy uncooked prawn crackers in a packet from the supermarket.

Serves 4

- 12 raw king prawns
- vegetable oil, for deep-frying
- 16 uncooked Asian prawn crackers
- ¼ cup (35 g) plain flour
- 1 egg
- 2 tablespoons milk

SALT-AND-VINEGAR DIPPING SAUCE

- 2 tablespoons malt vinegar
- 1 tablespoon extra virgin olive oil
- 1 tablespoon soy sauce
- 1 teaspoon brown sugar
- a few drops of fish sauce, to taste

✱ SPECIAL EQUIPMENT
deep-fryer (optional)
slotted spoon
mortar and pestle or rolling pin

1 To make the dipping sauce, mix the vinegar, olive oil, soy sauce, brown sugar and fish sauce in a small bowl. Taste and adjust the flavour by adding more fish sauce if you like. Set aside. (Makes about 80 ml.)

2 Peel the prawns, removing the heads and shells, leaving on the tails. Make a small cut along the back to remove the intestinal tract. Rinse the prawns under cold running water and set aside to dry on paper towel. Cut into bite-sized pieces.

3 Preheat oil for deep-frying in a deep-fryer to 180°C (or in a heavy-based saucepan until a cube of bread browns in 30 seconds). Deep-fry the prawn crackers until they puff up, crisp and change colour. Remove with a slotted spoon and drain on paper towel, then leave to cool a little. Crush the prawn crackers with a mortar and pestle (or place in a ziplock bag and seal, then crush with a rolling pin).

4 Sprinkle the flour onto a plate. Whisk the egg and milk together with a fork in a wide shallow bowl.

5 Lightly dust each prawn in flour, then dip in the egg wash and coat with the prawn-cracker crumbs.

6 Deep-fry the prawns for 1–2 minutes or until they float to the surface of the oil (which means they're cooked). Remove with a slotted spoon and drain on paper towel.

7 Serve the popcorn prawns with the dipping sauce to the side.

Prawn risotto

Yes, I know my background is Greek, but I still love risotto. Everyone has their own idea of how to make it. The key to my recipe is to not stir the rice. That way, the starch in the rice doesn't make the risotto claggy. I like to see all the grains of rice loose and separate. Instead of making stock from the prawn shells, you could use the same quantity of fish stock.

Serves 4

- 40 g unsalted butter
- 1 tablespoon olive oil
- 1 onion, finely chopped
- 2 cloves garlic, crushed
- 1 cup (200 g) carnaroli rice (see page 201)
- 12 raw king prawns, peeled, cleaned and sliced, shells reserved for making stock
- mascarpone and chervil sprigs (optional), to serve
- sea salt and freshly ground black pepper

PRAWN STOCK

- reserved shells from the peeled prawns (see above)
- 1 tablespoon olive oil
- 1 cup (250 ml) dry white wine
- 1 tablespoon tomato paste
- 2 cloves garlic, chopped
- 2 golden shallots, chopped
- 1 litre water

✳ SPECIAL EQUIPMENT
fine-mesh sieve

1 To make the prawn stock, place the prawn shells in a medium-sized heavy-based saucepan and drizzle with the olive oil. Cook over medium heat for 15 minutes, stirring. Remove the pan from the heat and deglaze the pan with wine, stirring to remove any cooked bits stuck to the base of the pan.

2 Return the pan to medium heat, then add the tomato paste, garlic, shallot and water. Bring to the boil, then reduce the heat to low and simmer for 25 minutes. Remove from the heat, then strain the stock through a fine-mesh sieve into a saucepan and discard the solids. Keep the stock warm.

3 Heat half of the butter with the olive oil in a large heavy-based saucepan over medium–high heat. Add the onion and garlic and cook for 2 minutes or until soft. Add the rice and continue to stir for 2 minutes until it is translucent and lightly toasted.

4 Add 3 cups (750 ml) of the hot prawn stock, reduce the heat to low, then simmer gently for 12–14 minutes until all the liquid has been absorbed.

5 When the rice is tender to-the-bite, but ever so slightly firm in the centre (al dente), remove the pan from the heat and add the prawns and remaining butter. (The prawns should gently cook in the heat of the pan off the heat.) Mix well to achieve a creamy consistency and adjust the risotto by adding ½ cup (125 ml) extra stock, if you want it to be a bit looser. Check that the prawns are cooked (if not, continue to stir until the prawns are just cooked through).

6 Divide the risotto among plates or bowls, top with a spoonful of mascarpone (if using), then season with salt and pepper and scatter with chervil, if you like. Serve immediately.

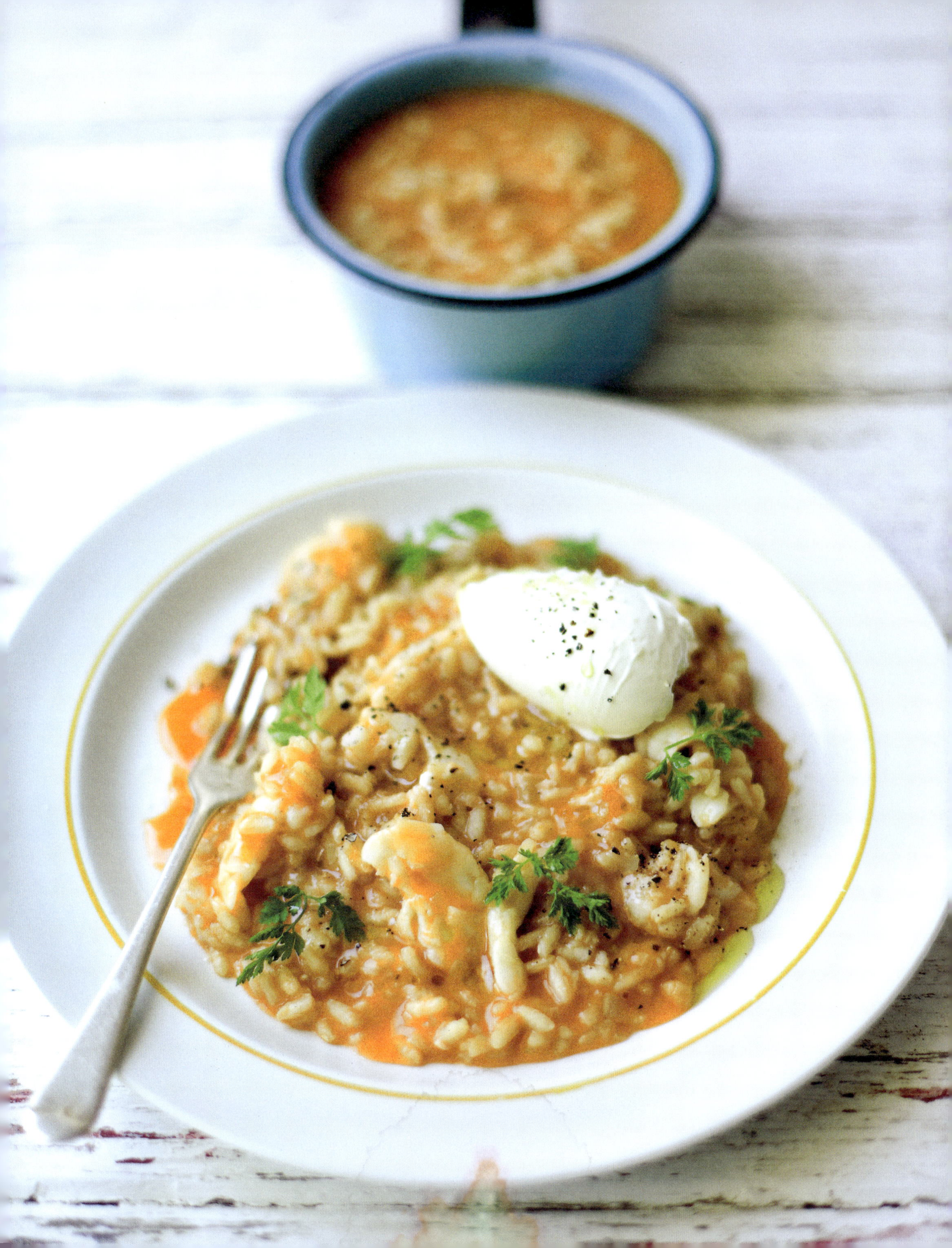

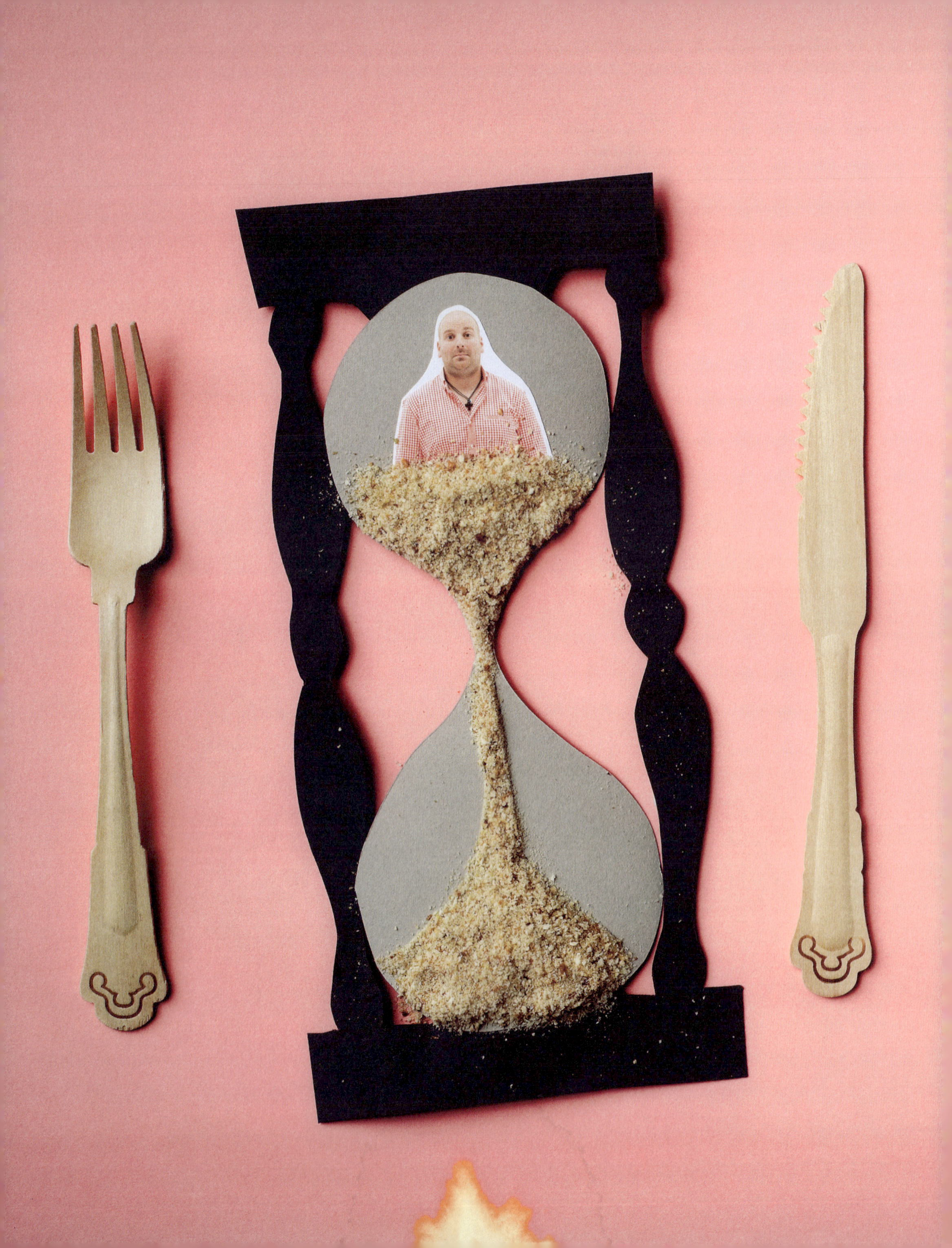

QUICK DINNERS

Sometimes we're in a rush and don't have a lot of time to spend cooking dinner. Although takeaway can seem like an easier option, here are some quick meal ideas that will be ready in next to no time. They're healthier and cheaper, too.

For dinner in a flash:

- To make an omelette, lightly beat 2–3 eggs with 1 tablespoon milk or water and cook in a non-stick frying pan over low heat for a few minutes until set. Fold in half and serve. You can add whatever vegetables you have at hand to flavour the egg mixture, such as grated carrot and zucchini (courgette), peas and corn, diced onion and freshly chopped herbs. Another favourite filling is shredded ham and cheese.

- To pan-fry a fish fillet, lightly dust it in plain flour. Melt a little butter in a non-stick frying pan and cook the fish over medium heat for a few minutes on each side, depending on the thickness of the fillet, until the flesh has turned opaque and is just cooked through. Squeeze over some lemon juice, season with salt and pepper and serve with a simple salad.

- Slice a chicken breast fillet in half widthways and flatten with a meat mallet. Brush with olive oil and chargrill over high heat for a few minutes on each side until cooked.

- For pan-fried lamb cutlets, cook in a little olive oil in a non-stick frying pan over medium–high heat. Remove and leave to rest. Add chopped garlic to the hot pan with a little more oil, some chopped cherry tomatoes and a tin of drained cannellini beans or chick peas. Cook for a few minutes until warmed through. Toss in some torn fresh herbs such as basil or flat-leaf parsley and season with salt and pepper.

Ham, tomato and cheese jaffles

My big brother Nick is an amazing tiler. He is passionate about his craft, which makes me realise that we both follow one basic rule: you must love what you do. Though he's a great tiler, my brother is a simple cook. I remember coming home from school and Nick making me toasted sandwiches in the jaffle machine. Great memories!

Serves 4

50 g unsalted butter, softened

8 thick slices good-quality bread

4 slices smoked ham off-the-bone

2 oxheart tomatoes, sliced

12 basil leaves

4 slices provolone cheese (see page 203)

✱ SPECIAL EQUIPMENT
   jaffle maker

1 Heat a jaffle maker according to the manufacturer's instructions. Working in batches if necessary, butter one side of each slice of bread, then place, buttered-side down, onto the jaffle maker.

2 Top each piece of bread with 1 slice of ham, some sliced tomato, 3 basil leaves and a slice of cheese. Butter the top piece of bread and place on top of the sandwich filling.

3 Close the jaffle maker and cook for a few minutes, until the bread has browned, the cheese has melted and the filling is toasty warm.

4 Serve immediately.

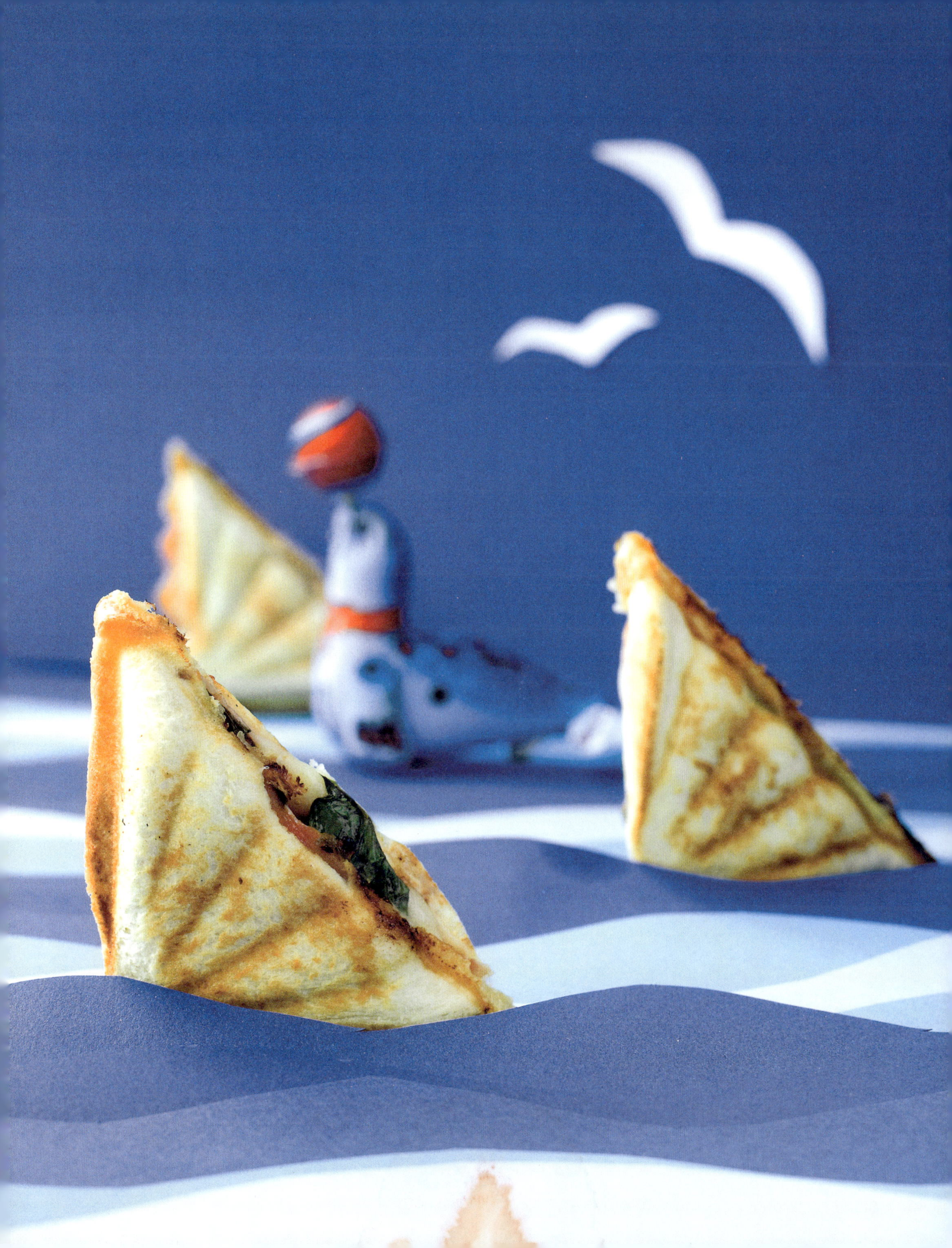

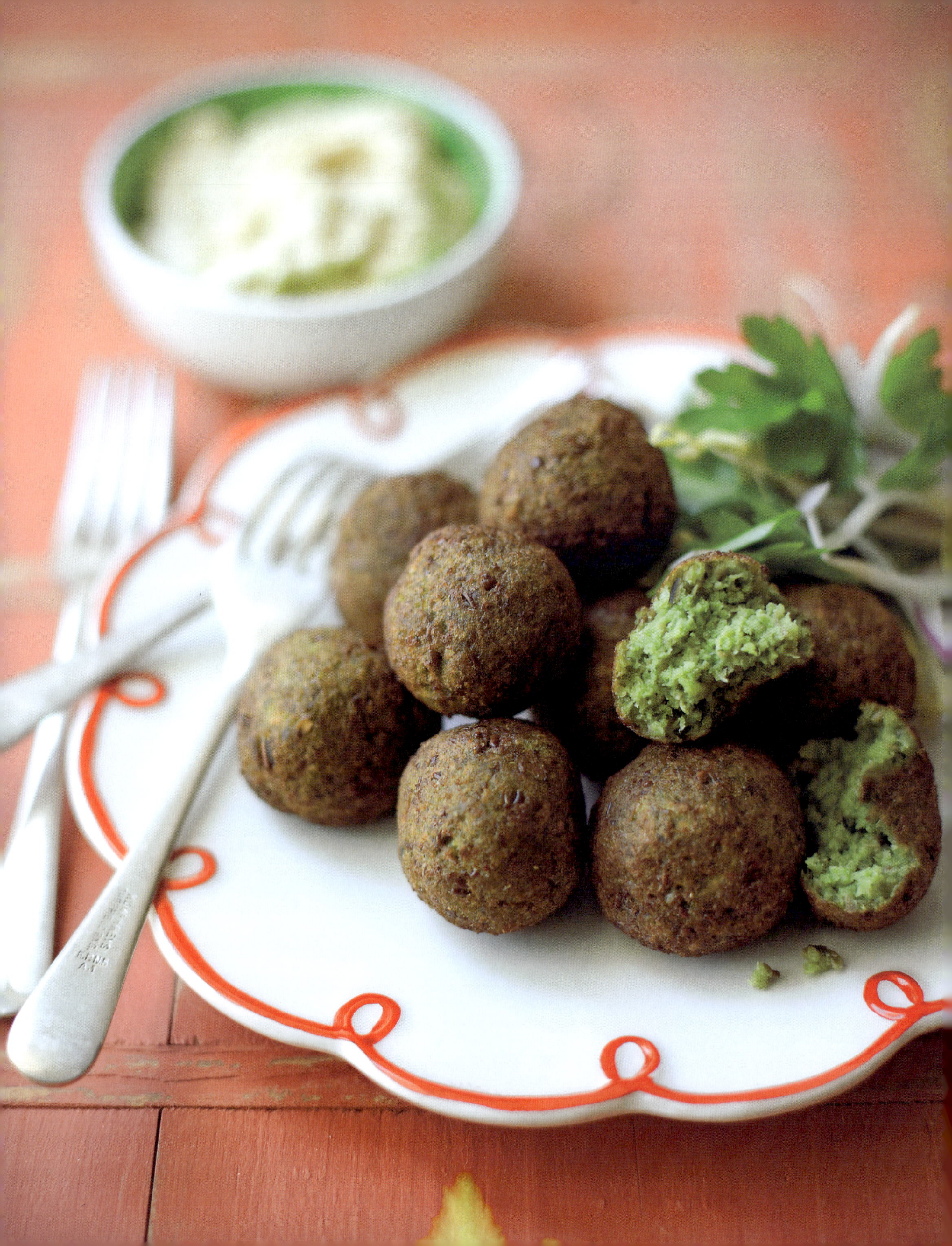

Alexandrian felafels

Dad was born in Alexandria, Egypt, to a Greek father and Italian mother, and I am sure that this influenced his palate, as well as mine. His mother, my Nonna Nicoletta, taught Mum how to make felafels, and I still love them.

Serves 4–6

200 g dried broad beans, soaked overnight in cold water

1 onion, coarsely chopped

2 cloves garlic, chopped

2 spring onions, thinly sliced

½ cup (small handful) flat-leaf parsley, chopped

½ cup (small handful) coriander, chopped

¼ cup (70 g) tahini (see page 203)

2 teaspoons ground cumin

2 teaspoons lemon juice

2 teaspoons olive oil

vegetable oil, for deep-frying

Hummus (see page 31), to serve

PARSLEY SALAD

1½ cups (2 handfuls) flat-leaf parsley leaves

1 small red (Spanish) onion, thinly sliced

100 g mung bean sprouts

50 ml extra virgin olive oil

juice of ½ lemon

✱ **SPECIAL EQUIPMENT**
food processor
deep-fryer (optional)
slotted spoon

1 Place the drained broad beans, onion, garlic, spring onion, parsley, coriander, tahini, cumin, lemon juice and olive oil in a food processor and process until the mixture is finely chopped. Transfer the felafel mixture to a bowl, then cover with plastic film and refrigerate for 2 hours.

2 Preheat oil for deep-frying in a deep-fryer to 170°C (or in a heavy-based saucepan until a cube of bread browns in 35 seconds).

3 Roll the felafel mixture into 3 cm balls. Deep-fry in batches, turning occasionally for 3 minutes or until golden brown. Remove with a slotted spoon and drain on paper towel.

4 To make the parsley salad, combine the parsley, onion, mung bean sprouts, olive oil and lemon juice in a bowl and toss to combine.

5 Serve the felafels with the parsley salad and hummus.

Pan-fried steak and mushrooms with garlic butter

People think that just because I own a two-hat-rated restaurant I must only eat fancy food. That's not the case. I still love the simple things in life. Give me a plate with steak, mushrooms and garlic butter, and you can't go wrong. As long as you don't overcook the steak!

Serves 4

4 × 180 g sirloin steaks

2 tablespoons olive oil

sea salt and freshly ground black pepper

MUSHROOMS WITH GARLIC BUTTER

200 g unsalted butter, chopped

2 cloves garlic, sliced

4 portobello mushrooms, stems trimmed

sea salt and freshly ground black pepper

roughly chopped flat-leaf parsley, to serve

1 Place the steaks on a plate and rub with olive oil. Season with salt and pepper and leave to come to room temperature.

2 Heat a large heavy-based frying pan or chargrill pan over high heat. Cook the steaks for 2 minutes on each side for medium–rare, turning once (for medium, cook the steaks for 3 minutes on each side) or continue until cooked to your liking. Make sure you only turn the steaks once.

3 Remove the steaks from the pan, cover loosely with foil and set aside on a plate to rest for 5 minutes.

4 Meanwhile, to make the mushrooms with garlic butter, add the butter and garlic to the pan, then reduce the heat to low. Fry the mushrooms for 5 minutes, turning until softened and cooked. Season to taste with salt and pepper and sprinkle with the parsley.

5 Place the steaks on serving plates, then add the mushrooms. Drizzle over the pan juices and serve immediately.

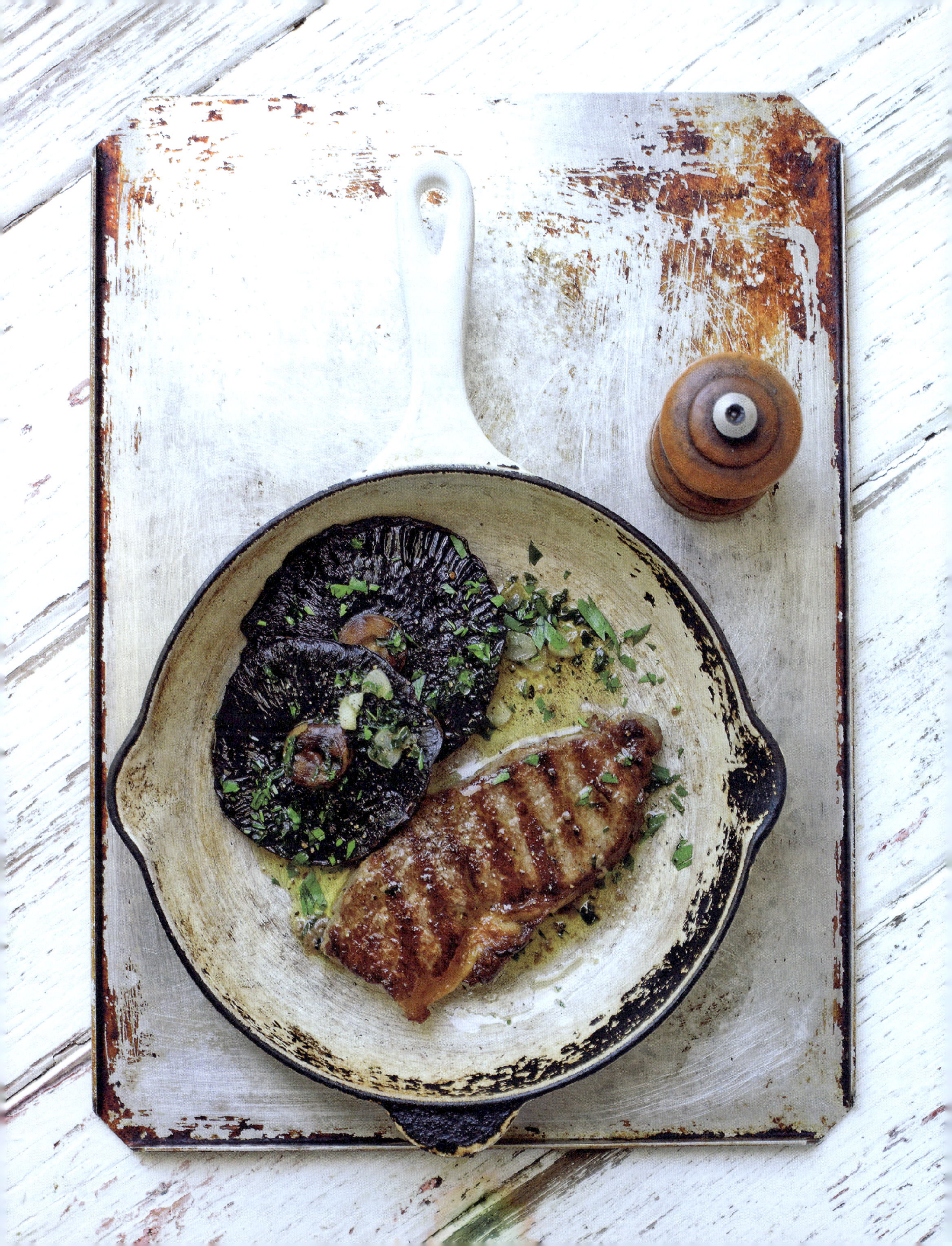

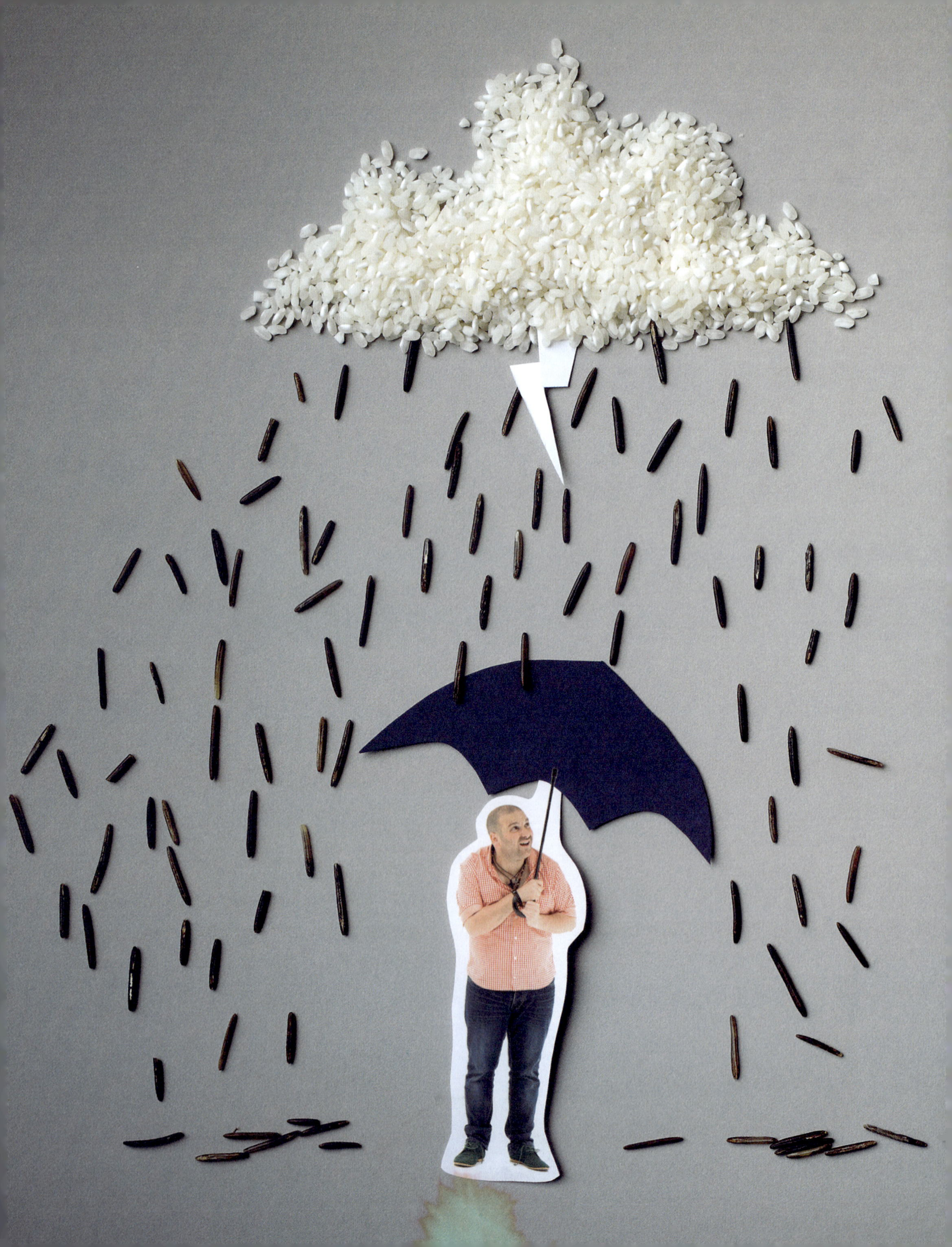

RICE

Rice is one of the most important cereal grains on the planet. This staple food is grown and harvested on every continent except Antarctica. More than 90 per cent of the world's rice is grown and eaten in Asia. To produce one kilogram of irrigated rice, it takes 5000 litres of water. Brown rice is rice that still has its outer coating, while white rice has been hulled, with its outer coating removed. There are thousands of varieties of rice, and they have many different uses.

Rice is so important to Asian diets that the words for 'rice' and 'food' are the same in several Asian languages. Rice triples in volume when cooked, so remember this when you choose your saucepan.

Rice can be divided into three main groups:

LONG-GRAIN RICE has long, slender kernels that produce light, fluffy rice. Varieties include basmati, jasmine and Thai fragrant rice.

MEDIUM-GRAIN RICE has short, wide kernels that are moist and tender when cooked. Arborio rice has large grains with white dots in the centre. It is most often used in risotto because of its creamy texture. Carnaroli and vialone are other Italian rice varieties used to make risotto.

SHORT-GRAIN RICE has short, round kernels that are soft and cling together when boiled. Japanese rice (such as koshikari used for sushi) is short-grained, as is Spanish rice (calasparra), used to make paella.

Mum's rice pilaf

Good food is not about using expensive ingredients. The cheapest and simplest ingredients can create the best dishes. Take this rice pilaf, for example. It is just delicious. If you have any leftover, eat it cold the next day with some yoghurt mixed through.

Serves 4

½ cup (125 ml) olive oil

50 g unsalted butter

1 cup (about 55 g) crushed egg vermicelli noodles

1 onion, finely chopped

1 clove garlic, sliced

1 cup (200 g) long-grain rice

2 cups (500 ml) water

sea salt

1 cup (80 g) flaked almonds

1 cup (150 g) currants

freshly ground black pepper

chopped coriander, to serve

1 Heat the oil and butter in a large saucepan over medium heat. Fry the crushed noodles for 2–3 minutes or until crisp and browned. Add the onion and garlic and continue cooking for 2–3 minutes or until softened. Add the rice and cook for a further 2 minutes. Add the water and a pinch of salt. Bring to the boil, then cover with a tight-fitting lid, reduce the heat to the lowest setting and cook for 10 minutes. Remove from the heat and leave to sit with the lid on the pan for another 10 minutes.

2 Meanwhile, preheat the oven to 160°C fan-forced (180°C conventional).

3 Toast the almonds on a baking tray for 5 minutes or until light golden. Set aside.

4 Remove the lid and fluff up the rice with a fork. Season with salt and pepper to taste. Stir through the currants, almonds and coriander. Serve.

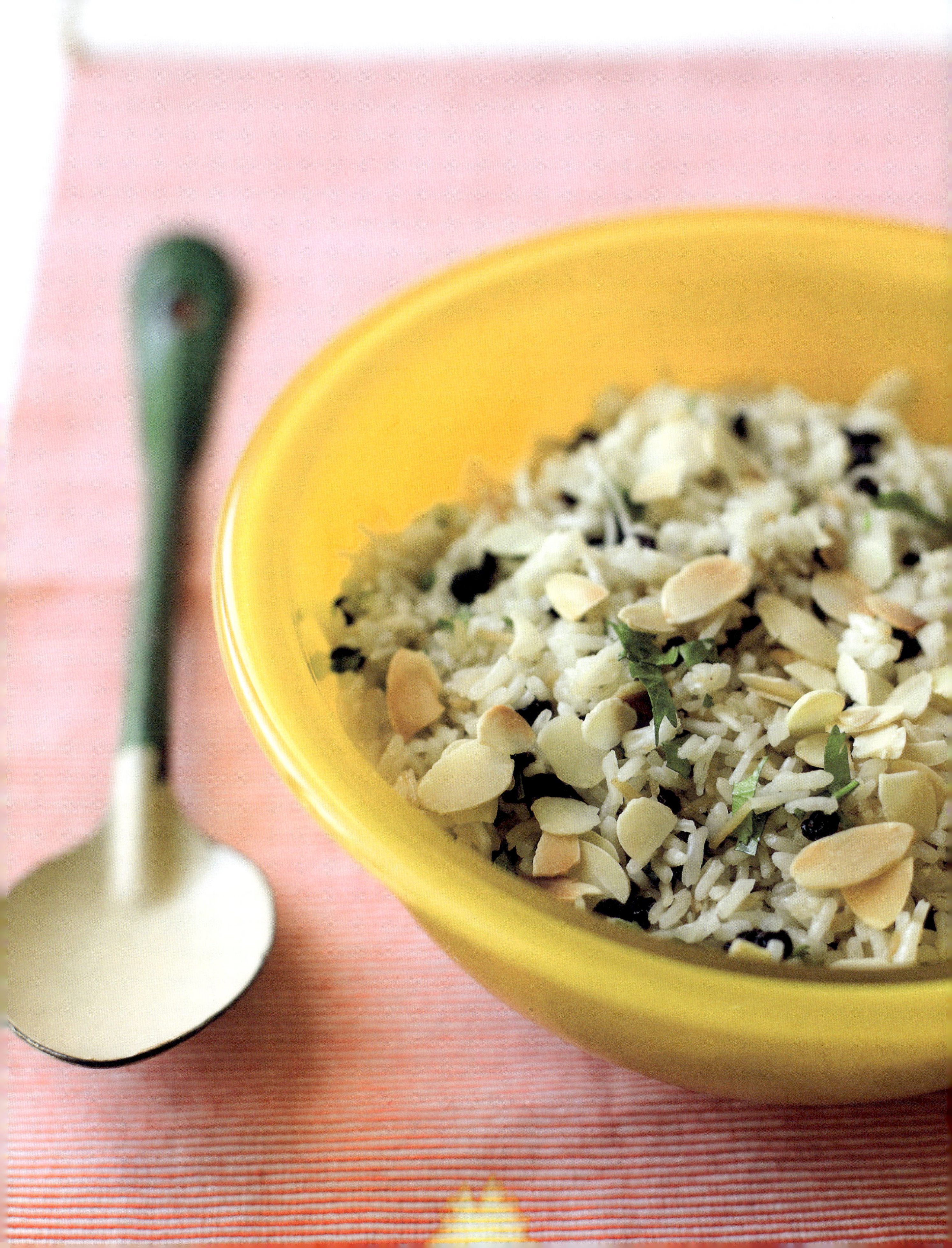

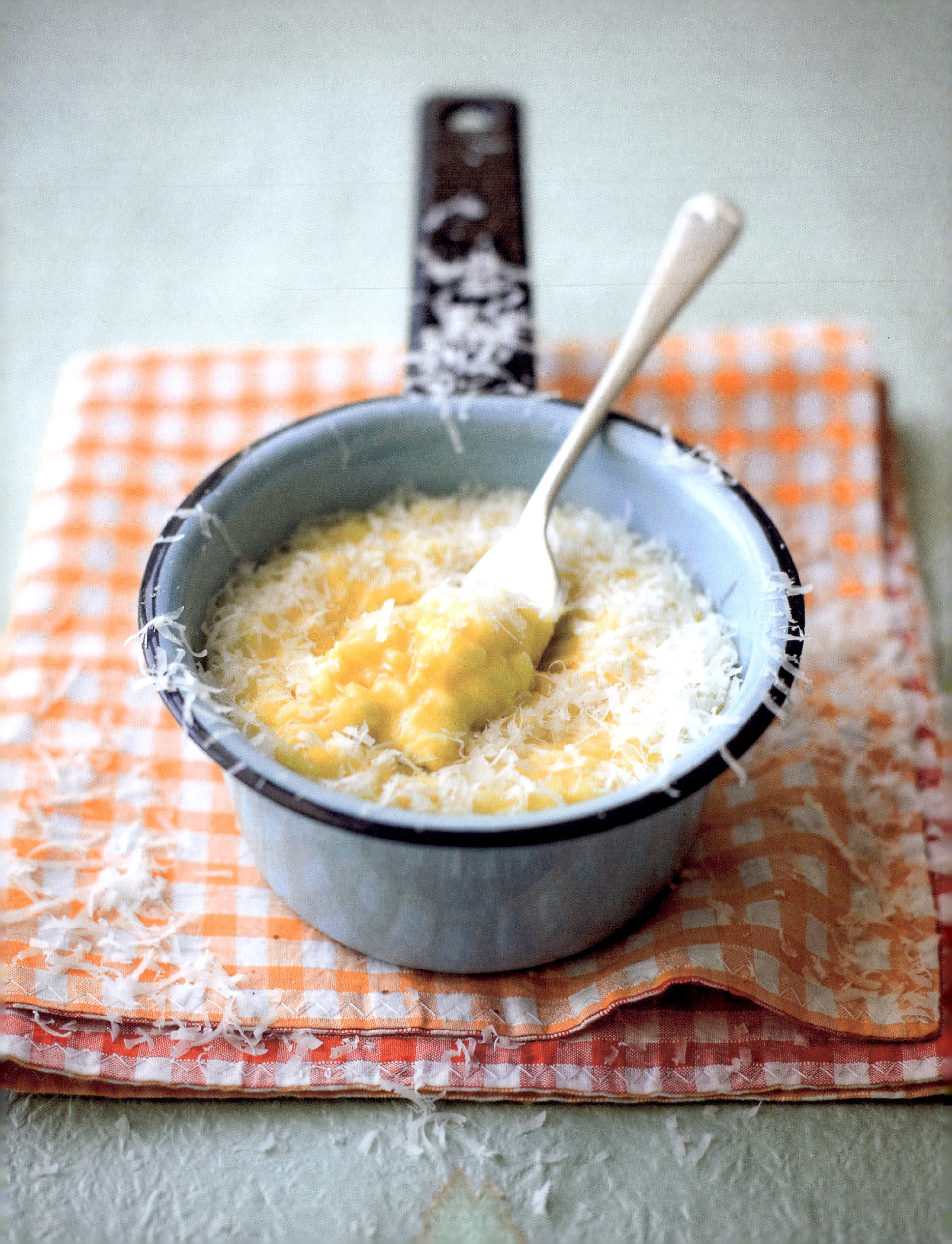

Pumpkin risotto my way

This is a great little entree. Some people think it's hard to cook risotto properly, but try this method and you'll see how easy it can be. There's no need to stir while the rice is absorbing the stock; just give it a quick stir when you add the sweet pumpkin puree at the end and you'll have a beautifully creamy risotto. When chestnuts are in season, roast a few and shave them over the risotto to add great flavour and texture.

Serves 4

400 g pumpkin, peeled, seeded and grated

60 g unsalted butter, softened

3 cups (750 ml) vegetable stock, plus ½ cup (125 ml) extra, as needed

1 tablespoon olive oil

1 onion, finely chopped

2 cloves garlic, crushed

1 cup (200 g) carnaroli rice (see page 201)

sea salt and freshly ground white pepper

grated parmesan, to serve

✱ SPECIAL EQUIPMENT
stick blender

1 Place the pumpkin and 40 g of the butter in a saucepan. Put the lid onto the pan and cook the pumpkin over low–medium heat for 10 minutes or until it is tender. Puree the pumpkin with a stick blender and set aside.

2 Heat the stock in a saucepan. Keep warm.

3 Heat the olive oil in a large heavy-based saucepan over medium–high heat. Add the onion and garlic and cook for 2 minutes or until soft. Add the rice and continue to stir for 2 minutes or until it is translucent and lightly toasted.

4 Add the hot stock to the rice, then reduce the heat to low and simmer gently for 12–14 minutes or until all the liquid has been absorbed. When the rice is tender-to-the-bite but ever so slightly firm in the centre (al dente), remove the pan from the heat and add the pureed pumpkin and remaining butter, then season to taste with salt and pepper. Stir well to achieve a creamy consistency and adjust the texture of the risotto with extra stock if you want a soupier result.

5 Divide the risotto among bowls or plates, then top with grated parmesan and serve.

Chocolate rice pudding

It doesn't matter what time of the day it is, a sweet tooth needs to be satisfied. Rice pudding is just the thing. Make sure the rice is cooked through though; there is nothing worse than crunchy rice.

Serves 4

1 cup (200 g) short-grain rice, washed

sea salt

400 ml water

850 ml milk

90 g caster sugar

1 vanilla pod, split lengthways, seeds scraped

⅓ cup (35 g) dutch-process cocoa (see page 202)

1 Place the rice, ½ teaspoon salt and water in a heavy-based saucepan. Bring to the boil over high heat, then stir and cover with a lid. Reduce the heat to low and cook for 15 minutes or until the liquid has been absorbed.

2 Place the milk, sugar, vanilla pod and seeds and cocoa in another saucepan, then stir and bring to a simmer over medium heat. Remove the vanilla pod. Add the milk mixture to the rice and cook over low heat for 20 minutes, stirring from time to time.

3 Remove the pan from the heat, cover with the lid and set aside for 5 minutes to cool a little.

4 Serve the warm chocolate rice pudding in bowls.

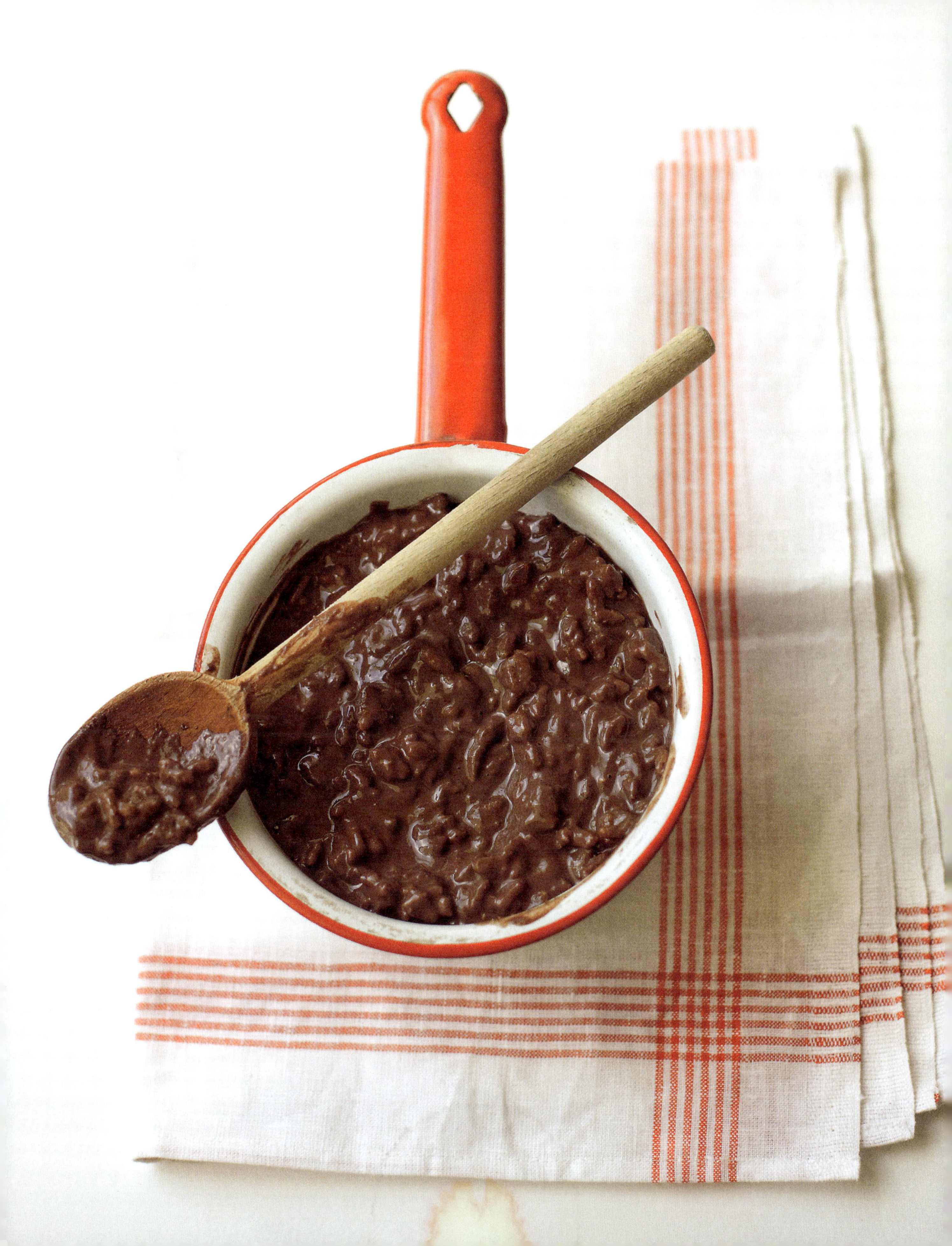

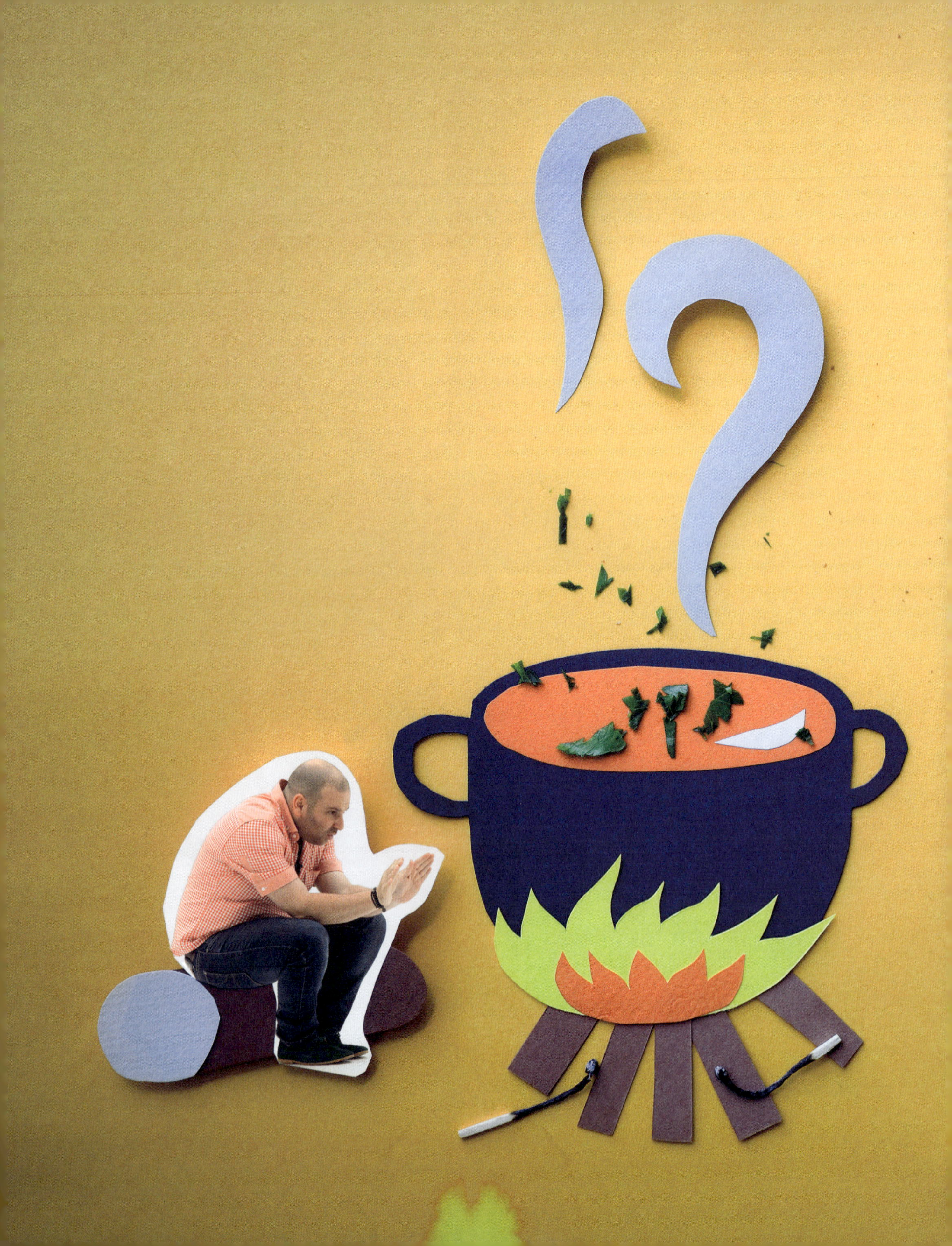

SOUP

Soups are popular the world over. In Australia we often associate them with winter, but they are also popular in tropical countries such as Malaysia, Thailand and Indonesia, where they are even eaten for breakfast!

Soups can be thin and clear (consomme, for example), thick and chunky (think minestrone or laksa) or pureed (such as pumpkin or potato and leek). Whatever the style of soup, it is usually made with some type of stock. This provides a base that gives depth of flavour to the soup. Chicken stock (see page 201) is the most versatile stock for making soup.

Mum's lentil soup

Who said that vegetarian food isn't tasty? The menu at one of my restaurants, Hellenic Republic, is made up of forty per cent vegetarian food. Pulses are a great ingredient and lentils are so healthy and delicious.

Serves 8

3 carrots

3 sticks celery

500 g brown lentils, rinsed under cold water

1 onion, halved

1 clove garlic

1 bay leaf

2 litres Chicken Stock (see page 201) or vegetable stock

2 tablespoons red-wine vinegar

2 tablespoons extra virgin olive oil

sea salt

Pita Bread (see page 10 or use purchased), to serve

1 Cut 1 carrot and 1 celery stick in half. Finely dice the remaining carrots and celery and set aside.

2 Place the lentils, halved carrot, halved celery, onion, garlic and bay leaf in a large saucepan. Cover with water and bring to the boil, then reduce the heat to low and cook for 10 minutes or until the lentils are tender.

3 Drain the lentils, then transfer to a baking tray lined with paper towel and leave to cool. Remove and discard the vegetables.

4 Preheat the oven to 160°C fan-forced (180°C conventional).

5 Place the diced carrot and celery on a baking tray and roast for 10 minutes or until tender but not browned. Remove from the oven and set aside.

6 Bring the chicken stock to the boil, then add the lentils, roast carrot and celery, red-wine vinegar and olive oil. Season to taste with salt.

7 Divide the soup among bowls and serve with pita bread.

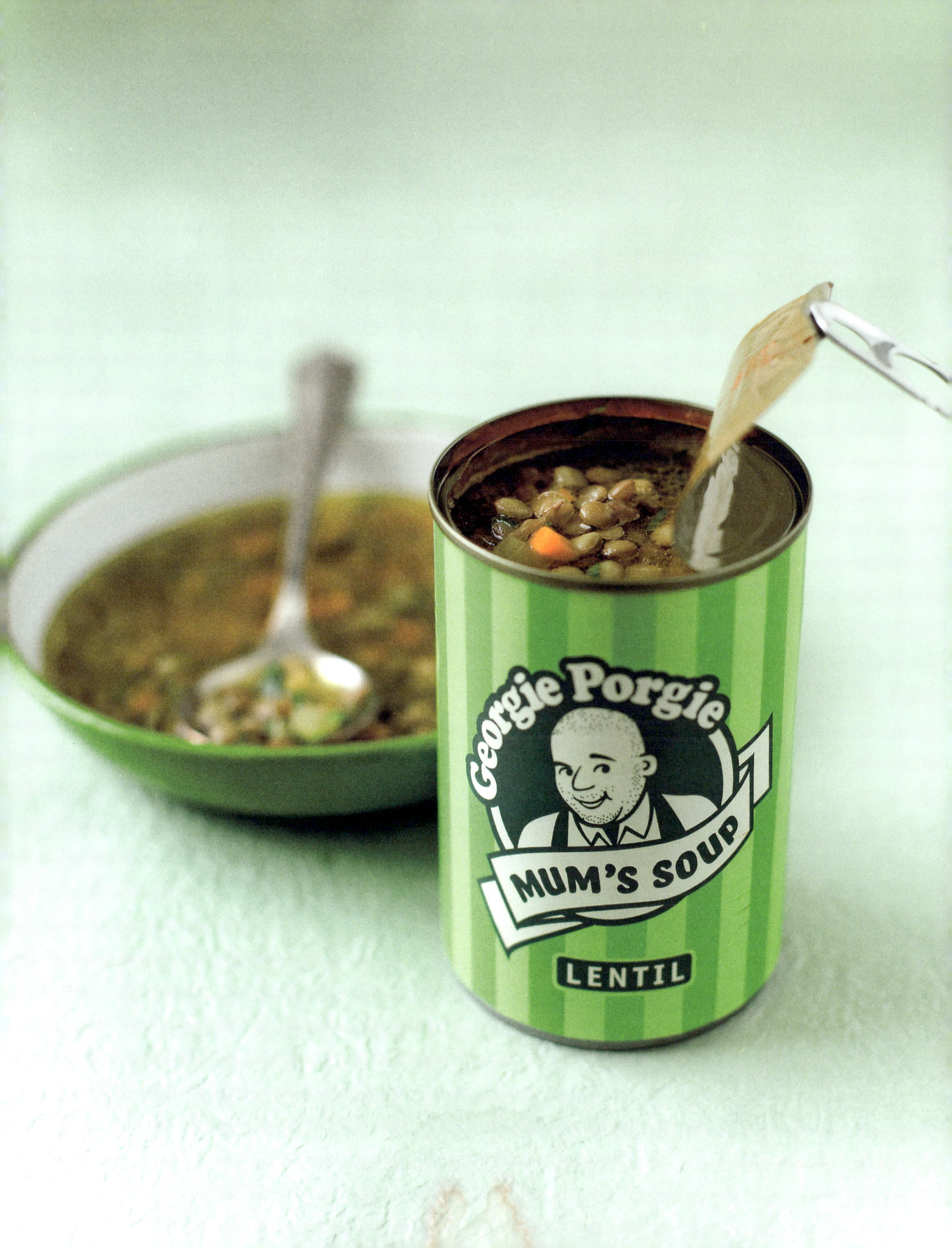
Georgie Porgie
MUM'S SOUP
LENTIL

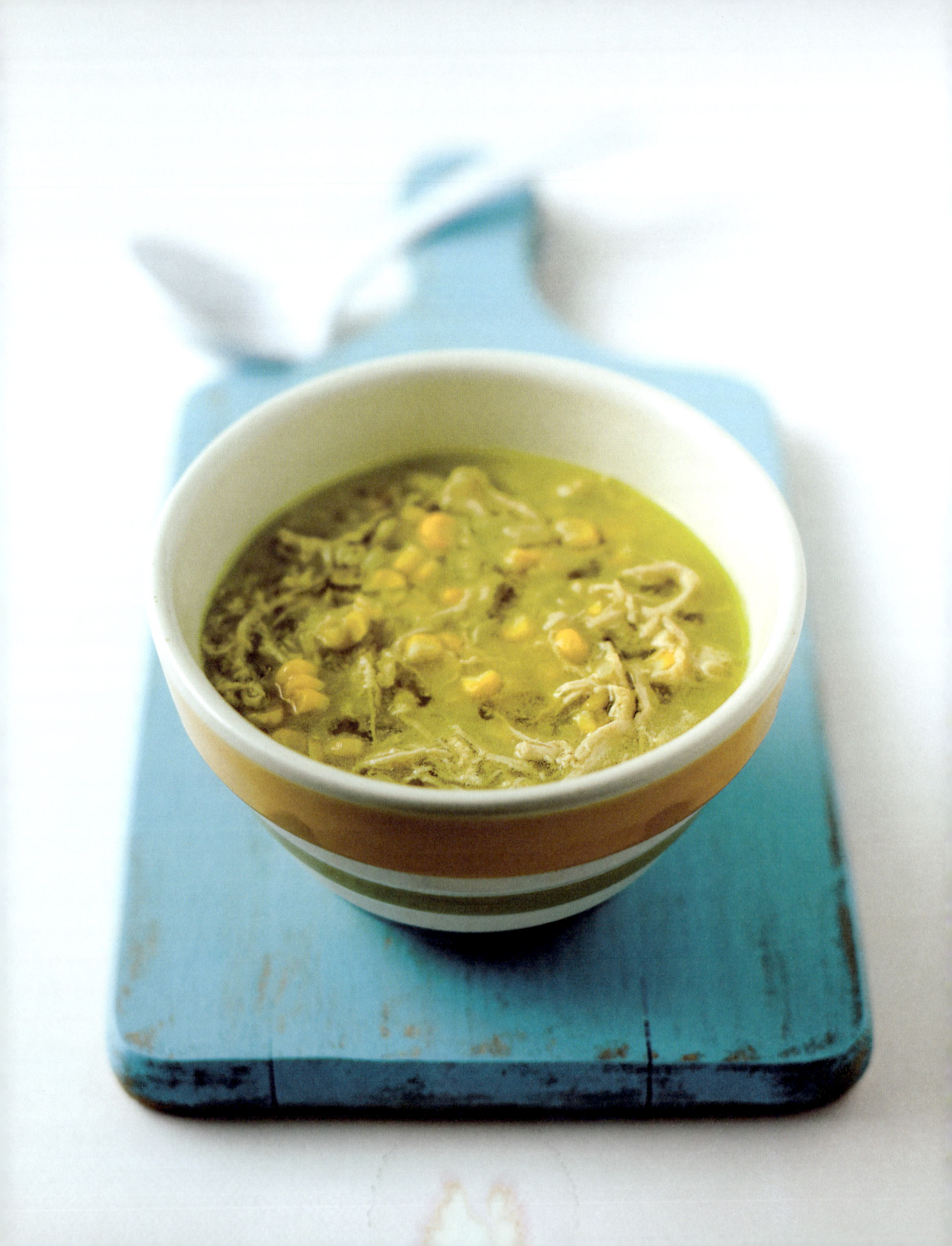

Chicken and sweetcorn soup

Sometimes the simple combinations are still the best – basil and tomatoes, chicken and sweetcorn, lamb and mint…

Serves 6

1 × 1.2 kg chicken

4 sweetcorn cobs, peeled, kernels removed, husks reserved

sea salt

3.5 litres water

1 tablespoon olive oil

3 golden shallots, sliced

20 g unsalted butter

2 cloves garlic, sliced

1 teaspoon chopped thyme

1 egg

1 cup (250 g) creme fraiche

freshly ground white pepper

✶ SPECIAL EQUIPMENT
stick blender

1 Wash the inside of the chicken under cold running water.

2 Place the chicken, corn husks and 2 teaspoons salt in a large saucepan and cover with the water. Bring to the boil, then reduce the heat to low and simmer for 1 hour, removing any scum that rises to the surface with a ladle. Remove the chicken from the stock and set the chicken aside to cool.

3 Strain the stock into a clean saucepan, then bring to the boil. Reduce the stock over medium heat for 30 minutes or until you have about 1 litre, skimming off and discarding any scum that comes to the surface.

4 Heat the oil and butter in a saucepan over medium–high heat, then cook the shallot and garlic for 5 minutes or until soft without colouring. Add the corn kernels and thyme and continue to cook for 3 minutes. Add the reduced chicken stock and simmer for 15 minutes.

5 Remove the pan from the heat, then remove 1 cup of the soup and set aside. Blend the remaining soup with a stick blender. Add the egg and creme fraiche and blend again.

6 Remove and discard the skin from the chicken, then remove the chicken flesh from the bones and finely shred the meat with your fingers. Discard the skin and bones.

7 Add the shredded chicken and reserved cup of soup to the pan, bring back to the boil, then remove from the heat and season to taste with salt and pepper. Ladle the soup into bowls and serve.

Pumpkin cappuccino

I did my apprenticeship at a three-hat restaurant where they served this dish as part of the *amuse-bouche* (something given to the customer before the first course to stimulate their appetite). The pumpkin soup sits high above the cup to resemble a cappuccino. So it's okay to make a mess!

Serves 6

100 g unsalted butter, chopped

50 ml olive oil

600 g pumpkin, peeled, seeded and grated (to yield 400 g)

a pinch freshly grated nutmeg

400 ml milk

200 ml thickened cream

sea salt and freshly ground black pepper

✱ SPECIAL EQUIPMENT
food processor
fine-mesh sieve
stick blender

1 Heat a wide-based saucepan over medium–high heat. Add the butter, olive oil and pumpkin and cook for 1 minute. Add the nutmeg and milk, then bring to the boil. Cover with a lid, reduce the heat to low and simmer for 8 minutes. Remove the pan from the heat.

2 Transfer the pumpkin mixture to a food processor and blend until smooth. Stir in the cream, then strain through a fine-mesh sieve into a clean saucepan. Season to taste with salt and pepper.

3 Gently bring the soup back to the boil over low–medium heat. Using a stick blender, carefully froth up the soup by holding the saucepan at a slight angle, with the blade two-thirds submerged in the soup.

4 Ladle the soup into cups and serve.

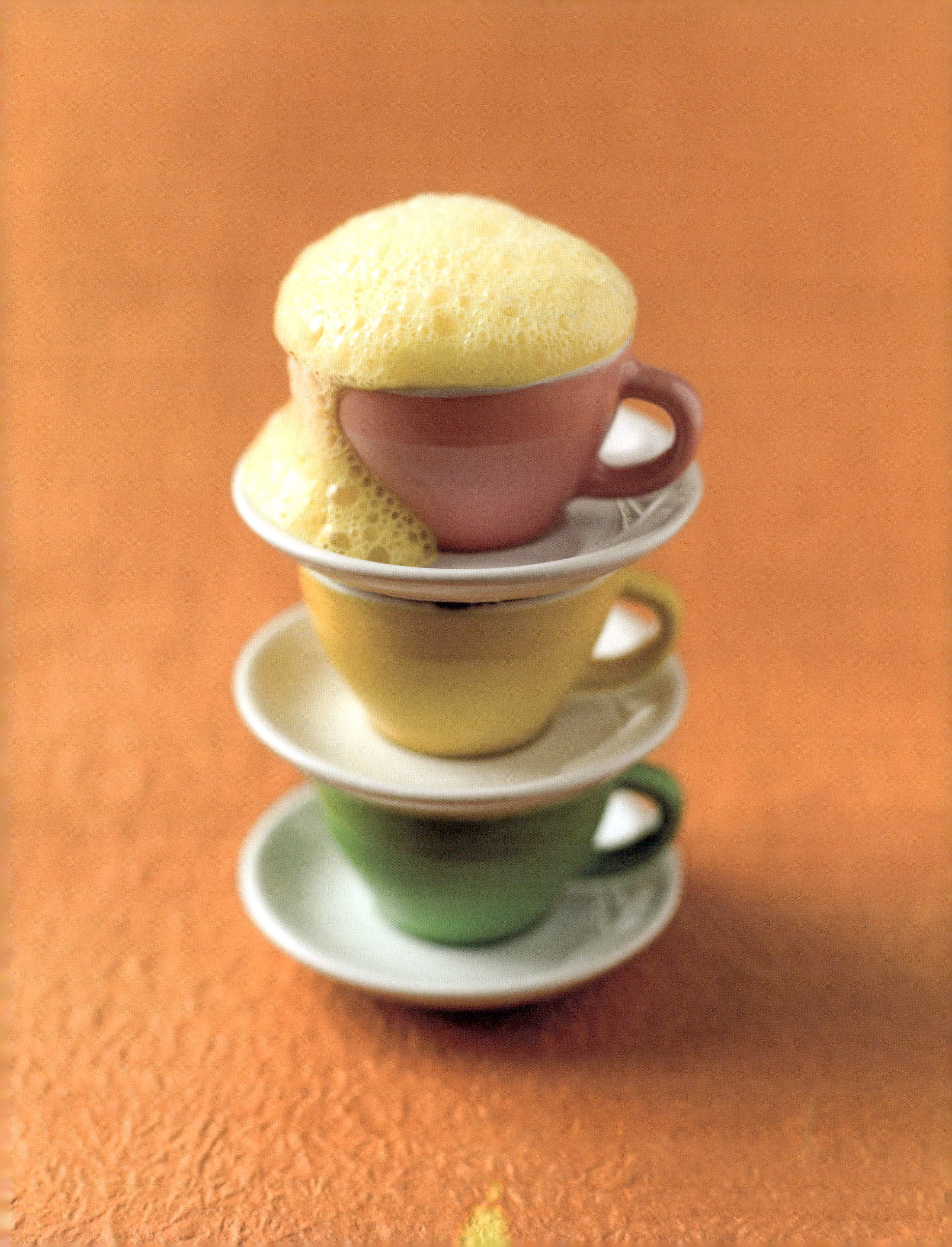

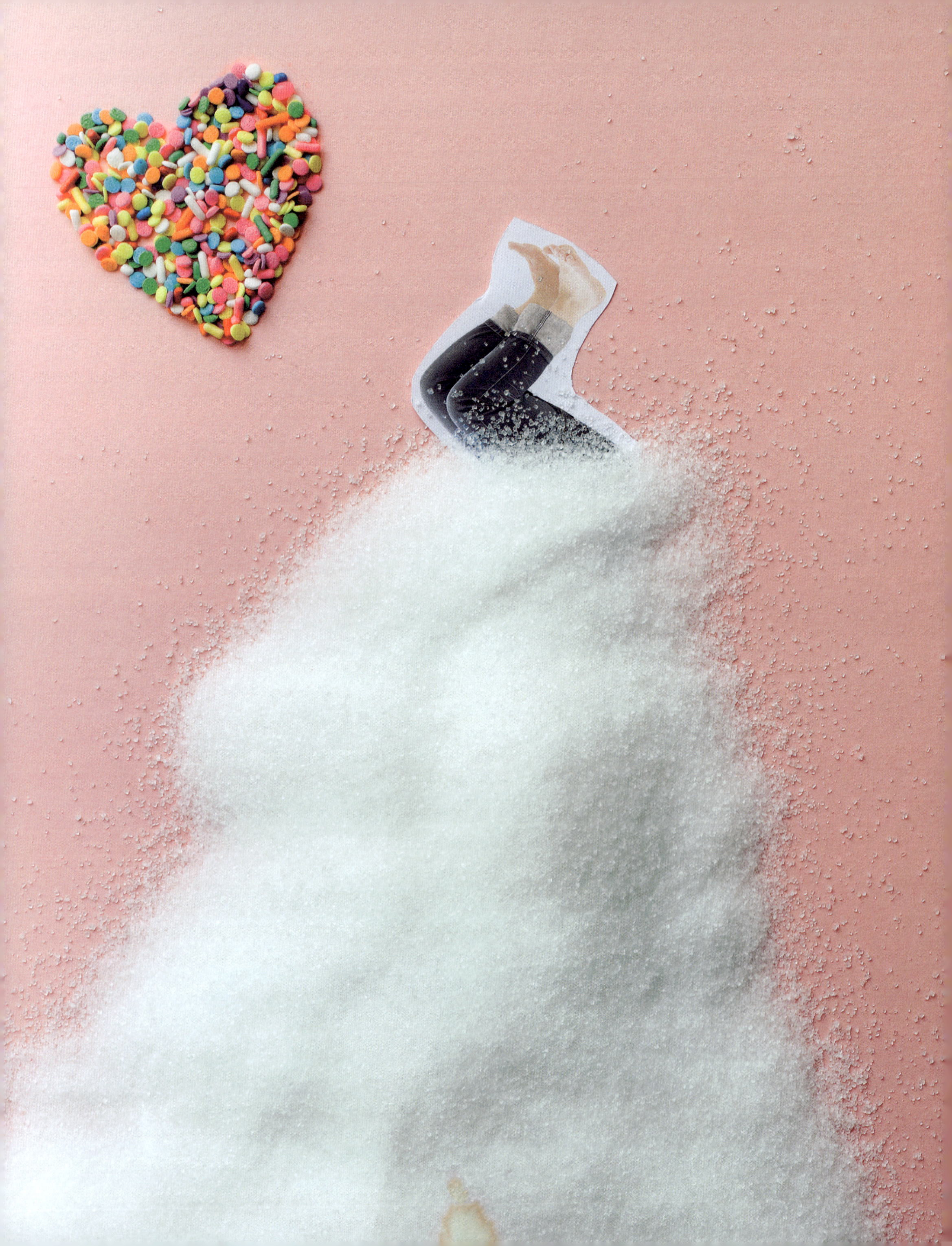

TREATS

Sugar, which is often used to make sweet treats, is a concentrated source of energy. We all need to be careful that we balance our energy intake with our level of activity. This is why sugar-rich foods are often called 'treats'.

Natural sugar comes from sugar cane and sugar beet. Molasses occurs naturally in sugar cane and sugar beet, giving the sugar a delicious flavour. Raw sugar has been processed minimally, with some molasses still present, making it a light brown colour. Demerara sugar is a type of raw sugar.

White sugar has been refined and filtered. Caster sugar is finely ground white sugar. Icing sugar or powdered sugar (sometimes called confectioner's sugar) is produced by grinding sugar very finely to form a powder. It is the key ingredient in icings and frostings.

Brown sugar is made by mixing white sugar crystals with molasses. Dark brown sugar contains more molasses. Muscovado sugar is very dark, with a deep, rich flavour. Molasses and golden syrup are syrup-form by-products of the sugar-refining process. Golden syrup is a key ingredient in Anzac biscuits.

Honey, made by bees using the nectar from flowers, is also a sweetener. Raw honey is known for its antibacterial properties and has been used for centuries to treat sore throats and coughs. It is even applied to cuts and sores to help them heal. Maple syrup (see Pancake-and-Maple-Syrup-Ripple Ice Cream on page 70) is made from the sap of black maple, red maple and sugar maple trees. Stevia is a herb that is about 200 times sweeter than sugar. Fructose is a type of sugar found in fruits and honey.

Triple chocolate muffins

You never leave my mum's house empty-handed. She always gives you food when you are there and food to take home with you. That's what food is all about: generosity of spirit. These muffins are perfect for sharing. Take them to school (or work) and give them to your friends.

Makes 12

1¾ cups (260 g) self-raising flour

½ cup (50 g) dutch-process cocoa (see page 202), sifted

¾ cup (165 g) soft brown sugar

1 cup (250 ml) milk

½ cup (125 ml) vegetable oil

2 eggs, lightly beaten

1 teaspoon vanilla extract

100 g dark couverture chocolate buttons (see page 202)

12 white chocolate Lindt balls or white chocolate buttons

✱ SPECIAL EQUIPMENT
  12-hole muffin pan or
    12 silicone muffin moulds
  12 paper muffin cases (optional)

1 Preheat the oven to 170°C fan-forced (190°C conventional). Line a 12-hole muffin pan with paper cases (or use 12 silicone muffin moulds, see opposite).

2 Combine the flour, cocoa and sugar in a large bowl.

3 Mix the milk, oil, eggs and vanilla in a medium-sized bowl.

4 Pour the milk mixture into the flour mixture and gently stir until just combined; don't over-mix or the muffins will be tough. Mix in the dark chocolate, then spoon enough of the batter into the muffin cases until they are three-quarters full. Add a white chocolate ball or button and top with a little more of the muffin batter.

5 Bake the muffins for 25 minutes or until a skewer inserted comes out clean.

6 Place the muffins on a wire rack and set aside to cool. (The muffins will keep in an airtight container for up to 3 days.)

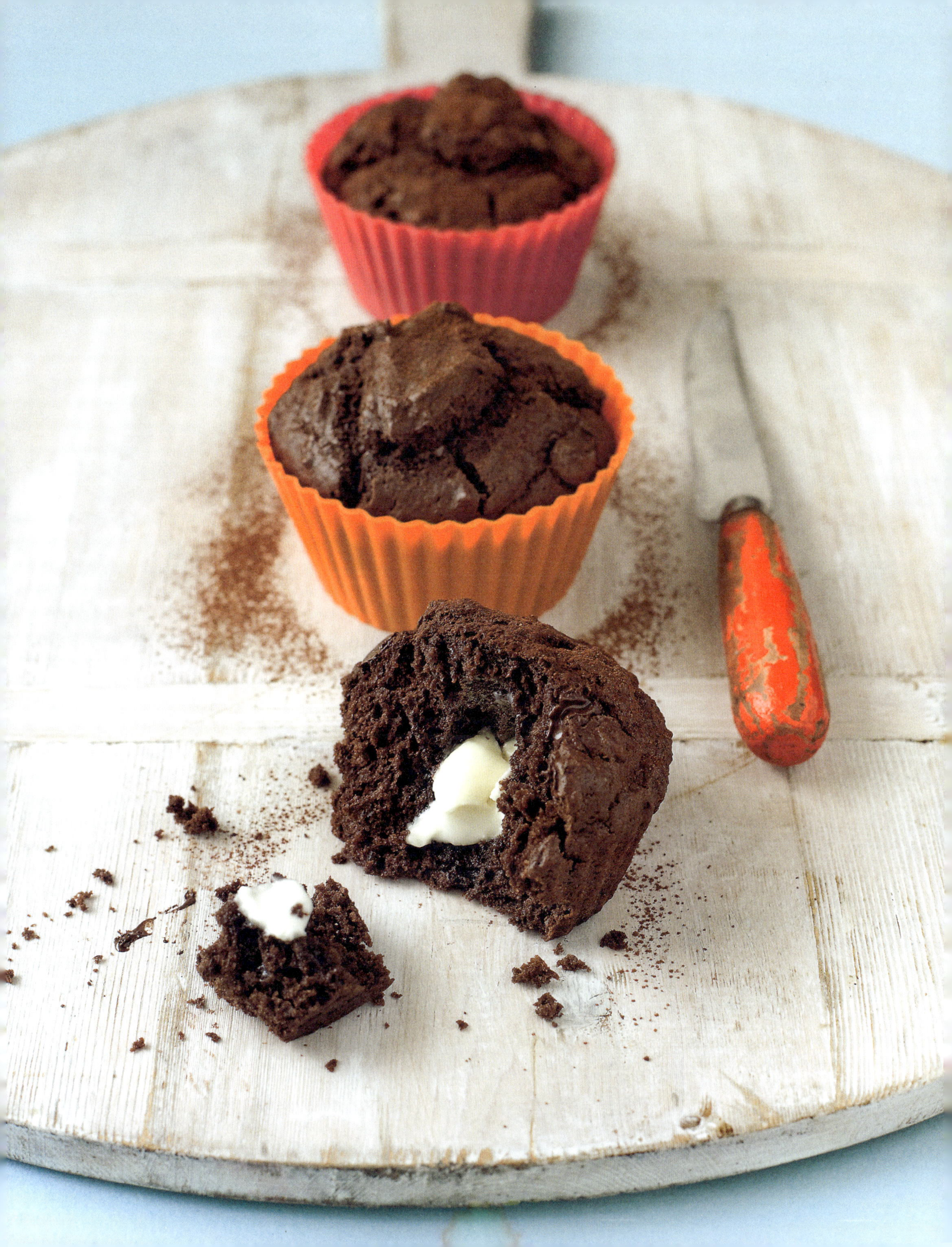

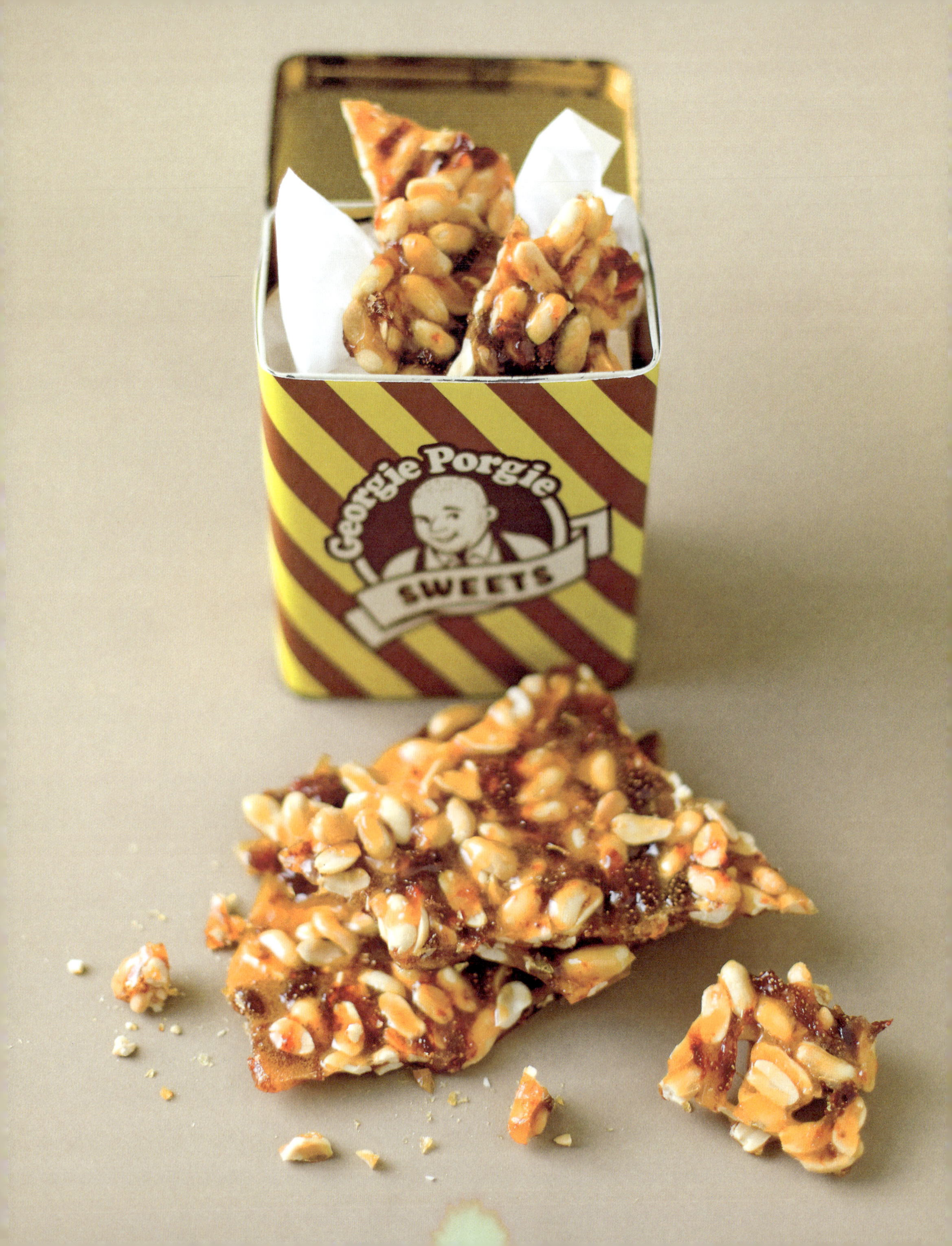
Georgie Porgie
SWEETS

Peanut butter and strawberry brittle

I think crunchy is one of the best textures in food. That's why I love this snack, which is not only crunchy but deliciously salty and sweet too. It celebrates one of my favourite flavour combinations, peanut butter and strawberries. It reminds me of all those peanut butter and jam sandwiches I ate for afternoon tea after school. If you don't have a sugar thermometer, use a wooden spoon to check the syrup. Let some of the mixture drip off the spoon. A strand of toffee will form after the drop when it is ready (hard-crack stage). You can also check by dropping some of the mixture into a small bowl of water. If it is ready, it will form a hard ball.

Makes a 30 cm × 20 cm slab

1 cup (220 g) caster sugar

½ cup (125 ml) corn syrup

½ cup (125 ml) water

200 g roasted salted peanuts

75 g dried strawberries, chopped

1 teaspoon bicarbonate of soda

✶ SPECIAL EQUIPMENT
baking tin (30 cm × 20 cm)
sugar thermometer (optional, see page 203)
large metal spoon

1 Line a 30 cm × 20 cm baking tin with baking paper.

2 Place the sugar, corn syrup and water in a saucepan over medium heat and stir until the sugar dissolves. Increase the heat to high and cook for 8–10 minutes to hard-crack stage (149°C on a sugar thermometer) or until the mixture starts to turn light brown. Remove the pan from the heat and immediately stir in the peanuts and strawberries. Carefully add the bicarbonate of soda; the mixture will foam up.

3 Pour the mixture into the prepared tin and spread out with the back of a large metal spoon to flatten the surface. Set aside to cool for 10 minutes.

4 Break the brittle into pieces to serve. Leftover brittle will keep in an airtight container for up to 1 week (if you can stop eating it!).

Upside-down pavlova

There is something really special about the combination of meringue, cream and passionfruit. It is crunchy, creamy, acidic and sweet. In a word – perfect. As to the argument about who invented it, the Kiwis or the Aussies, you know who I will be going for . . . the Aussies!

Serves 4

- 2 egg whites, at room temperature
- ½ cup (110 g) caster sugar
- ¼ teaspoon vanilla extract
- pulp from 16 passionfruit
- 200 g clotted cream (see page 202)
- mint sprigs (optional), to serve

* SPECIAL EQUIPMENT
electric mixer

1 Preheat the oven to 130°C fan-forced (150°C conventional).

2 Line a baking tray with baking paper. Beat the egg whites in the bowl of an electric mixer with the whisk attachment until stiff peaks form. With the motor running, add the sugar, a little at a time, until the sugar has dissolved. Beat in the vanilla extract.

3 Place heaped tablespoonfuls of the meringue mixture on the baking tray and bake for 45 minutes. Turn the oven off, then leave the door slightly ajar and allow the meringues to cool completely in the oven.

4 Divide half of the passionfruit pulp among 4 dessert glasses. Add a dollop of clotted cream to the glasses, then add the remaining passionfruit pulp and top with the chewy meringues. Garnish with mint sprigs, if you like.

5 Serve immediately.

Did you know?

- Sugar is sometimes used on construction sites to slow down the setting of cement.
- Caramelisation occurs when sugar is heated to the point where the molecules begin to break apart.
- 'Sugar' and 'sure' are the only words in the English language where 'su' is pronounced as 'sh'.

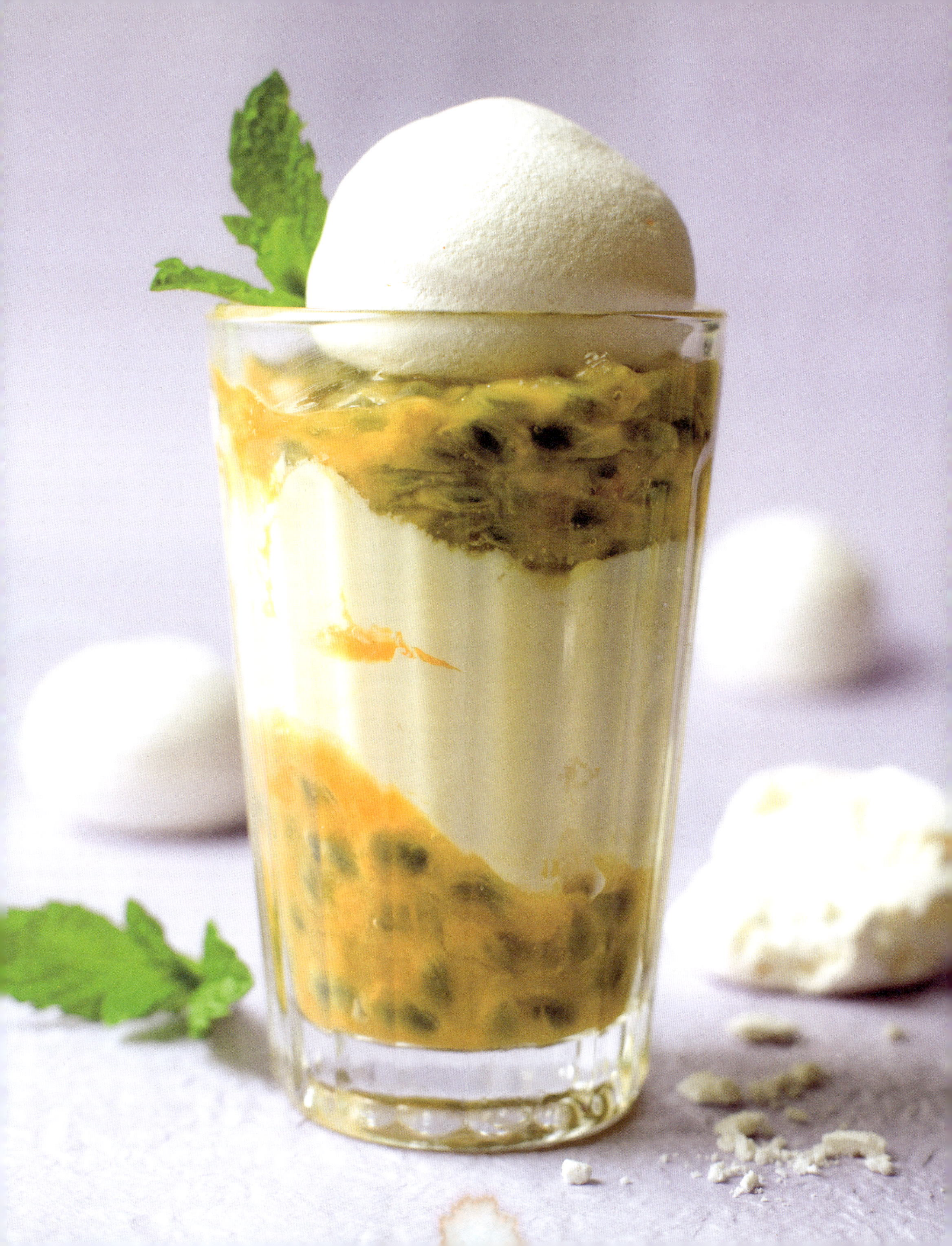

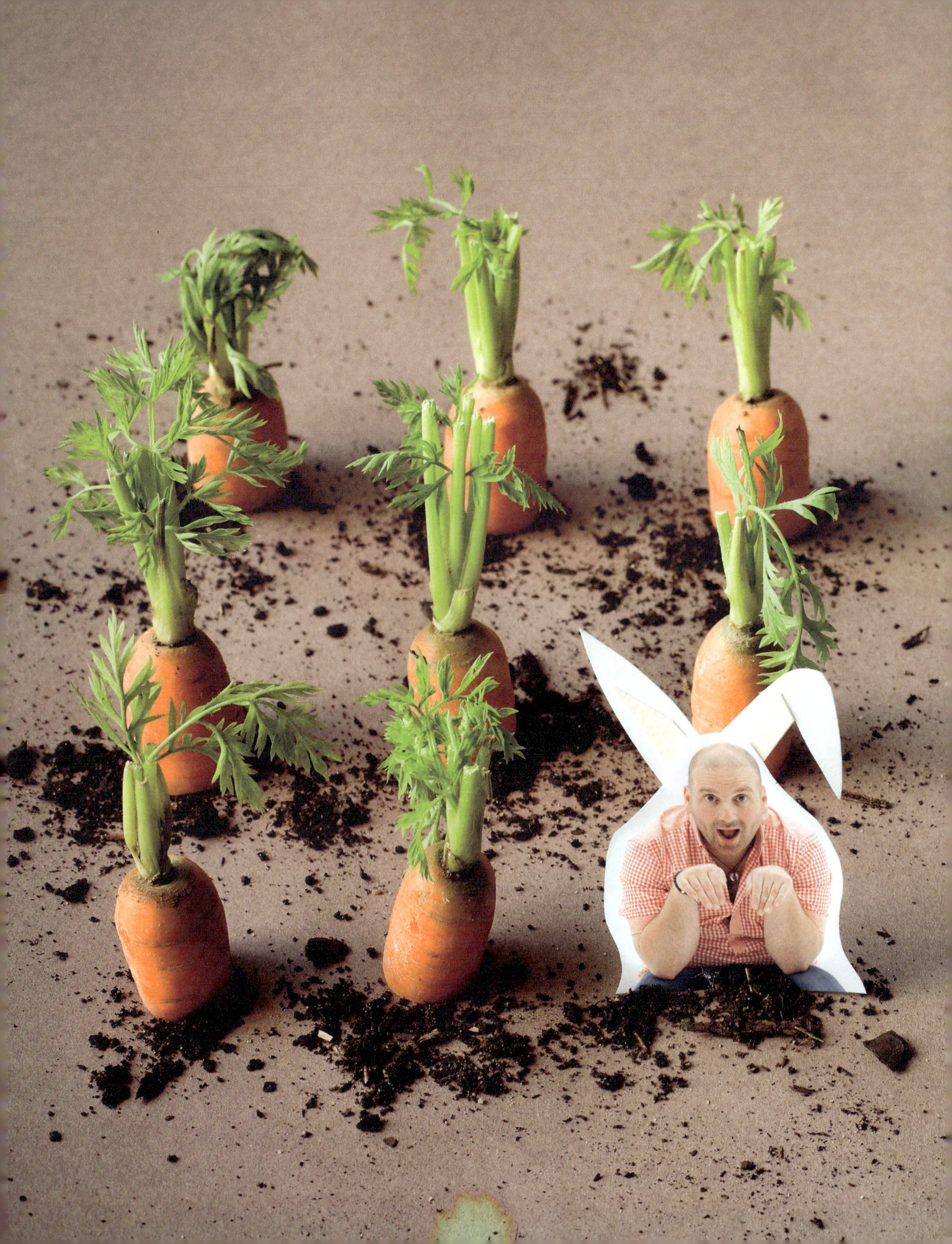

VEGETABLES

In Australia we are lucky to have so many different vegetables grown throughout the year. As we have so many climate zones, it is possible to have a year-round supply of Australian-grown produce at our fingertips. However, some vegetables reach their peak in a particular season when they will be abundant, ripe and full of flavour for you to enjoy. With all kinds of vegetables to try, vegetables are definitely not boring!

IN SUMMER look for avocado, beans, beetroot, cabbage, capsicum (pepper), carrot, celeriac, celery, cucumber, eggplant (aubergine), lettuce, peas, radish, rhubarb, silver beet, sweetcorn, tomato and zucchini (courgette).

IN AUTUMN try Asian greens, beetroot, broccoli, Brussels sprouts, cabbage, cauliflower, eggplant (aubergine), fennel, leek, parsnip, pumpkin, sweet potato and wild mushrooms.

IN WINTER use Asian greens, broccoli, Brussels sprouts, cabbage, carrot, cauliflower, celeriac, fennel, Jerusalem artichoke, kale, kohlrabi, silver beet, turnip and potato.

IN SPRING enjoy asparagus, broad beans, broccoli, cabbage, carrot, cauliflower, globe artichoke, leek, lettuces, peas, snow peas (mange tout), spinach, sugar snap peas and sweetcorn.

We are all encouraged to eat five serves of vegetables every day. Remember that your taste buds change as you get older, so if there's a food you didn't like when you first ate it, try it again later. You might change your mind.

Try cooking vegetables differently too, as this can make a huge difference to how they taste. Home-grown vegetables often taste better. Not only is it fun to grow them yourself, but it's also very convenient as you can go out and pick them fresh when you need them. Tomatoes and lettuce are easy to grow with only a little space.

Sweetcorn salad with labne

Sweetcorn is my all-time favourite vegetable. This dish is on the menu at The Press Club, and I really love it. Make sure the corn has a good char as this will add depth of flavour to the salad. If you prefer not to make your own labne (or don't have time), you can buy it from Middle Eastern food stores.

Serves 4

5 sweetcorn cobs, husks on

1 small red (Spanish) onion, thinly sliced

50 g smoked almonds, roughly chopped

sea salt and freshly ground black pepper

SHERRY VINAIGRETTE

2 tablespoons sherry vinegar

1 teaspoon Dijon mustard

⅓ cup (80 ml) extra virgin olive oil

sea salt

LABNE

125 g thick natural Greek-style yoghurt

¼ cup (3 tablespoons) finely chopped chives

¼ cup (3 tablespoons) finely chopped dill

¼ cup (3 tablespoons) finely chopped chervil

✻ SPECIAL EQUIPMENT
   fine-mesh sieve
   muslin

1 To make the labne, place the yoghurt in a fine-mesh sieve lined with muslin over a bowl in the fridge. Leave in the fridge overnight to drain the whey from the yoghurt so it thickens enough to be formed into balls of soft cheese.

2 The next day, place the chives, dill and chervil on a baking tray. Divide the drained yoghurt into eight, then roll into 2 cm balls with your hands and place on the tray of herbs. Roll the yoghurt balls around the tray so they are coated with herbs. (Makes 8 balls.)

3 Heat a barbecue flat plate or chargrill pan to high and cook the corn in their husks, turning over to colour evenly for 30 minutes.

4 Set the corn aside to cool. Peel off and discard the husks, then carefully slice the kernels off the cobs in large pieces. Place the corn in a bowl and discard the cobs. Set the corn aside.

5 To make the sherry vinaigrette, place the vinegar and mustard in a bowl, then whisk in the olive oil a little at a time until the mixture has thickened and emulsified. Season to taste with salt.

6 Mix the corn, onion and smoked almonds in a bowl, then drizzle with the sherry vinaigrette, season to taste with salt and pepper and place in a serving dish.

7 Serve immediately with labne to the side.

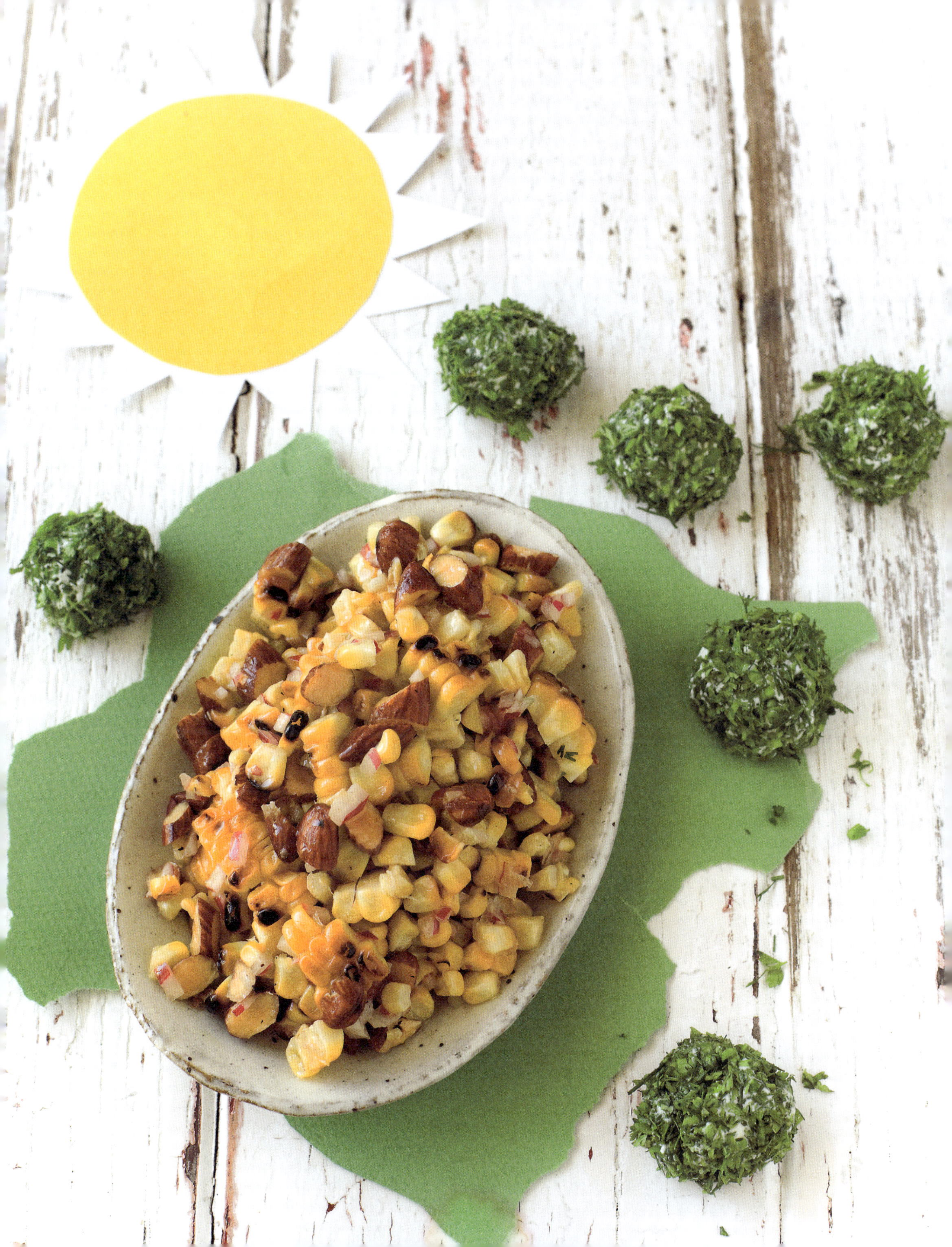

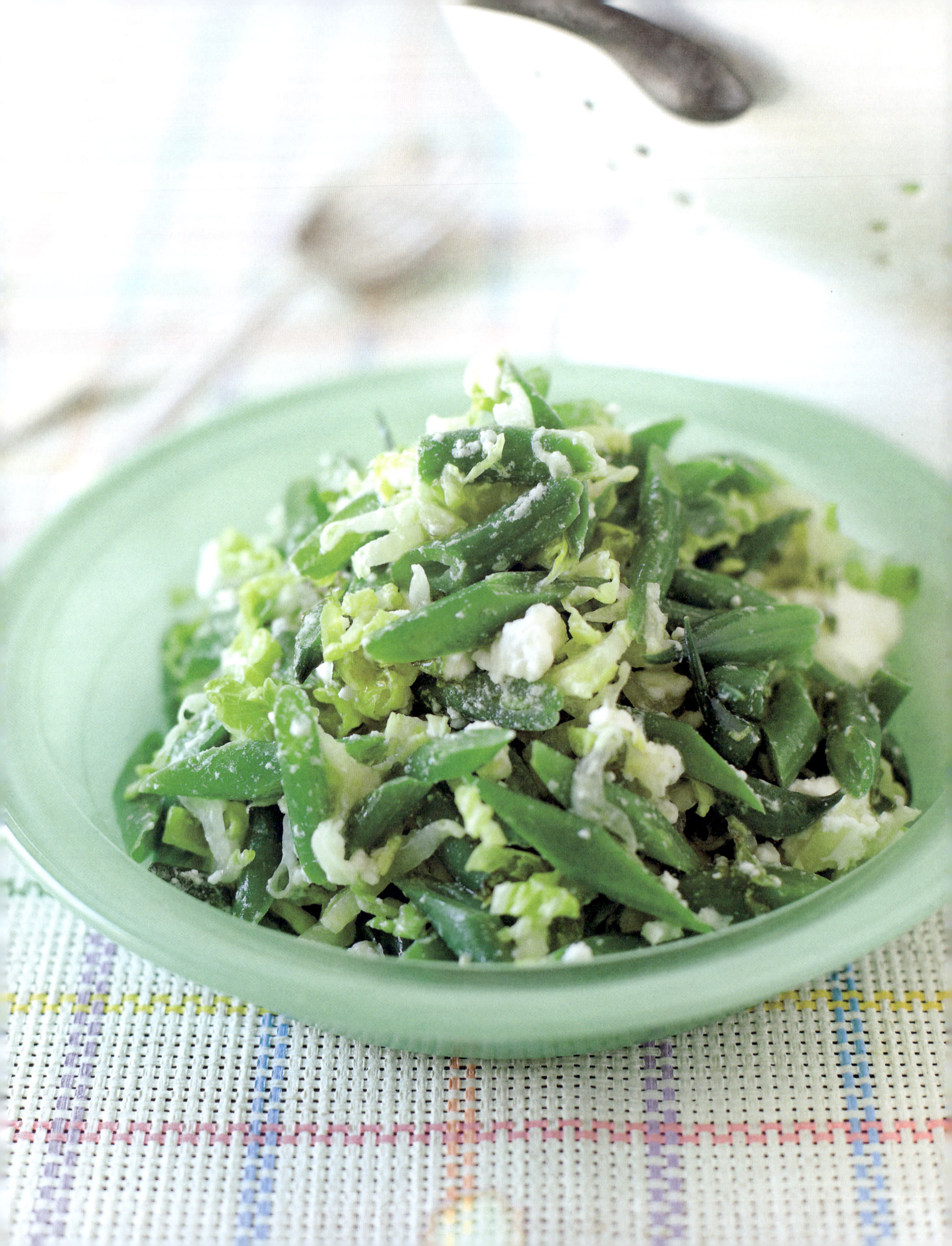

Green bean and feta salad

My head chef at The Press Club, Joe Grbac, serves this simple and tasty salad. Make sure you cook the beans through (I really hate crunchy beans).

Serves 4

300 g baby green beans

ice cubes

12 cos lettuce leaves, washed and dried

150 g feta, crumbled

extra virgin olive oil, for drizzling

1 Cut the beans into bite-sized pieces on the diagonal with a small sharp knife. Bring a medium-sized saucepan of water to the boil, then add the beans and blanch for 4 minutes or until tender. When the water returns to the boil, remove the beans and place them in a bowl filled with iced cold water. When the beans are cold, remove and drain.

2 Finely shred the cos leaves and place in a medium-sized bowl, then toss with the beans. Add the feta, then drizzle over a little olive oil.

3 Serve immediately.

Turned vegetables

This is another recipe that reminds me of my apprenticeship. I would spend hours each day practising this classic technique of shaping vegetables into seven-sided football shapes, working quickly using a special curved knife (pictured opposite). Although I used to hate doing this job when I was a young cook, now I get a certain pleasure from it. The technique is quite tricky (and a little dangerous) so don't try this until you are at least fourteen years old.

Serves 4

4 potatoes

4 swedes

2 large carrots

1 bulb garlic, cloves separated

1 tablespoon torn thyme

olive oil, for cooking

✱ SPECIAL EQUIPMENT
turning knife (see page 203)

1 Hold one potato vertically, then, using a turning knife (sharp knife with a curved edge), cut the top and bottom off. Cut the potato, top to bottom, in a curving motion, as if you were peeling the potato, creating a barrel shape. Next, rotate the potato so that you evenly cut every surface, to create a football shape. Repeat with the remaining potatoes and set aside.

2 Use the same method to prepare the swedes.

3 Preheat the oven to 180°C fan-forced (200°C conventional).

4 To turn a carrot, cut it in thirds lengthways into even 5–7 cm-long sections. Use the technique above to create a point at the top and bottom of the carrot, using the turning knife.

5 Place the turned vegetables in a roasting pan, scatter with garlic and thyme and drizzle with oil. Roast the vegetables for 30–40 minutes or until golden and cooked through.

6 Serve.

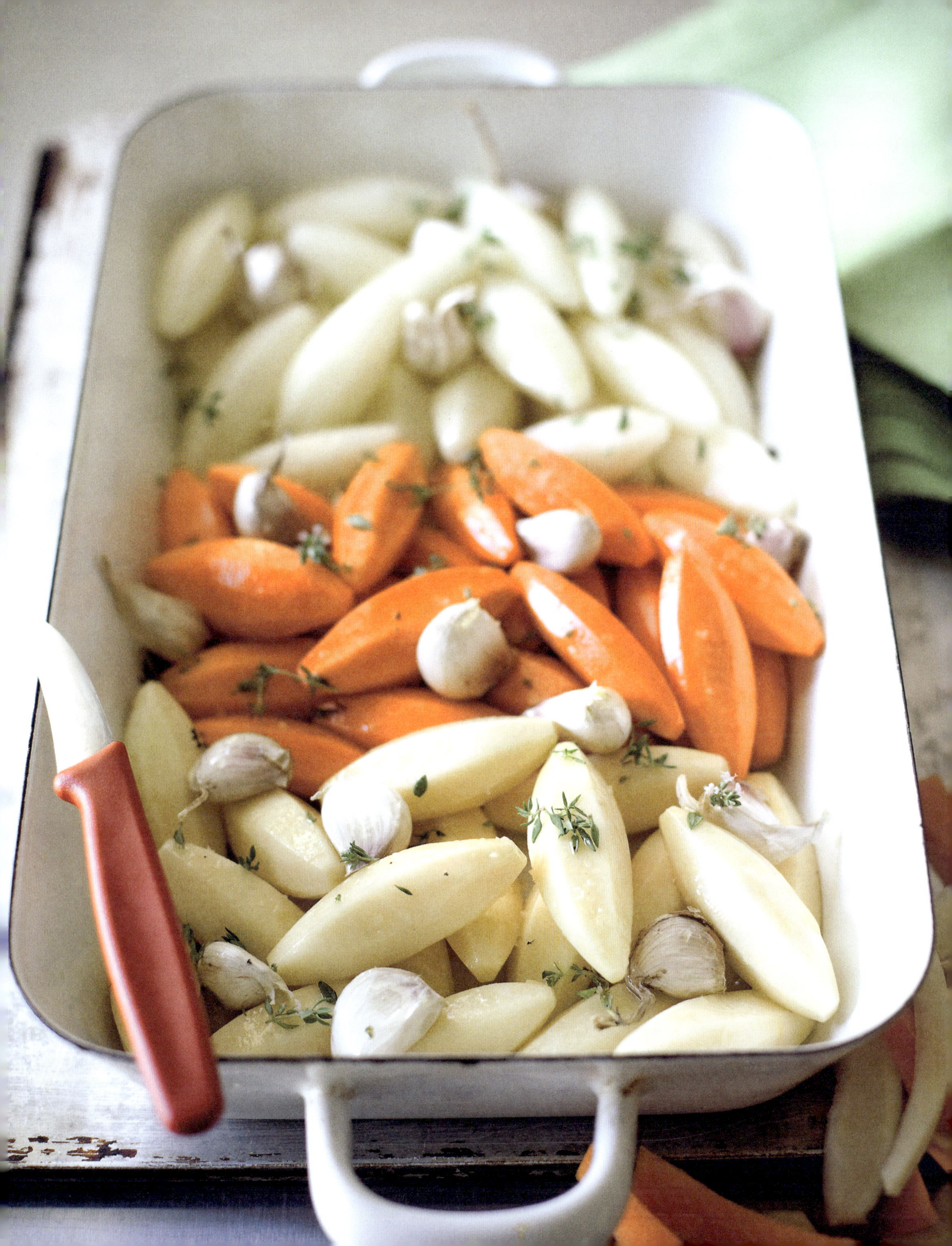

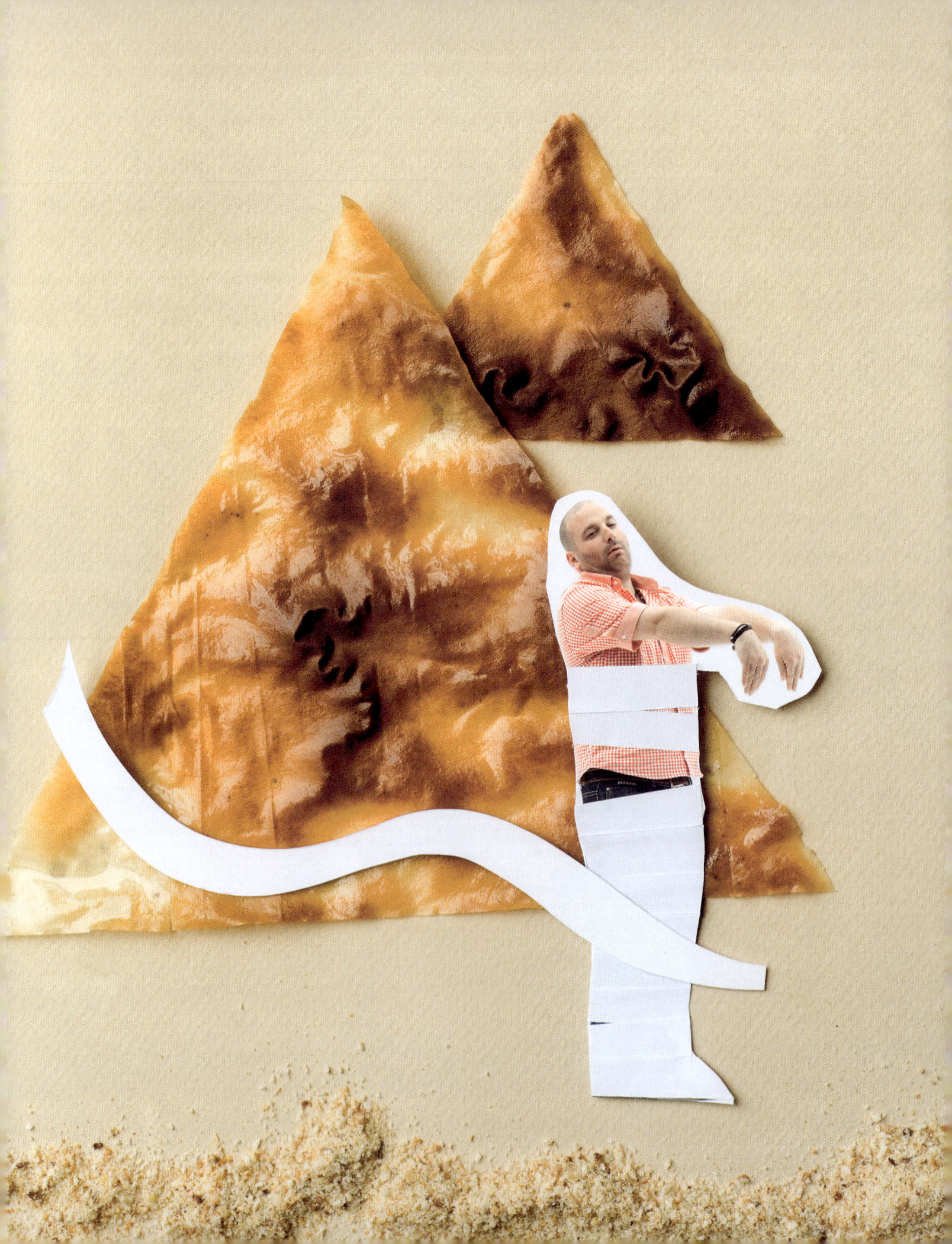

WRAPS

All around the world, people wrap food for cooking and eating. Wrapping provides protection for food, ensuring the contents stay together and remain moist as they cook. Wrapping also provides an easy and convenient way to eat food, as it makes it portable and you can use your hands, rather than cutlery, to eat it.

There are many types of wrappers. Some are edible and others are not. Edible wrappers include all types of pastry, from dumpling wrappers, wonton skins, spring-roll wrappers, gyoza wrappers and rice-paper wrappers to filo, puff and shortcrust pastry. Seaweed is used for nori rolls and other kinds of sushi. Fig leaves, lettuce, cabbage and vine leaves also work well as wrappers. Then there are different flatbreads, including pita, tortillas, mountain bread and naan.

Inedible wrappers include banana leaves, bamboo leaves, lotus leaves and corn husks. Foil and baking paper are also used for wrapping food when cooking.

En papillote is a French term that refers to the method of cooking where food is baked in a folded paper or foil parcel. The parcel holds in moisture to steam the food. This technique is particularly delicious using fish and chicken scattered with chopped herbs, drizzled with olive oil and topped with sliced lemon.

Greek salad cornets

This is ideal party food. You can fill the cornets with all sorts of ingredients to create your own flavour combinations. Try smoked salmon with creme fraiche, crispy beef with sweet chilli sauce or this yummy Greek salad. Just make sure your mixture isn't too wet as it will make the cornet pastry soggy.

Makes 16

8 spring roll wrappers (215 mm × 215 mm)

clarified butter (see page 201), melted, for brushing

GREEK SALAD FILLING

1 Lebanese cucumber, halved lengthways

1 ripe tomato, halved

6 kalamata olives, pitted and finely chopped

50 g feta, crumbled

small oregano leaves, to garnish

* SPECIAL EQUIPMENT
5 metal cornet cones (see page 203)
pastry brush

1 Preheat the oven to 180°C fan-forced (200°C conventional).

2 Cut each of the spring roll wrappers in half on the diagonal. Working in batches, cut each half into a semicircle and wrap it around a metal cornet cone. Brush the outside with melted clarified butter, then place the cone inside another cone to hold the wrapper in place. Repeat with the remaining cones, melted butter and pastry, stacking them inside the cones that are already wrapped.

3 Lay the stacks of cones on their sides on a baking tray and bake for 15 minutes or until crisp and lightly browned.

4 Remove the cornet wrappers from the oven, then remove the metal cones and leave the wrappers on a wire rack to cool.

5 While you wait for the cornet wrappers to cool, make the Greek salad filling. Use a teaspoon to remove and discard the cucumber seeds, then finely chop the flesh and place in a bowl. Remove and discard the tomato seeds, then finely chop the flesh and add it to the bowl, along with the olives and feta. Carefully spoon a little of the filling into each cone, then garnish with oregano.

6 Serve immediately so the cornet wrappers don't become soggy.

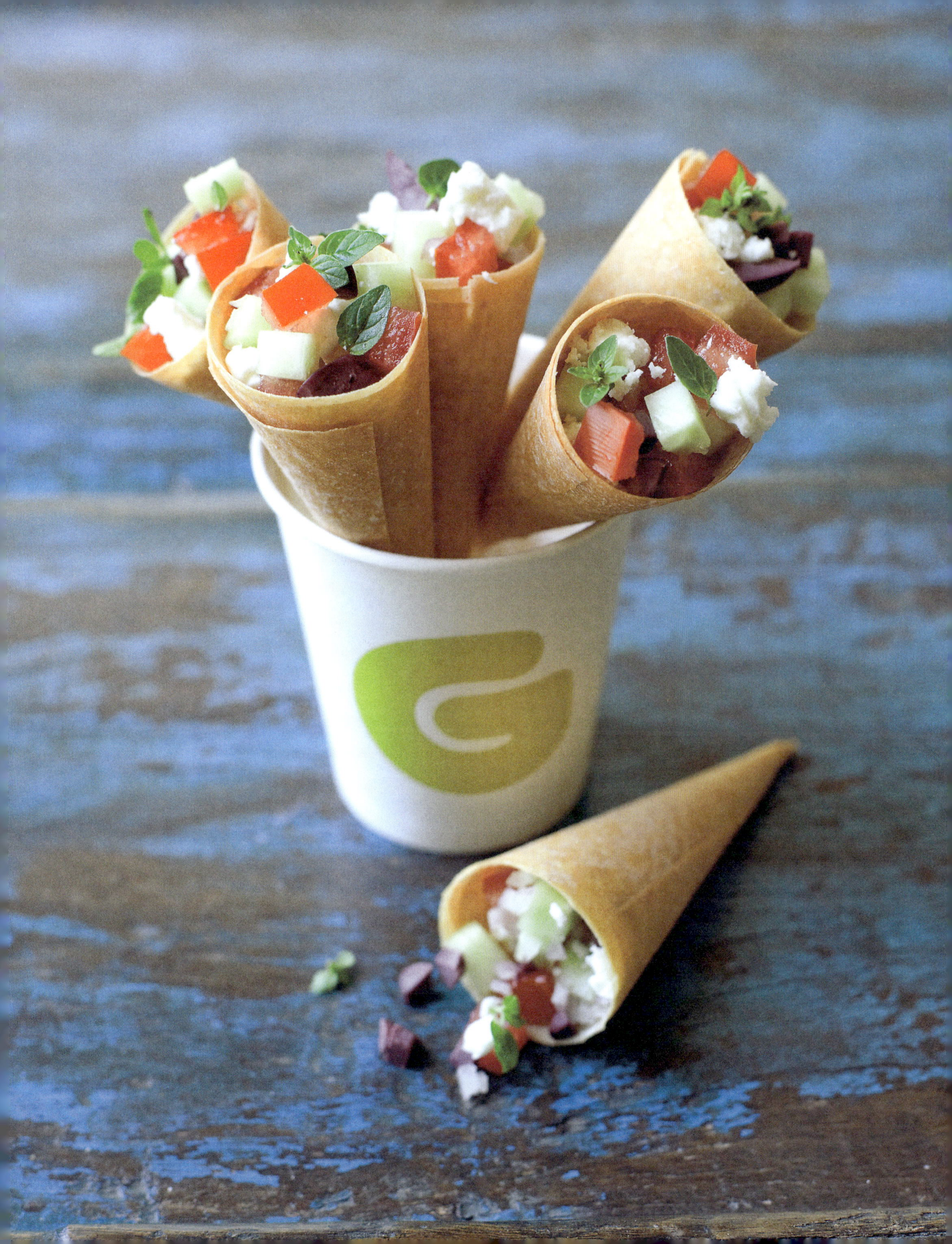

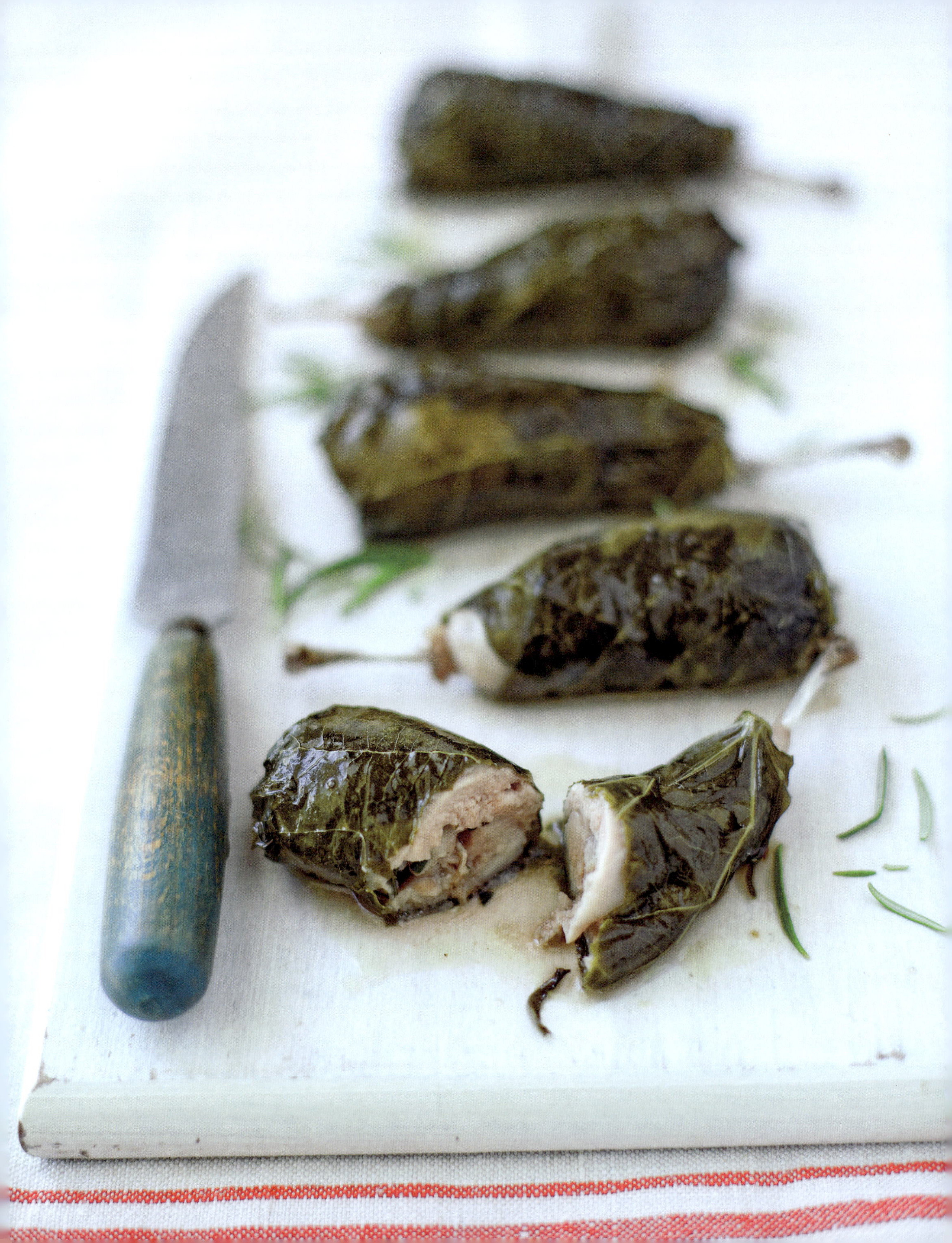

Quail wrapped in vine leaves

What Greek kid doesn't eat dolmades? You know: rice that has been flavoured with spices and wrapped in a vine leaf, then cooked. They are so yummy and a great healthy lunch snack. This quail dish is inspired by rice dolmades. That's what's so exciting about food – one idea can lead to another.

Serves 4

4 quail

2 tablespoons rosemary, finely chopped

125 g unsalted butter, softened

sea salt and freshly ground black pepper

8 preserved vine leaves

2 tablespoons olive oil

✱ SPECIAL EQUIPMENT
kitchen scissors

1 To butterfly the quail, use kitchen scissors to cut out the backbone. Next, cut through the breast bone. You will have 2 halves. Use your fingers to remove the small ribcage bones. Use the kitchen scissors to cut off the wings. Pat the quail dry with paper towel and set aside.

2 Mix the rosemary and butter in a small bowl until combined. Season to taste with salt and pepper and set aside.

3 Rinse the vine leaves under cold running water, then pat dry with paper towel. Lay the vine leaves on a chopping board.

4 Lay 1 quail half in the middle of each vine leaf, skin-side down, then spread 1 teaspoonful of rosemary butter over the flesh. Wrap the quail in the vine leaves so the leg sticks out the end (see opposite).

5 Preheat the oven to 180°C fan-forced (200°C conventional).

6 Heat a heavy-based frying pan over medium heat, then add 1 tablespoon of the olive oil and fry 2 of the wrapped quail halves for 1 minute on each side to seal. Repeat with the remaining quail, adding more oil to the pan if necessary.

7 Wrap each quail half in foil. Place on a baking tray and bake for 4–5 minutes or until cooked through.

8 Remove the quail parcels from the oven, unwrap the foil and serve.

Chocolate baklava

The argument still rages as to who invented baklava – the Turks, the Greeks or perhaps the Persians. Who cares? I have added chocolate to this baklava recipe just because I love chocolate and nuts together. Awesome. These gorgeous little parcels are best eaten on the day they are made.

Serves 6

250 g slivered almonds, chopped

150 g honey, plus extra for drizzling

125 g dark couverture chocolate buttons (see page 202)

2 teaspoons ground cinnamon

6 sheets filo pastry

50 ml clarified butter (see page 201), melted

✷ SPECIAL EQUIPMENT
pastry brush

1 Preheat the oven to 180°C fan-forced (200°C conventional).

2 Place the almonds, honey, chocolate and cinnamon in a bowl, then stir to combine and set aside.

3 Lay 1 sheet of the filo on a clean bench. Brush the filo with butter, then fold in half and brush again with butter.

4 Spread one-sixth of the almond mixture along the short edge of the filo. Fold in the sides to cover the filling, then roll up tightly. Place the filo parcel seam-side down on a baking tray lined with baking paper.

5 Repeat this process with the remaining pastry, butter and chocolate filling.

6 Bake the chocolate baklava for 6 minutes or until crisp and golden.

7 Leave to cool, then drizzle with extra honey and serve.

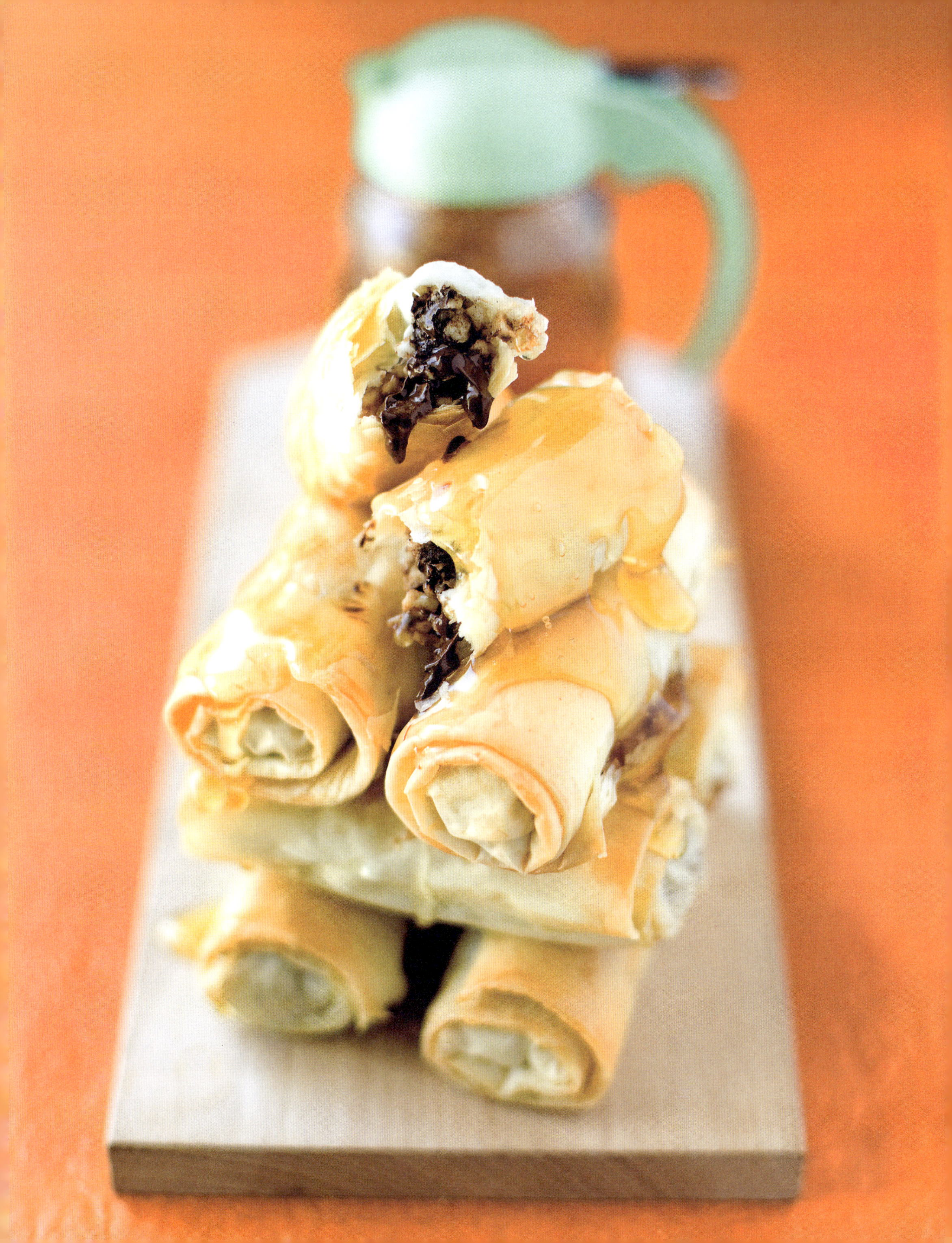

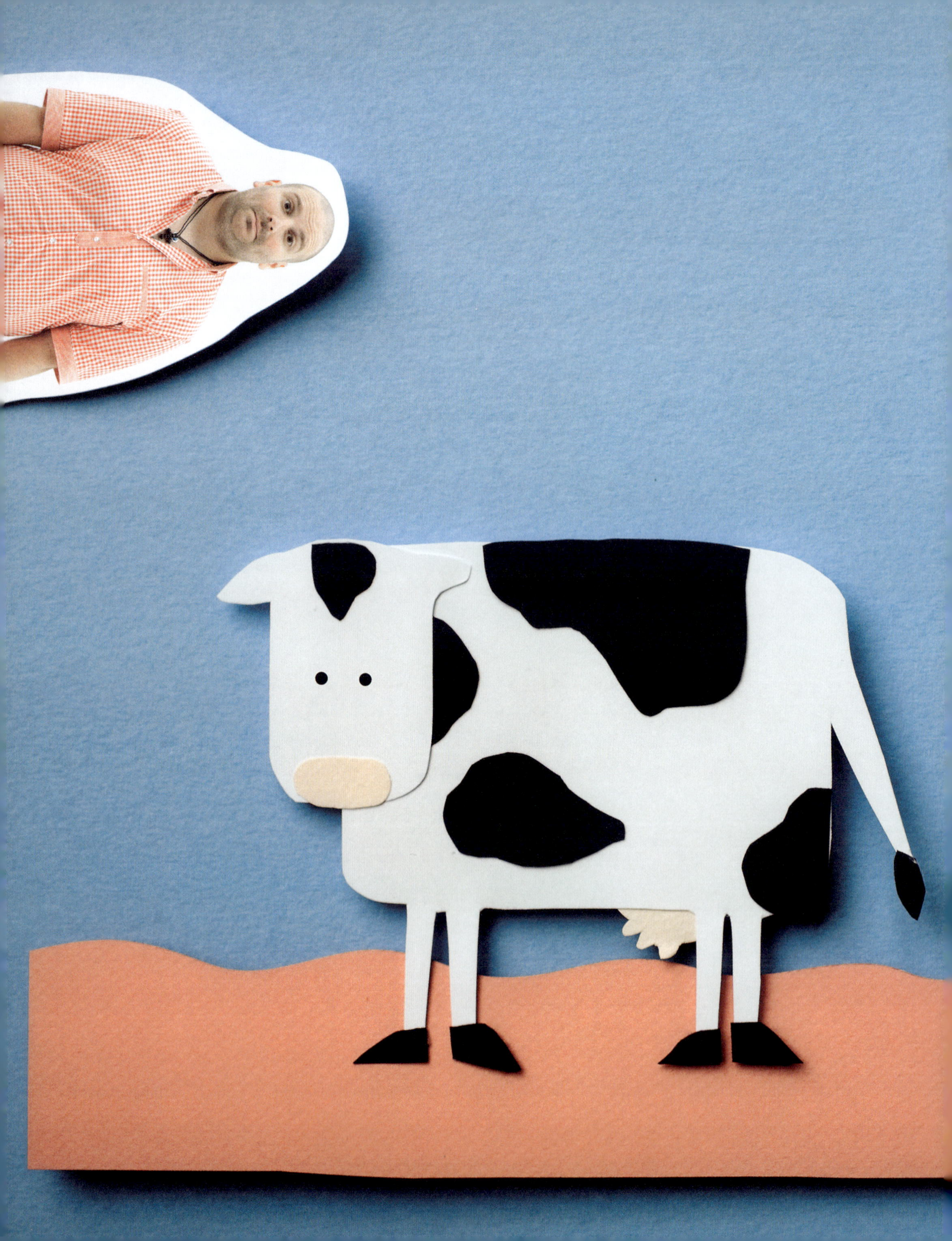

yoghurt

People have been making and eating yoghurt for at least 4500 years. Originating from Central Asia, India and Southern and Central Europe, yoghurt is now a popular and convenient snack food almost everywhere. It is most often made from cow, sheep or goat's milk, but the milk of mares, buffaloes, camels and even yaks can also be used. Many people believe that the first batches of yoghurt were created by accident as nomadic people migrating to Europe carried bags full of goat's milk.

Yoghurt is made by adding a bacterial culture to milk. Typically, the milk is heated to about 80°C, then cooled to 45°C. A good bacteria is then added, which helps it to ferment. (The bad bacteria is destroyed by heating the milk.) This temperature is maintained for four to seven hours to allow the milk to ferment. Fermentation produces lactic acid, which reacts with milk to give yoghurt its creamy texture and characteristic tang.

Yoghurt can be used to make smoothies, marinades, salad dressings, soups, dips and stews. Because it is naturally sour, yoghurt is commonly eaten with fruit or honey.

Homemade yoghurt with honey and walnuts

When I am working in Mykonos, I wake up every morning and sit down to a bowl of yoghurt with honey and walnuts. It's a cracker of a breakfast that leaves you feeling so healthy and satisfied.

Makes 1 litre

1 litre full-cream milk

1 tablespoon honey, plus extra for drizzling

1 cup (250 g) natural Greek-style yoghurt (you'll need to use one with live cultures)

1 cup (100 g) walnut halves

1 Heat the milk in a medium-sized saucepan until it froths around the edges; do not let it boil. Pour into a medium-sized ceramic bowl and leave to cool until the side of the bowl is cool enough to touch with your hands; this will take about 30 minutes.

2 Whisk the honey and yoghurt into the milk, then cover tightly with plastic film and wrap in a small blanket or towel. Leave to sit at room temperature for about 8 hours for the yoghurt to form. Refrigerate until required.

3 Just before serving, preheat the oven to 160°C fan-forced (180°C conventional).

4 Place the walnuts on a baking tray and roast for 5 minutes or until they brown slightly and smell delicious. Remove and set aside to cool. Roughly chop the walnuts and set aside.

5 Divide the yoghurt among bowls or glasses, then scatter the walnuts over and drizzle with honey. Serve. (Leftover yoghurt can be stored in an airtight container in the refrigerator for up to 2 weeks.)

Did you know?

- Eating yoghurt gives you healthier gums.

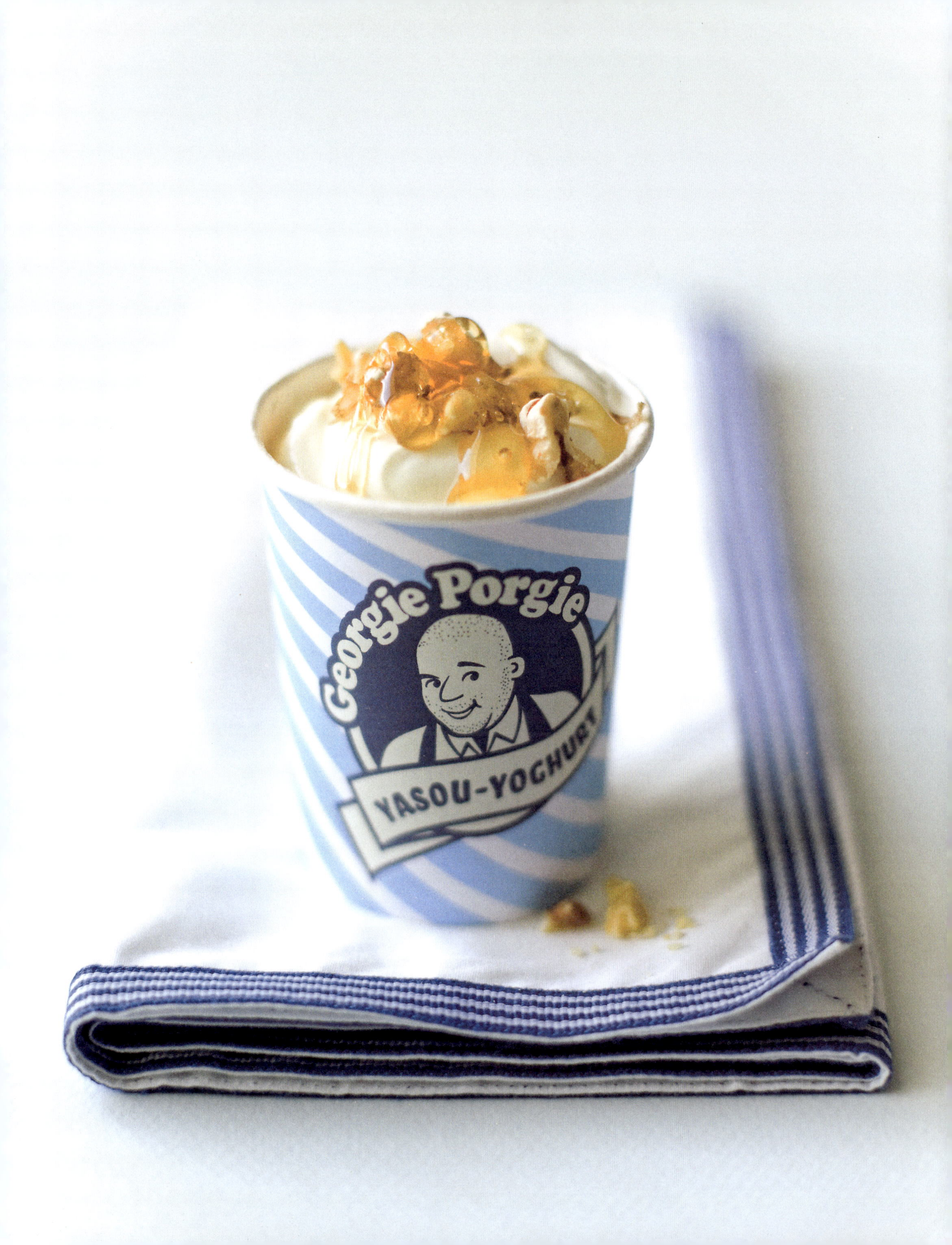
Georgie Porgie
YASOU-YOGHURT

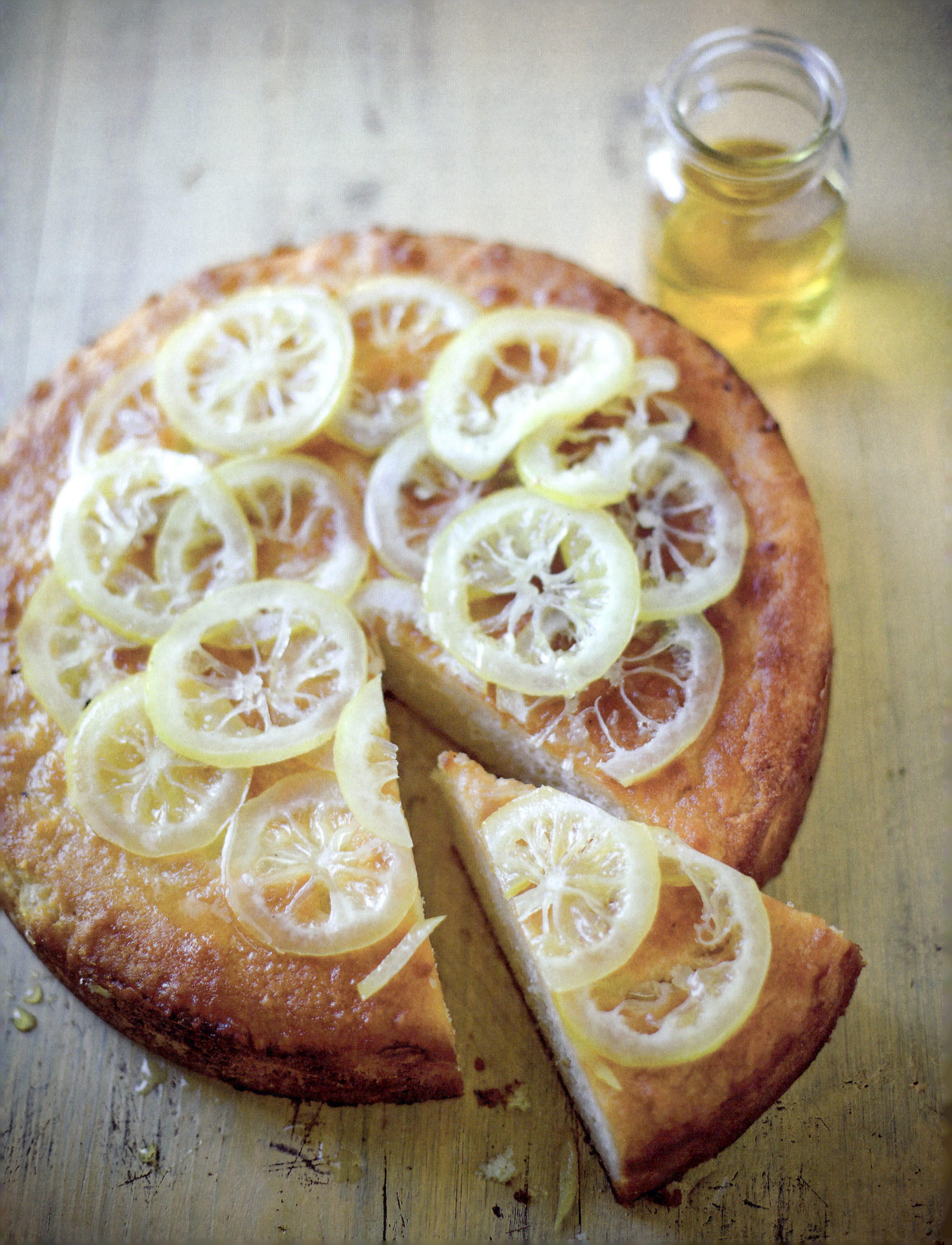

Yoghurt and lemon syrup cake

The beauty about a cake is that you can share it with friends. This lovely, moist cake has a delicious lemony tang and is great served with a pot of tea. To ensure the cake absorbs the syrup, pour it over while the cake is still hot. Although this is terrific eaten while still warm, it just gets better with age.

Serves 8

125 g unsalted butter, softened

250 g caster sugar

2 eggs

1 cup (250 g) natural thick Greek-style yoghurt

1 teaspoon vanilla extract

finely grated zest of 2 lemons

¼ cup (60 ml) lemon juice

400 g self-raising flour

½ teaspoon bicarbonate of soda

LEMON SYRUP

1 cup (220 g) caster sugar

1 cup (250 ml) water

⅓ cup (80 ml) lemon juice

2 lemons, well scrubbed and thinly sliced widthways

* SPECIAL EQUIPMENT
   23 cm springform cake tin
   electric mixer
   flexible spatula
   large metal spoon
   bamboo skewer

1 Preheat the oven to 180°C fan-forced (200°C conventional).

2 Grease and line a 23 cm springform cake tin with baking paper.

3 Cream the butter and sugar in the bowl of an electric mixer until light and fluffy. Add the eggs, one at a time, and continue to mix until combined. Add the yoghurt, vanilla, lemon zest and juice and continue to mix. Add the flour and bicarbonate of soda and gently fold through with a flexible spatula.

4 Spoon the batter into the prepared cake tin and smooth the surface with the back of a large metal spoon; the mixture will be quite firm.

5 Bake for 45 minutes or until the cake is cooked through when a skewer inserted in the centre comes out clean.

6 Meanwhile, to make the lemon syrup, combine the sugar, water and lemon juice in a small saucepan and cook over low heat, stirring with a wooden spoon to dissolve the sugar. Add the lemon slices and simmer for 10 minutes to soften the lemon. Set aside to cool.

7 When the cake is cooked, remove it from the oven and poke it all over with a bamboo skewer to make lots of small holes; this helps the syrup soak into the cake. Slowly pour the cooled lemon syrup over the hot cake until it has all been absorbed.

8 Decorate the top of the cake with the candied lemon slices. Leave the cake to cool in the tin, then remove it from the tin.

9 Slice the cake and serve. (Leftover cake will keep in an airtight container for up to 1 week.)

Yoghurt snow

Life can sometimes be too serious. That's why I love food, because it allows you to enjoy the whimsical side of life. This yoghurt 'snow' (granita) is a case in point.

Makes about 1 litre

1 litre milk

½ cup (180 g) honey

1 cup (250 g) natural thick Greek-style yoghurt

✻ **SPECIAL EQUIPMENT**
27 cm × 19 cm plastic container

1 Place the milk and honey in a medium-sized saucepan and heat gently over low heat, stirring with a wooden spoon until the honey has dissolved. Remove the pan from the heat and add the yoghurt. Stir well and set aside until cool.

2 Transfer the yoghurt mixture to a plastic container (mine is 27 cm × 19 cm) or stainless-steel tray, cover with plastic film and place in the freezer to freeze.

3 Using a large metal fork, stir the mixture every 20 minutes or so, scraping the edges and breaking up any chunks of ice as the mixture freezes. Just before serving, mash the granita with a fork once again.

4 Divide the yoghurt snow among bowls and serve. (Leftover granita can be stored in an airtight container in the freezer for up to 1 week.)

Did you know?

- You can make a simple homemade cheese, called labne (see page 164), by draining natural Greek-style yoghurt in muslin and refrigerating. The yoghurt will form a solid (curd) and drained liquid (whey).

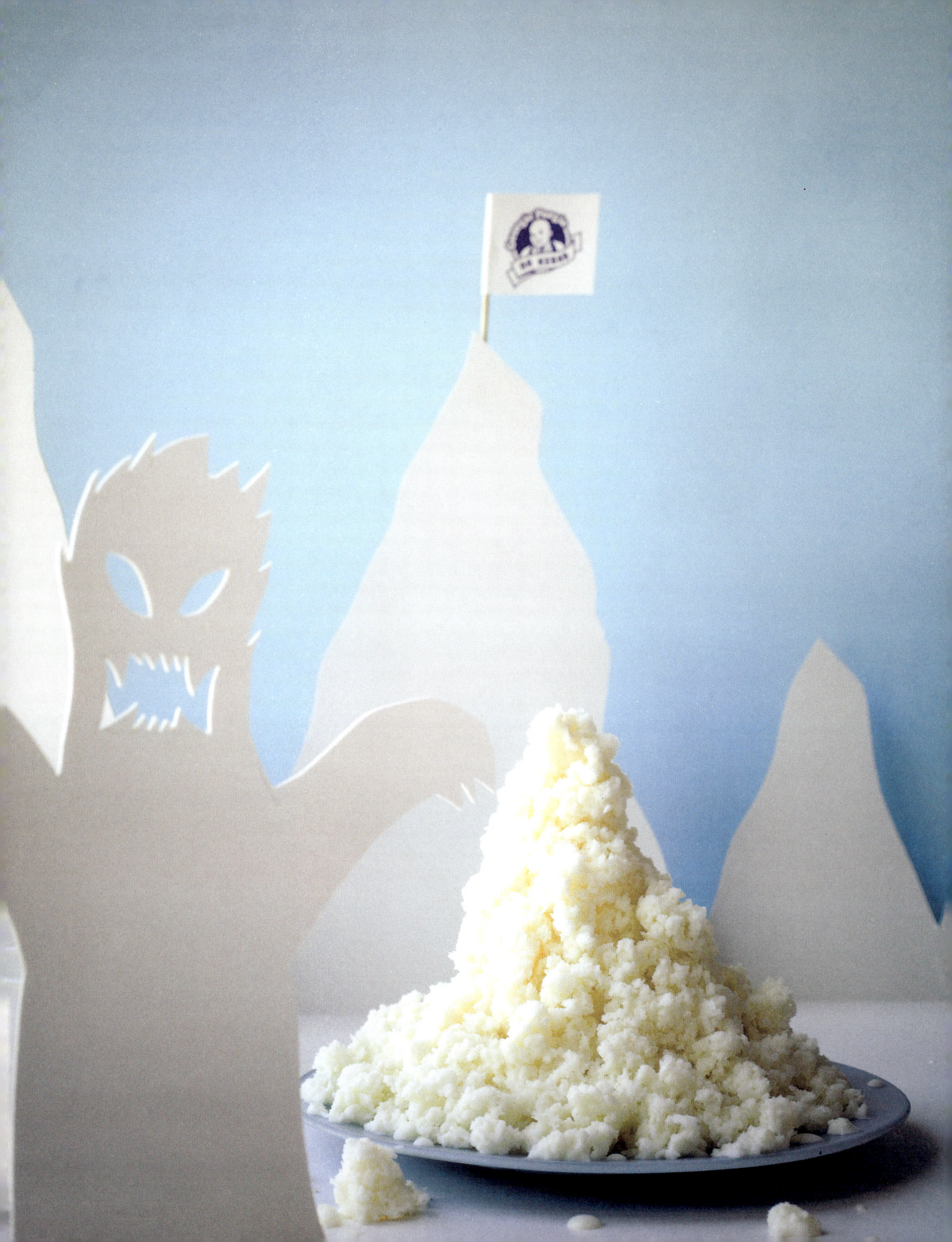

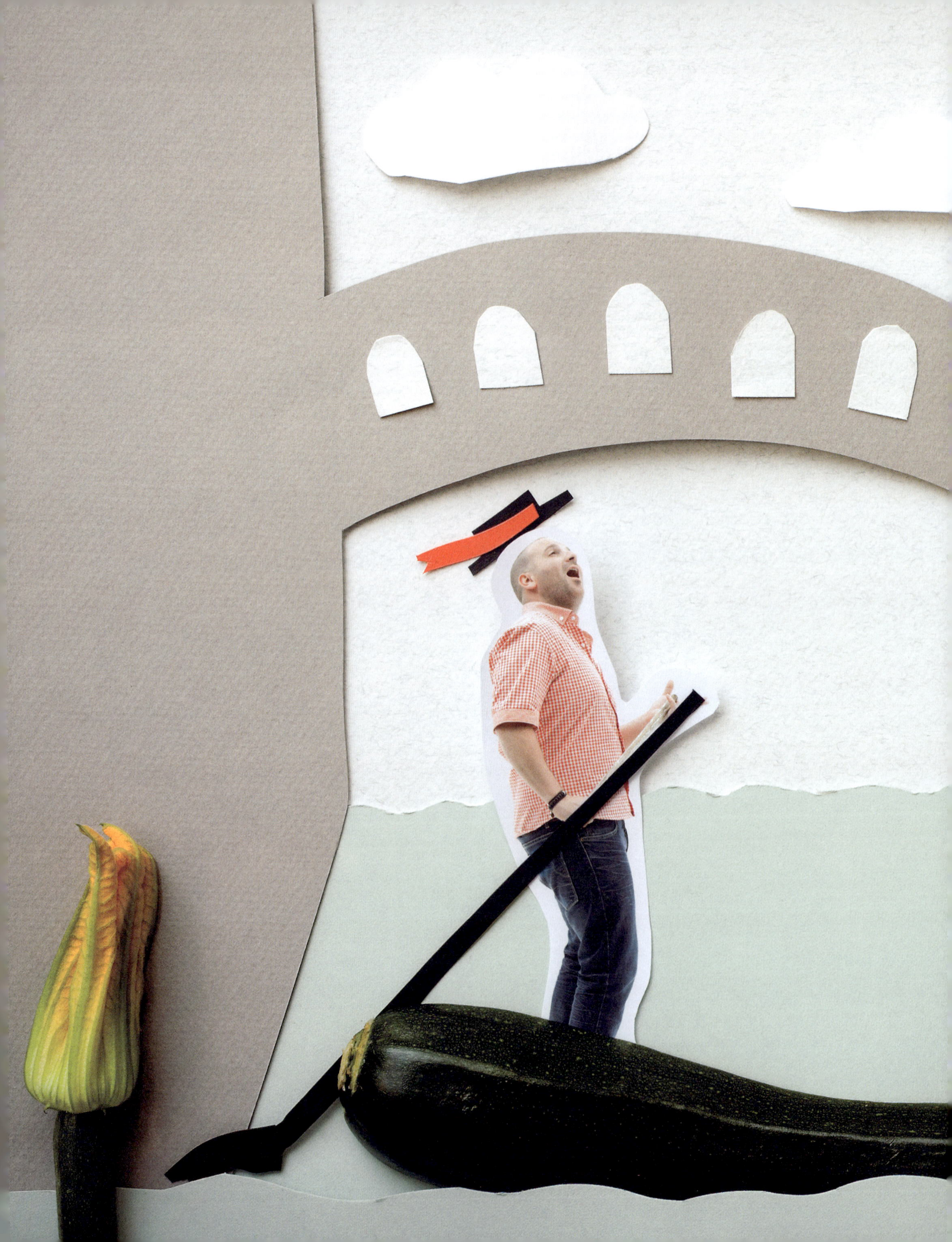

ZUCCHINI

Zucchini (also known as courgette) is a form of squash that is at its seasonal best during summer. It belongs to the same family as pumpkins, watermelons and squashes. Zucchini skins can be green, yellow or almost black. The flesh is often soft and succulent, with many small seeds. The small, pale green Lebanese zucchini are mostly grated and added to omelettes, filo fillings and fritters, or used for stuffing.

Choose zucchini that feel heavy for their size with firm, glossy, tender skins. They are very fragile and should be handled with care as small punctures will lead to decay. Store them in a plastic bag in the refrigerator for no longer than three days.

To prepare zucchini, wash them under cold running water and cut off both ends. They can be steamed, boiled, grilled, barbecued, baked or fried. They can also be eaten raw, such as sliced or shredded in a salad (see page 192) or as a crudite (vegetable stick) to serve with dips. Zucchini flowers are also edible. They are often filled with a stuffing, then deep-fried, sauteed or baked, or used in salads, soups and pasta sauces.

Zucchini fritters

When I eat these fritters, I think of being by the sea in Greece. After swimming all day, there's nothing better than sitting in a tavern eating crispy zucchini fritters.

Makes 16–20

- 2 (about 500 g) zucchini (courgette), coarsely grated
- salt
- 1 clove garlic, finely chopped
- 1 tablespoon finely grated lemon zest
- 60 g kefalograviera cheese (see page 202), finely grated
- 2 eggs, beaten
- ½ cup (75 g) plain flour
- sea salt and freshly ground black pepper
- ½ cup (125 ml) olive oil
- lemon wedges, to serve

1 Place the grated zucchini in a colander, then add 1 teaspoon salt and leave to drain for 10 minutes. Squeeze out any excess moisture from the zucchini with your hands and transfer it to a large bowl. Add the garlic, lemon zest, cheese and eggs. Stir in the flour until just combined. Season with a little salt and pepper.

2 Pour enough olive oil into a heavy-based non-stick frying pan to cover the base. Heat over medium heat, then, working in batches, place 2 tablespoonfuls of the zucchini mixture in the pan. Repeat, spacing the fritters a few centimetres apart to allow room to spread out and turn. Cook the fritters for 2–3 minutes on each side or until golden and cooked through.

3 Remove the fritters and drain on paper towel. Season with a little extra salt and serve with lemon wedges to the side.

Did you know?

- While zucchini are treated as vegetables in cooking, they are actually a fruit.

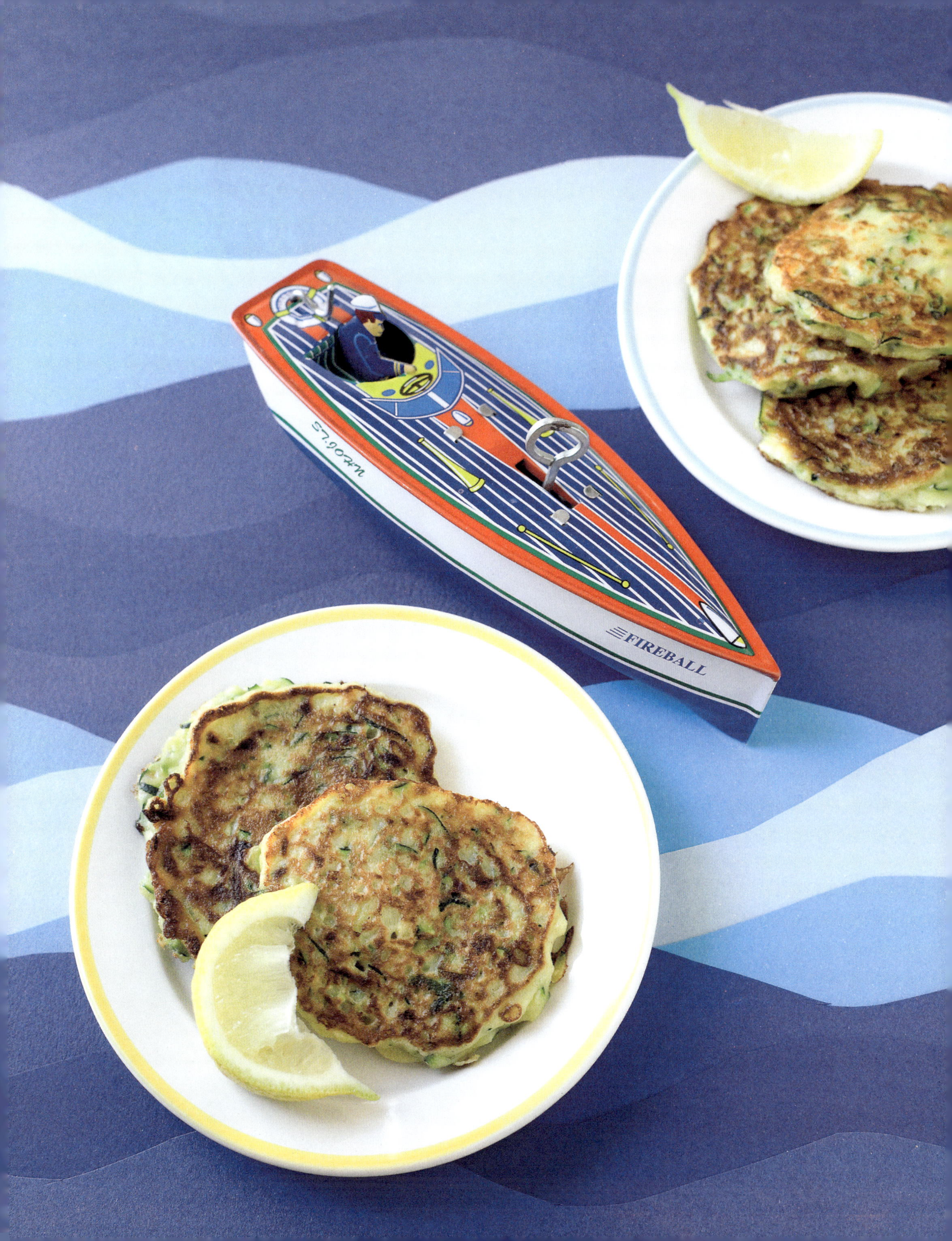
FIREBALL

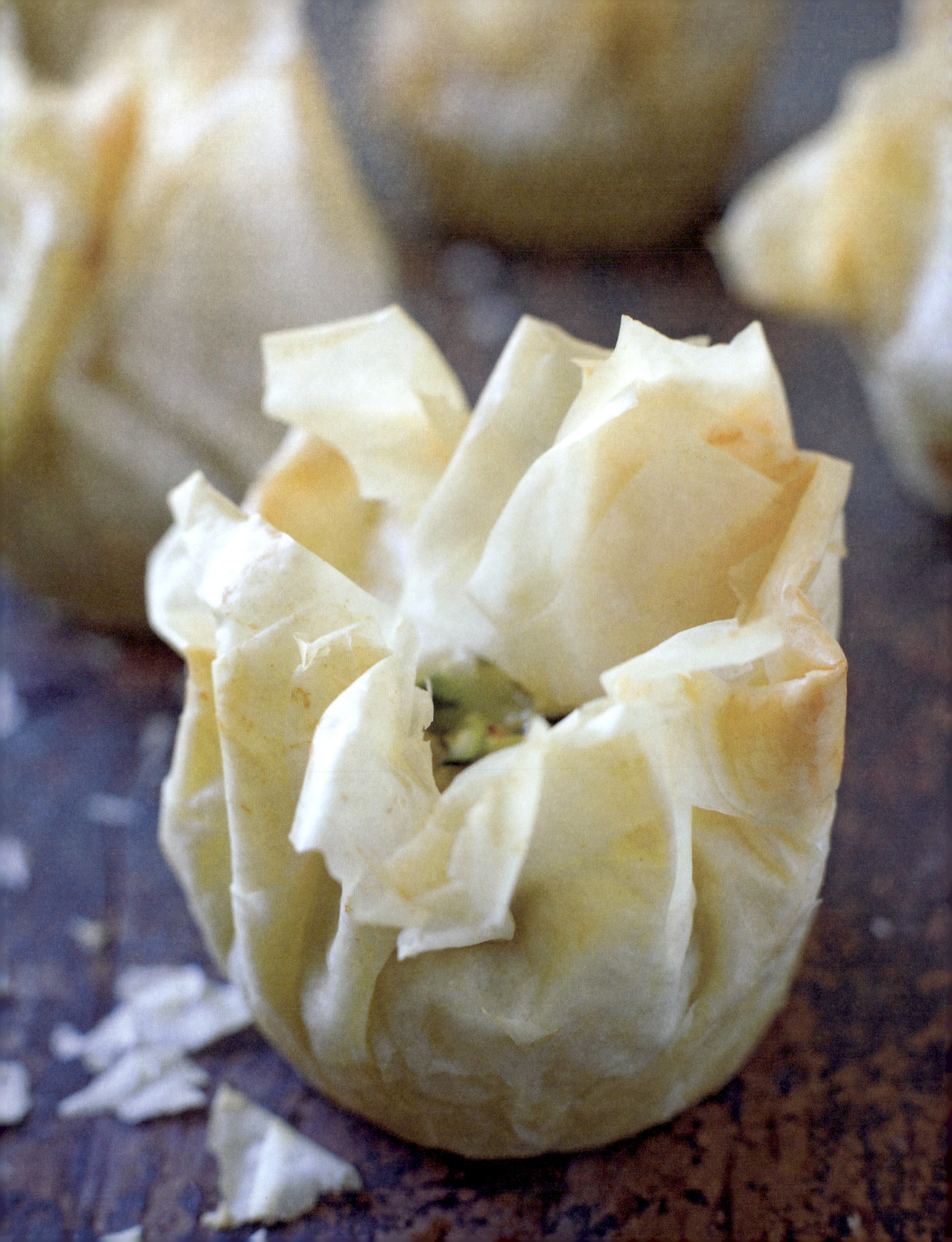

Zucchini, bacon and cheese pies

Ever since I was a child, I have eaten filo-based pies and pastries. My mum would often fill them with a mixture of Greek cheeses such as feta and kefalograviera and wild greens like nettles that she had foraged from the roadside. Here I have used zucchini and added some bacon for a decidedly non-Greek touch. Try them – not only are they easy to make, they are delicious as well.

Makes 12

- 2 (about 500 g) zucchini (courgette), coarsely grated
- salt
- 2 tablespoons olive oil
- 1 onion, finely chopped
- 2 tablespoons long-grain rice
- 2 rashers bacon, rind removed, finely chopped
- 1 clove garlic, thinly sliced
- ½ cup (100 g) feta, crumbled
- ½ cup (40 g) grated parmesan
- 3 eggs, beaten
- 4 large mint leaves, shredded
- freshly ground black pepper
- 125 g clarified butter (see page 201), melted
- 12 sheets filo pastry

✱ SPECIAL EQUIPMENT
  12-hole muffin pan
  pastry brush

1 Place the grated zucchini in a colander, then add 1 teaspoon salt and leave to drain for 10 minutes.

2 Preheat the oven to 200°C (180°C fan-forced).

3 Meanwhile, heat the olive oil in a large frying pan over low heat and gently fry the onion, rice, bacon and garlic for 2 minutes. Transfer to a large bowl to cool completely.

4 Squeeze out the zucchini with your hands to remove excess moisture and add to the onion mixture. Add the feta, parmesan, eggs and mint and season to taste with salt and pepper. Mix well to combine.

5 Place the filo sheets on a chopping board and use a sharp knife to cut them in half lengthways. Cut each length into 3 to make 6 square shapes per sheet.

6 Brush a 12-hole muffin pan with clarified butter, then add a square of filo. Brush with the butter and place another sheet of filo over the top so the corners of the filo are at a different angle (see opposite). Continue until you have 4 layers. Repeat with the remaining filo and clarified butter; all 12 holes will be lined with filo cups.

7 Divide the zucchini mixture among the filo-lined muffin holes. Take 2 squares of filo and scrunch them up tightly. Place on top of the filling in each muffin hole. Repeat this process with the remaining filo sheets until all the tops are covered. Brush the scrunched filo liberally with clarified butter.

8 Bake the pies for 35 minutes or until the filo is golden.

9 Leave the pies to cool for a few minutes before carefully removing from the pan and serving.

Zucchini flower salad

Zucchini flowers are considered a delicacy. The female flower blossoms on the end of the zucchini, whereas the male flower grows directly on the stem and is slightly smaller than the female. The pistils and stamens should be removed before cooking. For a bit of fun, I like to place two chive lengths on the capsicum and feta puree to look like bunny ears, but this is purely optional.

Serves 4

2 red capsicums (peppers)

80 g feta

1 tablespoon extra virgin olive oil, plus extra for drizzling

1 tablespoon red-wine vinegar

4 zucchini (courgette) flowers, with baby zucchini attached

lemon juice, to taste

black sea salt (optional, see page 201) or sea salt and freshly ground black pepper

✱ SPECIAL EQUIPMENT
food processor

1 Preheat the oven to 180°C fan-forced (200°C conventional).

2 Place the capsicums on a baking tray and roast for 30 minutes or until softened and collapsed. Remove the capsicums from the oven and place in a bowl, then cover with plastic film and leave to sweat (this makes the skins easier to peel). When cooled, peel off the skins and remove and discard the seeds.

3 Place the capsicum in a food processor with the feta, olive oil and vinegar, then process until smooth. Set aside. (Makes about 1 cup (250 ml). Store any leftover puree in an airtight container in the fridge for up to 3 days.)

4 Gently remove and discard the stamens and pistils from the zucchini flowers, then gently shred the flowers. Thinly slice the zucchini and place in a bowl. Drizzle with olive oil and lemon juice and toss gently.

5 Place a spoonful of the capsicum and feta puree on a serving plate, then arrange the zucchini flowers and sliced zucchini alongside. Season with salt and pepper and serve.

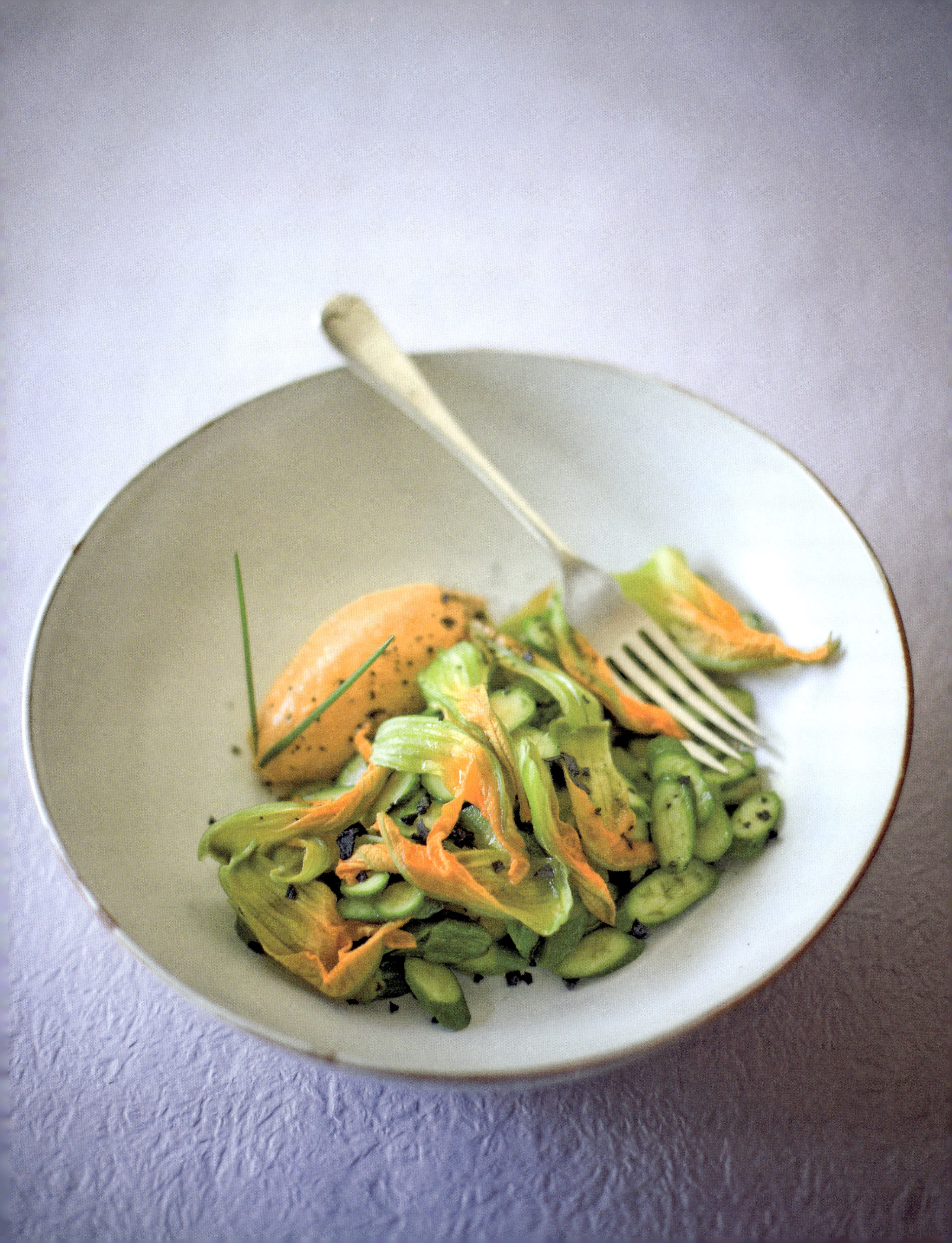

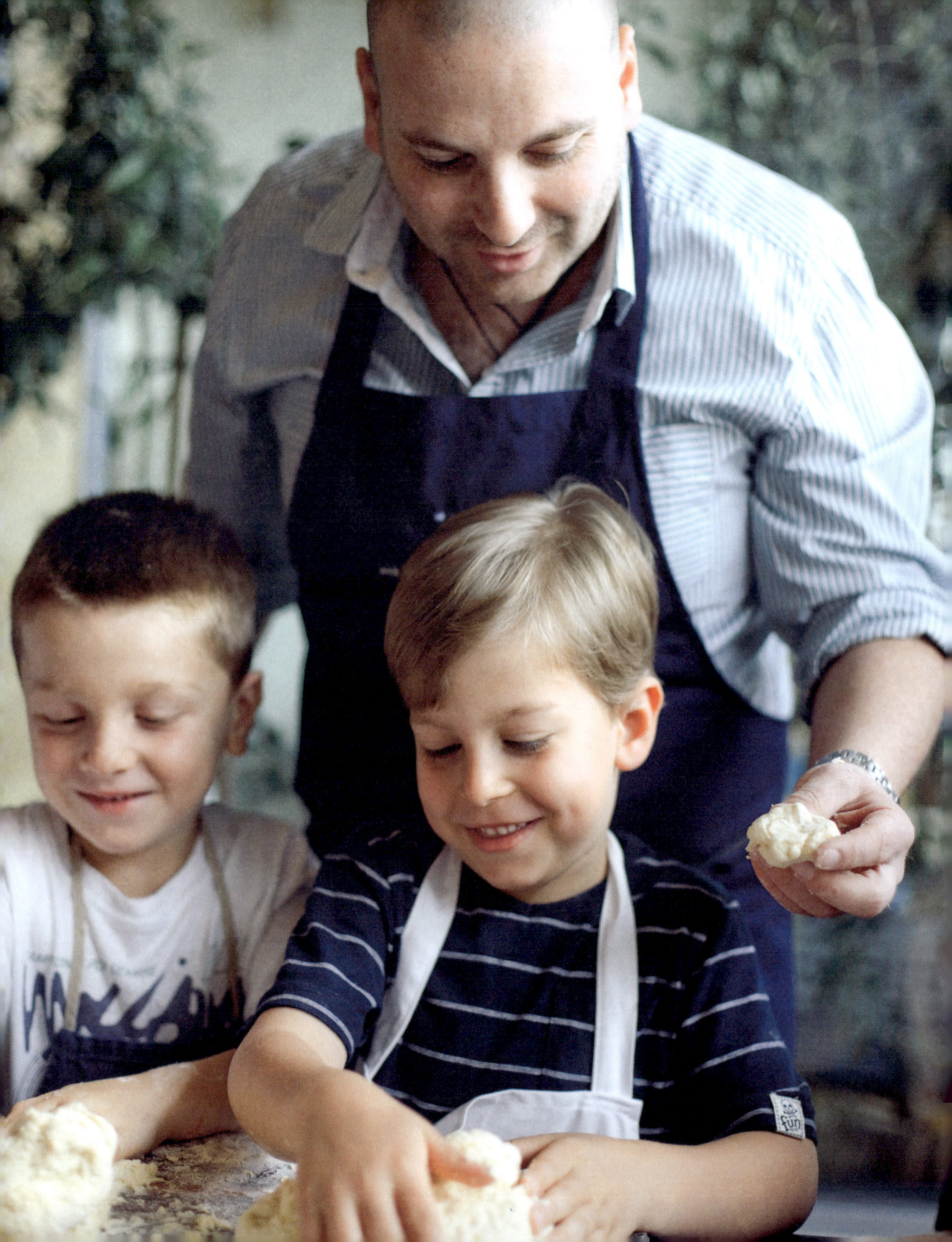
fun

Kitchen basics

Notes for parents

Teaching children to cook takes time and patience. However, while it may be quicker and easier for you to cook on your own, there are many benefits to sharing the kitchen with your kids. Not only will they be able to assist you with meal preparation, but they will eventually be able to cook the family meal completely by themselves, giving them a great sense of achievement. Cooking with your kids is not just about teaching kitchen skills for life, but about helping them to develop confidence. Both will stand them in good stead when they eventually leave home. (And as an added bonus, you get to enjoy the results of their labour!)

I hope you enjoy making many recipes from this book and collect happy memories from teaching your children how to cook. Here are my tips for getting started:

- Cook together when you have plenty of time, so that you can really enjoy the experience. Weekends and school holidays, when you are less rushed and tired, are good.
- When starting out, supervise your child closely until you know what they can manage on their own. Later on, you can read each recipe and identify the parts your child can manage safely alone, then work through the rest together. Encourage them to do as much as possible unaided.
- Before you begin, assemble all the ingredients and equipment you will need.
- Don't worry about the mess, but ask your child to clean benches and tidy as they go. This is what all good cooks and chefs do.
- Be patient. It may take a while for your child to master a skill. Persevere and remember that it will become easier with practice.
- Encourage your child to read the following section on kitchen safety.

Kitchen safety

Cooking is great fun, but it is important to remember that some things in the kitchen can be dangerous. Make sure the floor is dry and free from spills and obstructions to prevent slipping and tripping. To avoid accidents, always clean up spills as you go.

SHARP THINGS

- Knives, peelers and graters are all sharp, so be careful when using them.
- Good-quality sharp knives are best. Small hands are best suited to small knives.

Once basic knife skills and confidence have developed, larger knives can be used to tackle bigger jobs.

- Always pick up a knife by its handle. Remember, the sharp end of the knife should always face away from you.
- Blunt knives can be dangerous as it is harder to cut with them. Keep your knives sharp.
- When holding an ingredient that is to be cut, protect your fingers by tucking in your fingers to avoid the sharp blade.
- Place knives on their sides, not edge up.
- Ensure that you are standing at the correct bench height when using knives. A sturdy footstool may be required for younger kids.
- Use a chopping board to protect the bench surface. It can be secured by placing a moistened paper towel or dishcloth underneath. This prevents the board from slipping and moving.
- Never leave sharp knives in the sink for washing up – anyone reaching in unawares could cut themselves. Clean knives by wiping the blade while still holding the handle. Use hot soapy water.

HOT THINGS

- Remember that ovens and stovetops can get very hot. Adults should supervise young children when using this equipment.
- Always use oven mitts when touching hot cooking equipment. You'll need oven mitts for the microwave too, if you don't use special microwave dishes.
- Saucepan handles can also get hot. Use oven mitts.
- Make sure saucepan handles are safely facing away from the edge of the bench and stovetop so they can't accidentally be knocked.
- When taking lids off hot pans or dishes, stand back as the steam can burn.
- Oil and butter reach very high temperatures, so you need to be very careful when cooking with them. Wet food can cause fat to spatter, so add it carefully to the pan, using tongs if necessary. Cook with dry hands to prevent water dripping into hot fats. This can cause the fat to spit and possibly burn you.
- Fat is flammable and catches fire easily. Do not try to douse fat fires with water as this will cause the fat to spatter everywhere. Have a fire blanket in the kitchen for this purpose.

ELECTRICAL APPLIANCES

- Check appliances for any damage to power cords before using.
- Keep electrical cords away from the oven, stovetop and sink.
- Switch off appliances before you unplug them.
- Unplug by pulling out the plug, not by pulling on the cord.
- Don't touch electrical appliances or plugs with wet hands.
- Keep the electrical components of equipment away from water. To clean them, wipe them down with a damp cloth and dry with a tea towel.
- Don't put your fingers inside electrical equipment, as the blades are sharp. Always keep fingers away from the blade, especially when the equipment is plugged in.

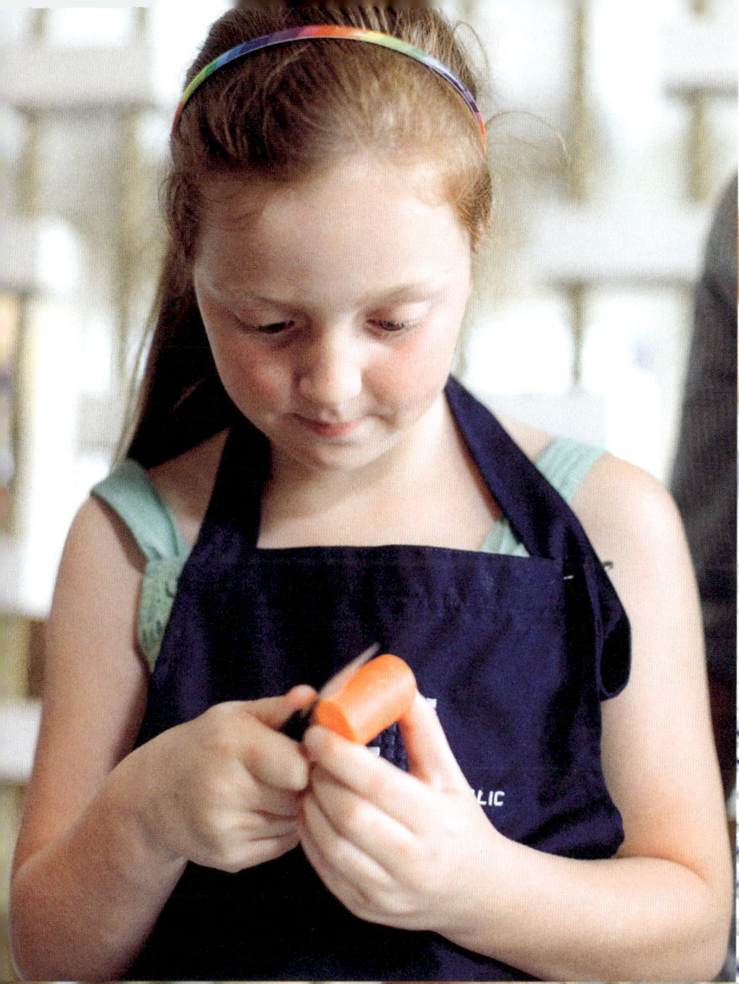
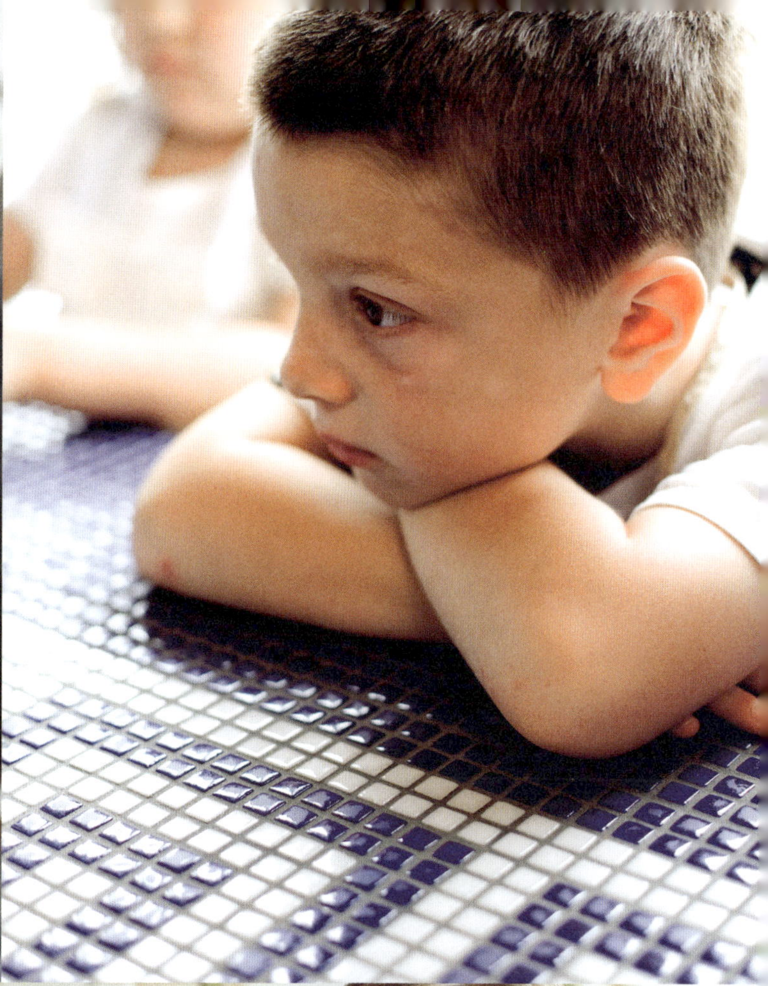
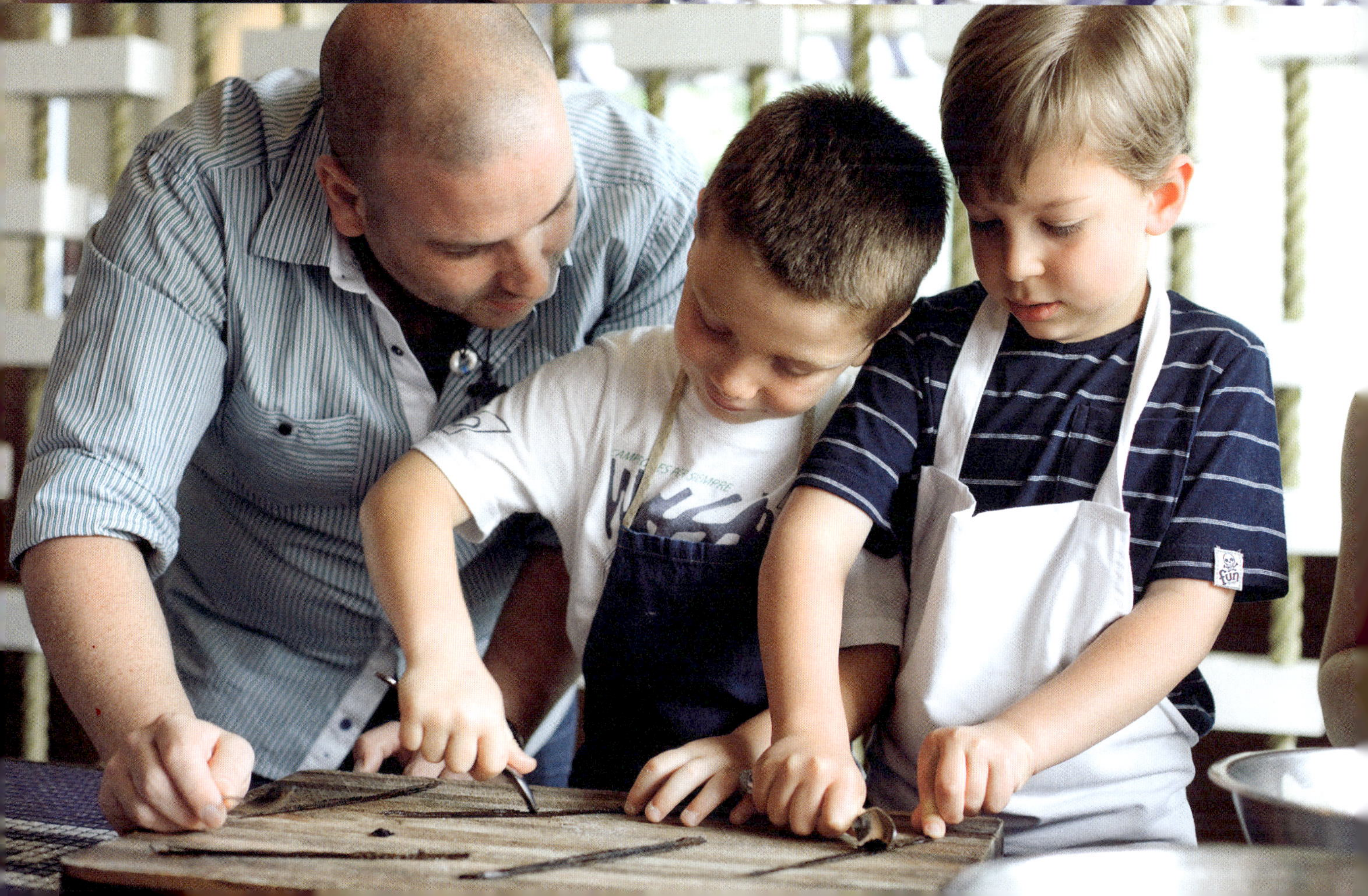

- Stick blenders must be turned off and unplugged before cleaning. Don't be tempted to bring your mouth to the blade to taste, as the blades are really sharp!

- Don't try to get toast out of the toaster with a knife or fork. If the toast is burnt and stuck, always turn off the power at the wall switch and unplug the toaster first, then allow the toast to cool down before getting an adult to remove it.

Ready, set, cook

- Read the recipe through from start to finish. Make sure you understand what the terms mean and what the ingredients are. Read the recipe as many times as you need to before starting.

- Make sure you have all the ingredients in the quantities that you need. (Parents: when planning, write a shopping list and get the kids involved. This is all part of the fun.)

- Allow enough time to prepare the food as well as cook it, so you're not rushing. (Parents: remember that it takes a little longer when kids are starting out.)

- Assemble all the equipment you need and place it safely on the bench.

- Before you begin cooking, roll up your sleeves and wear an apron. Make sure you are wearing appropriate footwear.

- Wash your hands in warm soapy water and dry them well. Wet hands can be slippery. Wipe down the kitchen bench too. (Parents: small children will need a sturdy stool or step to be at correct bench height.)

- Recipes are written with the ingredients listed in the order they will be used. Divide the ingredients into sections for each step. Place them in a particular spot on the bench with any utensils needed for measuring, stirring, chopping, etc.

- Follow each step of the recipe before moving on to the next one.

- Keep your preparation area clean by wiping down and tidying as you go. This is good practice, and also makes cleaning up at the end easier. (Parents: be sure to include the kids in the clean-up as a cooking session is never complete until all the dishes are washed and put away.)

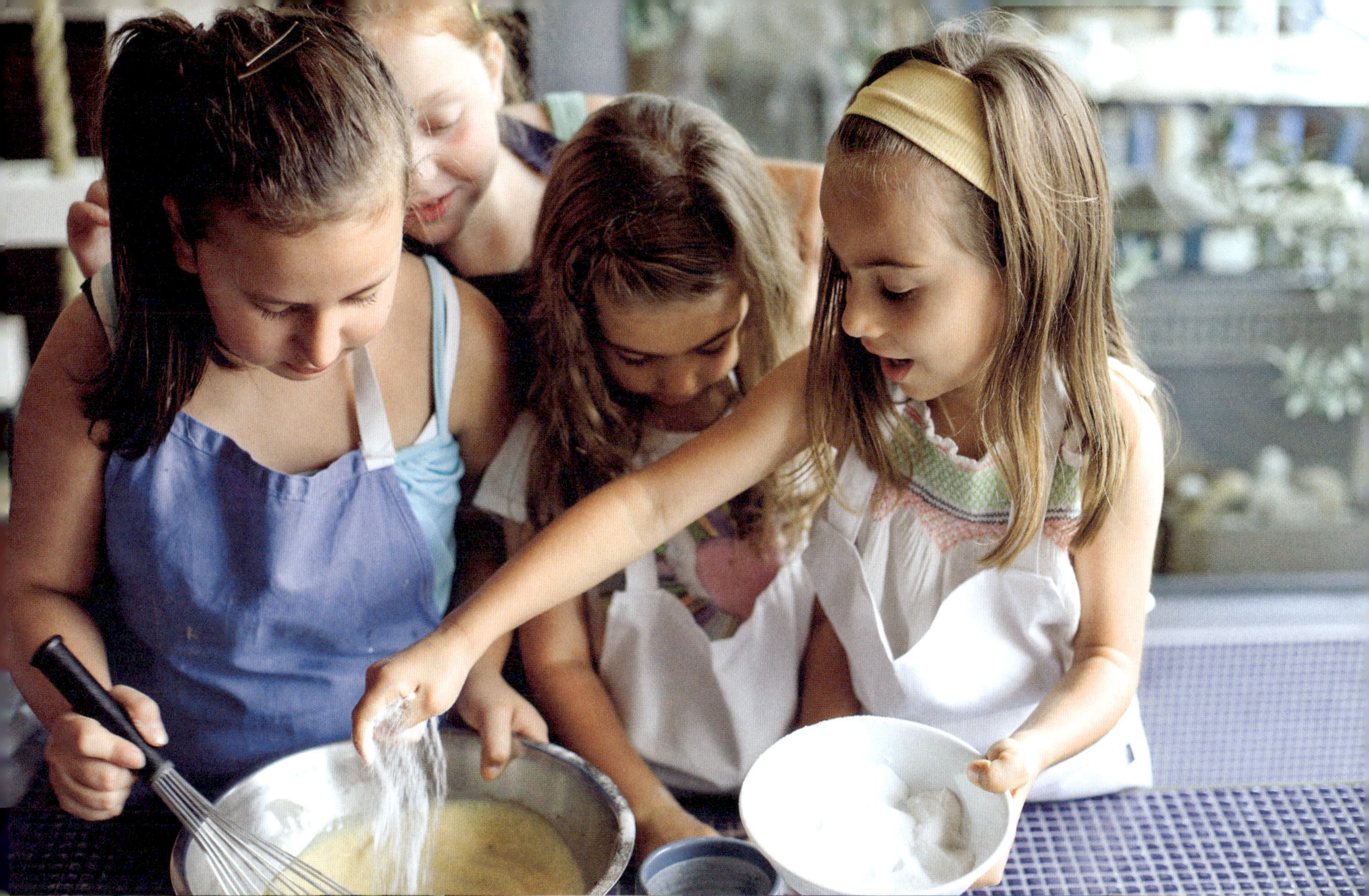

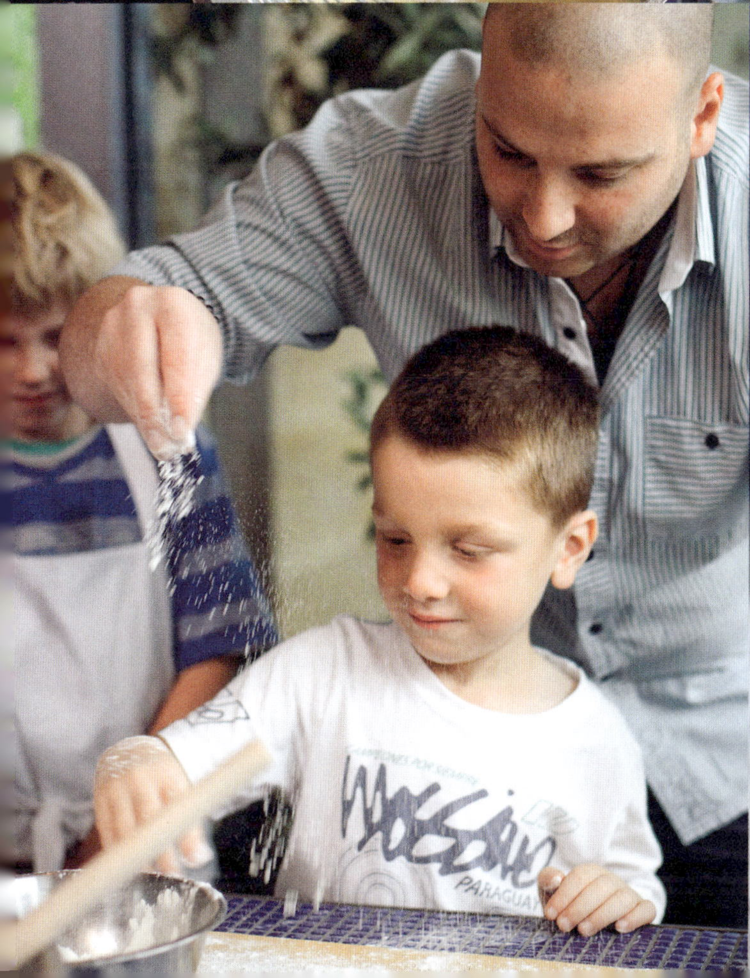

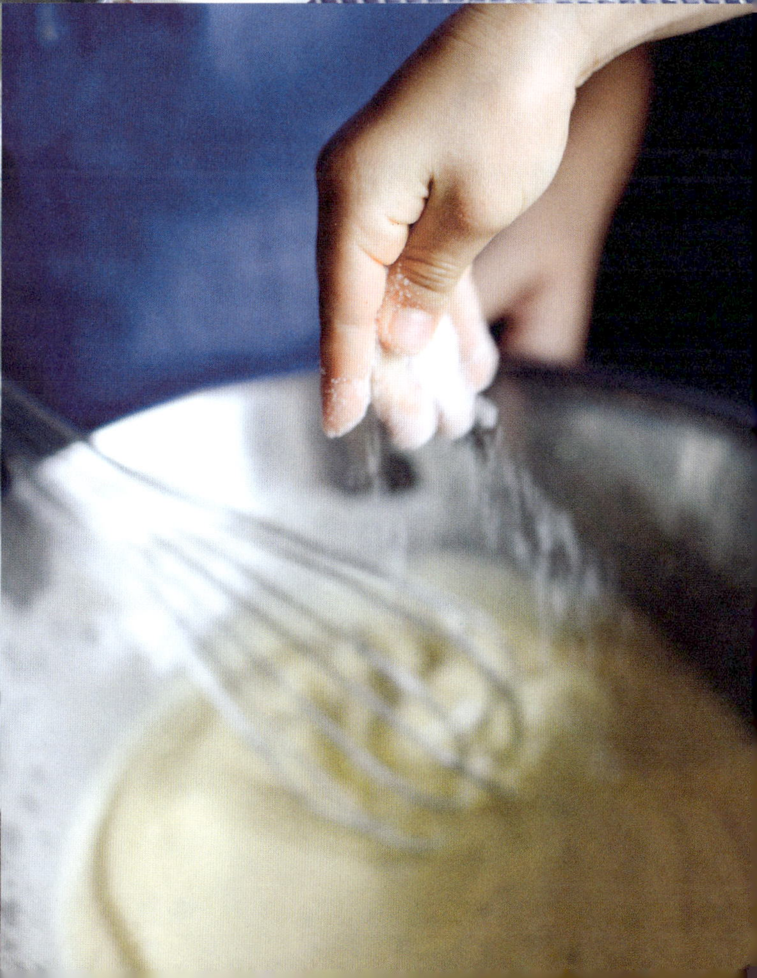

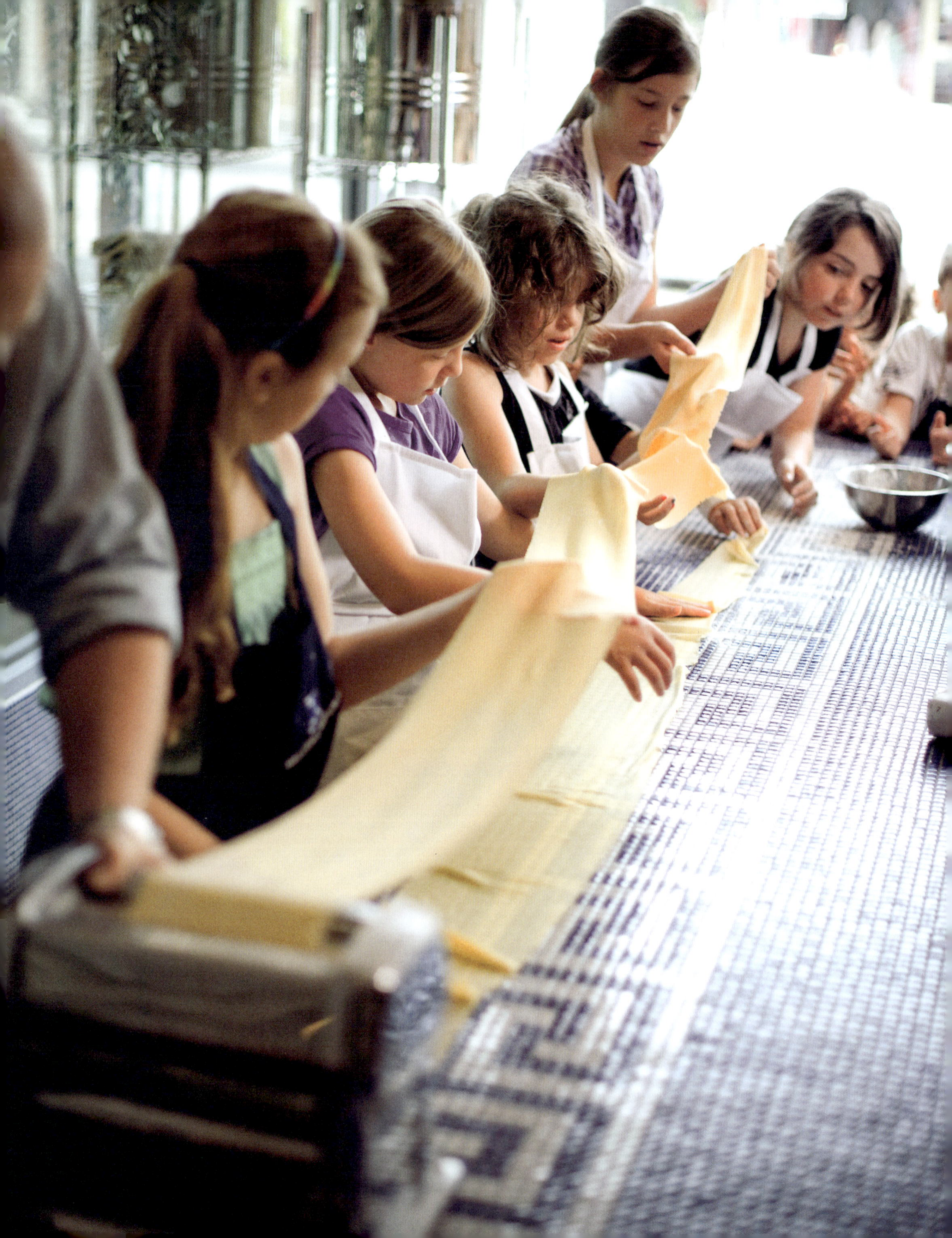

Glossary

Asian spiral vegetable cutter
Used to cut vegetables into spirals. Available from Asian food stores.

Black sea salt
This mined mineral salt is available in large crystalline pieces. Its distinctive sulphurous aroma adds a unique note to dishes it is added to. Available from herbies.com.au.

Buffalo mozzarella
This creamy fresh mozzarella is made from the milk of domesticated water buffaloes rather than cows.

Carnaroli rice
An Italian medium-grain rice. I prefer to use it for making risotto as it is longer, has a firmer texture and contains more starch than arborio rice.

Chicken stock
To make your own chicken stock, place 1.5 kg roughly chopped chicken bones, 750 g halved chicken wings, 1 roughly chopped onion, 1 roughly chopped celery stick, the roughly chopped white part of 1 leek, 6 stalks flat-leaf parsley, 2 sprigs thyme, 1 bay leaf and 10 black peppercorns in a large stockpot, then add 4 litres cold water. Bring to a simmer, then reduce the heat to low to maintain the stock at a constant gentle simmer for 3 hours, topping up with water occasionally to keep all ingredients submerged. Skim any rising foam and scum regularly from the surface within the first 30 minutes. (Skimming the surface and keeping the stock at a simmer results in a clear stock. Boiling results in a cloudy stock.) When cool enough to handle, strain the stock through a colander lined with a damp muslin into a clean container. Chill in the refrigerator overnight. Remove the solidified fat from the surface. Transfer to an airtight container, then label, date and refrigerate for up to 3 days or freeze for up to 3 months.

Citric acid
This weak acidulant occurs naturally in vegetables and fruits, especially citrus fruits such as lemons and limes. Used to preserve foods and add a sour taste, it is available in powder form from larger supermarkets.

Clarified butter
Pop unsalted butter into a microwave-safe container and microwave on medium for 90 seconds. Remove and allow the milk solids and butterfat to separate. Skim off the butterfat and reserve, discarding the milk solids.

Clotted cream
A rich, thick cream with a slightly caramelised flavour containing between 48 and 60 per cent butterfat.

Cornichons
Small pickled cucumbers. Available from specialty food stores and delis.

Dariole moulds
Small flowerpot-shaped cooking vessels made from stainless-steel, aluminium or plastic. They are used to give moulded desserts such as custards, creams and jellies a uniform shape. Available from specialty cookware stores.

Dark couverture chocolate buttons
It is determined by law that this grade of chocolate must contain a minimum of 32 per cent cocoa butter and 54 per cent combined total of cocoa solids and cocoa butter. The more cocoa butter and solids a chocolate contains, the less sugar it has. This gives it a more chocolatey flavour.

Dutch-process cocoa
This is the powder remaining after the cocoa butter has been removed from cocoa beans. Dutch-process cocoa powder is unsweetened cocoa treated with an alkali to neutralise its acids.

Five spice powder
A Chinese ground-spice mixture containing cassia, cloves, fennel, star anise and Sichuan pepper (or ginger or cardamom). Available from the spice section of larger supermarkets.

Freekah
This increasingly popular grain is made from wheat harvested while still young, then sun-dried and set on fire to separate the straw and chaff from the seeds. It is then roasted and thrashed to crack it into smaller pieces. Available from specialty food stores and health food stores.

Gelatine leaves (gold and titanium strength)
Gelatine is a setting agent derived from collagen. It comes in powder or leaf form and is used to set jellies, mousses and sweets. The leaves come in different grades – titanium, gold and silver – according to how easily they set. Titanium-strength leaves are the strongest and silver are the weakest, with gold somewhere in between. Gelatine leaves must be soaked in water prior to use. Available from specialty food stores and good delis.

Haloumi
A Cypriot-style cheese traditionally made from goat's or sheep's milk. It has a high melting point, making it suitable for grilling and frying. Available from larger supermarkets and good delis.

Kecap manis
A sweet, sticky Indonesian soy sauce available from Asian food stores and selected supermarkets.

Kefalograviera cheese
Originating in Greece and Cyprus, this hard, salty cheese is traditionally made from sheep's milk. It is commonly used for cooking, although it is also appreciated as a table cheese. Available from Greek food stores and good delis.

Mayonnaise
To make your own mayonnaise, place 2 egg yolks and 2 teaspoons Dijon mustard in a small bowl. Using a hand-held electric mixer, blend until well mixed. Gradually pour in 1 cup (250 ml) vegetable oil, drop by drop at first and then in a slow, steady stream, blending continuously with the mixer until all the oil is incorporated and the sauce emulsifies. Stir in 2 teaspoons white-wine

vinegar and season to taste with sea salt and freshly ground white pepper. (Store in an airtight container in the fridge for up to 1 week. Makes about 250 ml.)

Metal cornet cones
Also called metal baking cones. Pastry is wrapped around the metal cone and then baked to make edible cones for stuffing. Available from specialty cookware and baking stores.

Ovens
My recipes were tested using a fan-forced oven. If using a conventional oven, check the manufacturer's instructions and adjust the oven temperature (usually 20°C higher for a non fan-forced oven) and cooking time accordingly. Preheat your oven well before baking or roasting.

Panko breadcrumbs
A large Japanese-style dried breadcrumb that remains light and crisp when fried. Available from larger supermarkets and Asian food stores.

Provolone cheese
A semi-hard southern Italian cow's milk cheese that comes in mild, sharp and smoked versions. I have used mild provolone in the recipes in this book.

Salted white cod roe paste
Salted and cured cod roe used to make the Greek dip taramosalata. Available from Greek food stores and delis.

Semolina
Made from milled durum wheat flour. The milling process separates the bran, germ and starch, and semolina is made from the sifted starch component of the wheat as it is ground into flour.

Shredded pickled beetroot
Available in jars from larger supermarkets.

Sterilised jars
To sterilise jars, wash the jars and lids in hot, soapy water, then rinse well and dry in a 130°C fan-forced (150°C conventional) oven for at least 10 minutes.

Strong '00' plain flour
The strength of flour refers to the amount of gluten it contains. '00' is a super-fine Italian flour grade with a high protein content, traditionally used for making pasta. Available from larger supermarkets.

Sugar thermometer
The best are digital probe thermometers which give immediate and precise readings. Alternatively, use a sugar thermometer that clips to the side of the pan for continuous monitoring. To test your thermometer, place it in a pan of water and bring the water to the boil. The thermometer should read 100°C in boiling water. Don't use infrared thermometers for sugar work, as they will measure water vapour, not syrup.

Tahini
A thick paste with a nutty flavour, made from ground sesame seeds. It is often used in Middle Eastern cooking. Available from larger supermarkets.

Turning knife
A small, sharp knife with a curved blade used for cleaning and shaping vegetables.

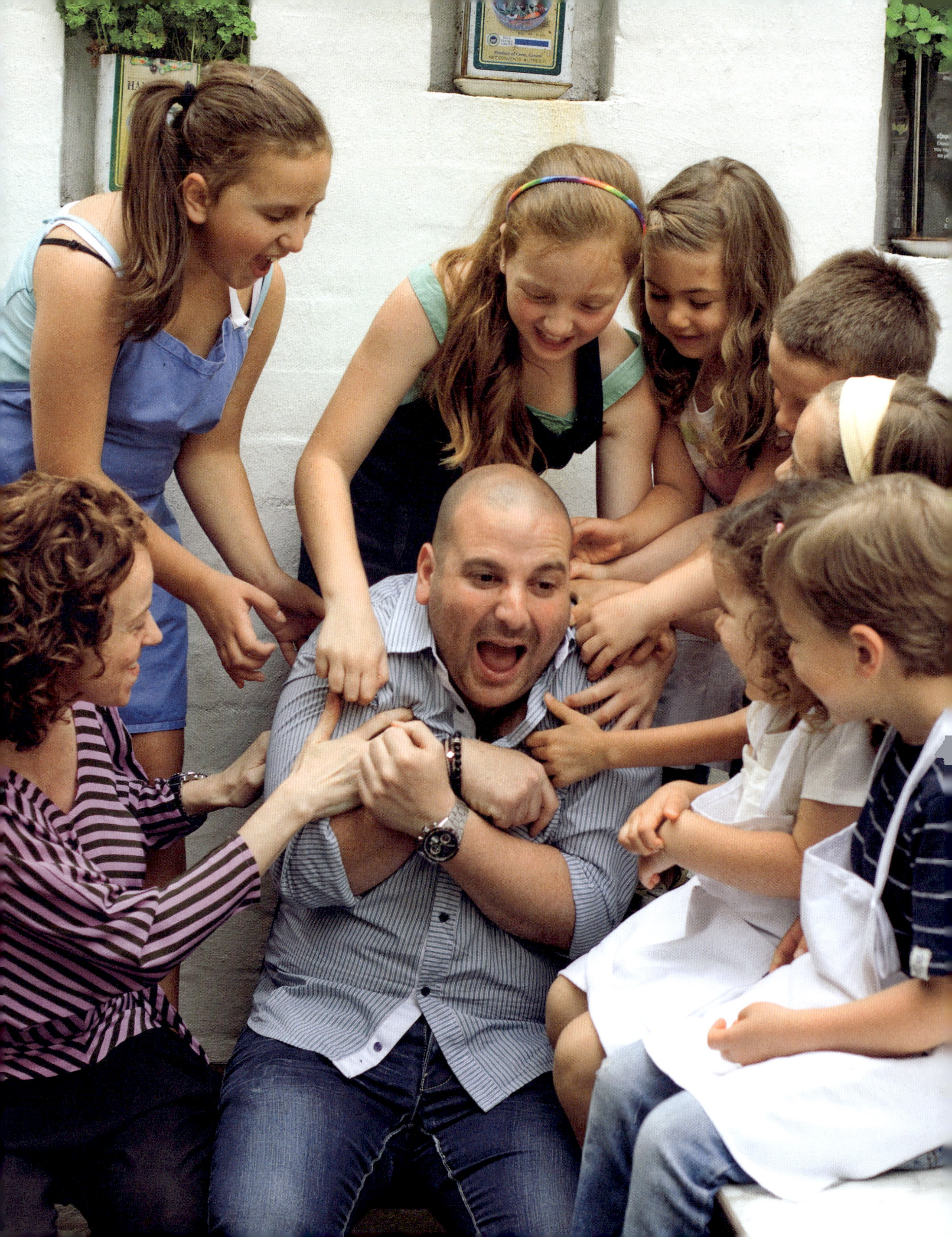

Thank you

I firstly need to thank my beautiful girl, Natalie, for giving me the idea to write a cookbook that kids would enjoy and also that would bring out the inner kid in me. I love and thank you, Nat, and I can't wait for our little one!

I need to thank Caroline Velik, who I believe is one of Australia's best food stylists. She has worked so hard on this book and has helped to make it possible for me. Thanks to photographer Mark Chew and his assistant Rebecca, who make my food come alive on the page. Mark, you rock!

Big thanks also go to Travis McAuley, my business partner and head chef from Hellenic Republic, who works so hard at the restaurant and still finds the time to cook with me.

Huge thanks to Lauren Calleja, my executive assistant but more importantly my friend, for keeping me in line and on time.

To all my nieces, nephews, godsons and goddaughters – I love you guys so much. We are family, and family is everything! To my family, thank you for supporting me and understanding my dream. I love you all!

Special thanks to my publisher, Julie Gibbs, and to all the team at Penguin, especially Ingrid Ohlsson, Megan Pigott, Daniel New, Evi Oetomo, Kathleen Gandy, Ariane Durkin, Jane Morrow, Kim Noble and the many more behind the scenes for believing in my ideas and being patient.

To all my 300-plus staff in all the restaurants, thank you for representing me every day so I am able to make books like these. Without you I am nothing; together we are strong!

Also, to my business partners who believe in me and support my every move, I thank you. I also need to acknowledge my *MasterChef Australia* family. Love you guys.

To all the young cooks out there who come to my restaurants, believe in what I say and love food, I thank you. You are the next generation and I am so proud to know that we are in good hands. There is only one secret to good cooking:

YOU MUST FIRST LOVE, THEN COOK, THEN CELEBRATE.

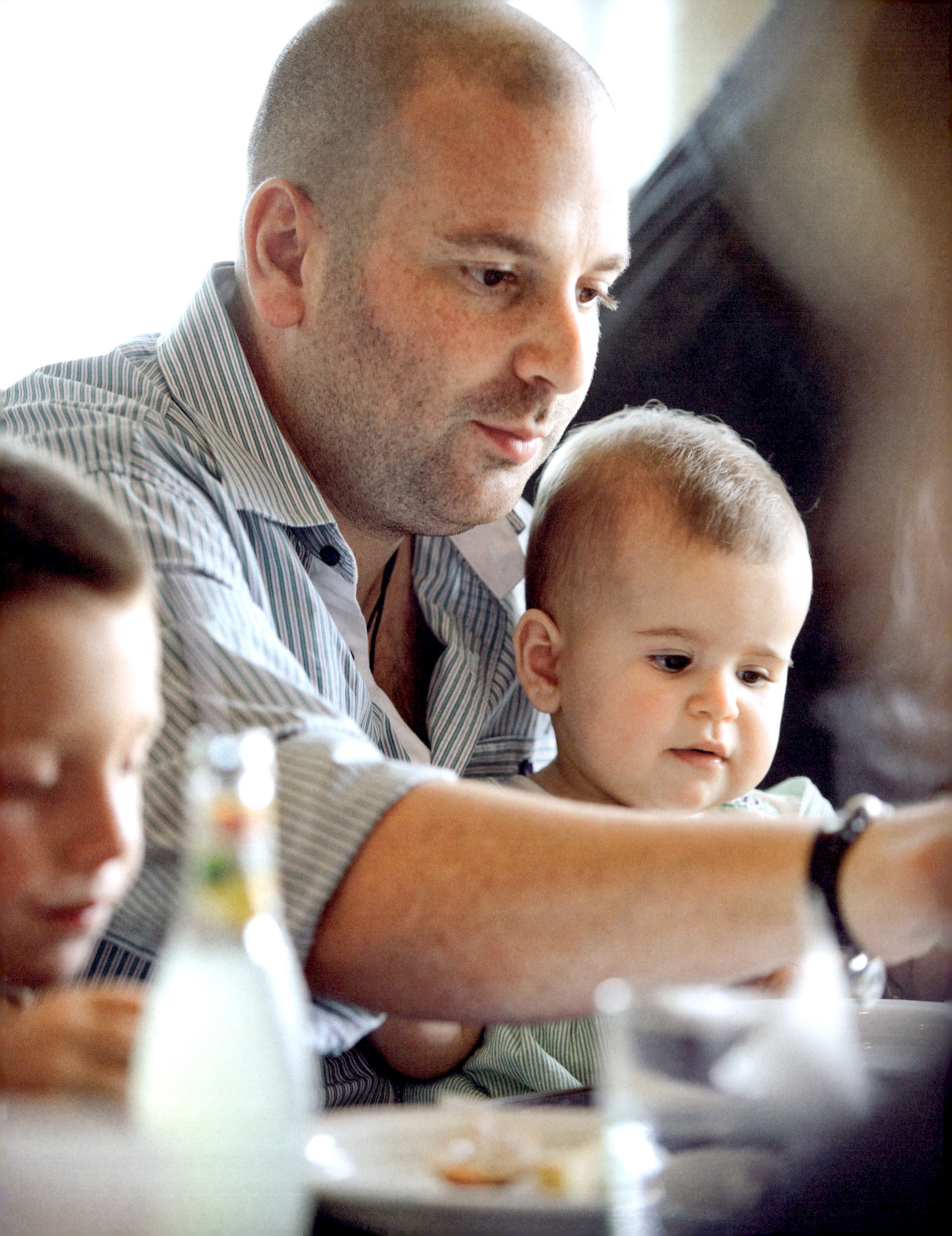

Index

A
Alexandrian felafels 135
amuse-bouche 152
apples
   Apple and rhubarb puree 2
   Apple tarts with frangipane cream 5
   Compressed apple with slow-roasted pork belly 6
Avocado tzatziki 32

B
bacon
   Zucchini, bacon and cheese pies 191
baklava
   Chocolate baklava 176
batter 43
beans, dried
   Alexandrian felafels 135
beans, green
   Green bean and feta salad 167
Bechamel sauce 112
beef
   Pan-fried steak and mushrooms with garlic butter 136
beetroot
   Roasted beetroot and yoghurt salad 64
berries
   Peanut butter and strawberry brittle 159
Best-ever spaghetti bolognese 92
brains
   Crispy fried lamb's brains 44
Braised chicken with potato, tomatoes and cinnamon 24
bread
   Damper 9
   Flatbread filled with feta and mint 13
   Homemade peanut butter on toast 55
   leavening agents 9
   Mini chocolate tsoureki 14
   Pita bread 10
   in salads 59
breadcrumbs 43
brittle
   Peanut butter and strawberry brittle 159
butter
   Clarified butter 88, 201
   ghee 88

C
cakes
   Fudgy chocolate brownies 76
   Yoghurt and lemon syrup cake 183
celery
   Mum's slow-cooked lamb with celery 87
cheese
   Flatbread filled with feta and mint 13
   Green bean and feta salad 167
   Ham, tomato and cheese jaffles 132
   Hamburger with haloumi 96
   My Yia Yia's Cypriot ravioli 111
   Nonna Nicoletta's spaghetti with fresh ricotta and parmesan 108
   Real chicken parma 21
   Watermelon and feta salad 60
   Zucchini, bacon and cheese pies 191
chick peas
   Hummus 31
chicken
   buying 17
   Braised chicken with potato, tomatoes and cinnamon 24
   Chicken breast fillets 131
   Chicken drumettes with homemade barbecue sauce 18
   Chicken stock 201
   Chicken and sweetcorn pie 22
   Chicken and sweetcorn soup 151
   jointing 17
   Real chicken parma 21
chocolate
   Chocolate baklava 176
   Chocolate marshmallow souffles 40
   Chocolate rice pudding 144
   Fudgy chocolate brownies 76
   Hot chocolate 14
   Mini chocolate tsoureki 14
   Triple chocolate muffins 156
Clarified butter 88, 201
Cocktail sauce 124
Compressed apple with slow-roasted pork belly 6
Condensed milk fool with lemon granita 56
Court bouillon 44

Creme brulee 39
Crispy fried lamb's brains 44
Crumbed calamari 48
custard
    Creme brulee 39
    for ice cream 67
Cypriot eggless ravioli
  dough 111
Cypriot grain salad 63

D
Damper 9
dippers 27
    Fried whitebait 32
dips
    Avocado tzatziki 32
    Hummus 31
    Taramosalata 28
dressings
    Sherry vinaigrette 164
    see also mayonnaise

E
eggs
    buying and storing 35
    Creme brulee 39
    Eggs with soldiers 36
    freshness 35
    Greek-style Scotch eggs 47
electrical appliances 196, 198

F
fats and oils safety 196
felafels
    Alexandrian felafels 135
fish
    Fish fillets 131
    Fried whitebait 32
Flatbread filled with feta
  and mint 13
flowers in salads 59
Frangipane cream 5
Fried whitebait 32
fritters
    Alexandrian felafels 135
    Crispy fried lamb's brains 44
    Crumbed calamari 48
    Greek-style Scotch eggs 47
    Zucchini fritters 188

Fruit skewers with fairy floss 104
Fudgy chocolate brownies 76

G
getting started 195, 198
ghee 88
gnocchi
    Potato gnocchi 120
Golden thread prawns with
  cocktail sauce 124
grains
    Cypriot grain salad 63
granita
    Lemon granita 56
Grbac, Joe 167
Greek salad cornets 172
Greek-style Scotch eggs 47
Green bean and feta salad 167

H
ham
    Ham and pineapple pizza 52
    Ham, tomato and cheese
      jaffles 132
    Real chicken parma 21
Hamburger with haloumi 96
Homemade barbecue sauce 18
Homemade peanut butter
  on toast 55
Homemade yoghurt with
  honey and walnuts 180
honey 155
    Homemade yoghurt with
      honey and walnuts 180
    Yoghurt snow 184
Hot chips with taramosalata 116
Hot chocolate 14
hot things (safety) 196
Hummus 31

I
ice cream
    Pancake-and-maple-syrup-ripple
      ice cream 70
    Raspberry ice cream 72
    types 67
    Vanilla-bean ice cream 69

J
jaffles
    Ham, tomato and cheese
      jaffles 132
jelly
    Liquorice allsorts jelly 79
    Milk jelly with fudgy chocolate
      brownies 76
    Passionfruit jelly 80

K
Keftedes 95
kitchen basics
    bench height 196
    chopping boards 196
    electrical appliances 196, 198
    fats and oils 196
    getting started 195, 198
    hot things 196
    knife safety 195–6
    preparation area 198
    recipes 195, 198
    safety issues 195–8
    sharp things 195–6

L
Labne 164, 184
lamb
    cuts 83
    Greek-style Scotch eggs 47
    Lamb cutlets 131
    Lamb doner kebabs 84
    Lamb kebabs with tomato
      salad 103
    Mint-crusted lamb racks 88
    Mum's slow-cooked lamb
      with celery 87
lemon
    Lemon granita 56
    Yoghurt and lemon syrup
      cake 183
lentils
    Mum's lentil soup 148
Liquorice allsorts jelly 79

M
Maggie Beer's sour-cream pastry 22
maple syrup

Pancake-and-maple-syrup-ripple
   ice cream 70
Mayonnaise 36, 203
   Cocktail sauce 124
   Star-anise mayonnaise 44
   Tartare sauce 100
Meat sauce for pasta 112
Meringue 160
Milk jelly with fudgy chocolate
  brownies 76
mince 91
   Best-ever spaghetti bolognese 92
   Greek-style Scotch eggs 47
   Hamburger with haloumi 96
   Keftedes 95
   Lamb doner kebabs 84
   Meat sauce for pasta 112
   uses 91
Mini chocolate tsoureki 14
mint
   Flatbread filled with feta
     and mint 13
   Mint-crusted lamb racks 88
muffins
   Triple chocolate muffins 156
Mum's lentil soup 148
Mum's rice pilaf 140
Mum's slow-cooked lamb
  with celery 87
Mushrooms with garlic butter 136
My Yia Yia's Cypriot ravioli 111

N

Nonna Nicoletta's spaghetti with
  fresh ricotta and parmesan 108
nuts
   Chocolate baklava 176
   Homemade peanut butter
     on toast 55
   Homemade yoghurt with
     honey and walnuts 180
   Peanut butter and strawberry
     brittle 159

O

Omelette 131
oven mitts 196

P

Pancake-and-maple-syrup-ripple
  ice cream 70
Pan-fried steak and mushrooms
  with garlic butter 136
Parsley salad 135
passionfruit
   Passionfruit jelly 80
   Upside-down pavlova 160
pasta
   Best-ever spaghetti bolognese 92
   cooking 107
   Cypriot eggless ravioli dough 111
   making 108
   Meat sauce for pasta 112
   Nonna Nicoletta's spaghetti
     with fresh ricotta and
     parmesan 108
   My Yia Yia's Cypriot ravioli 111
   Pastitsio 112
   sauces 107
   storing 107
   Whole egg pasta dough 108
Pastitsio 112
pastries
   Apple tarts with frangipane
     cream 5
   Chocolate baklava 176
   Prawns wrapped in
     kataifi 100
pastry
   Maggie Beer's sour-cream
     pastry 22
pavlova
   Upside-down pavlova 160
peanut butter
   Homemade peanut butter
     on toast 55
   Peanut butter and strawberry
     brittle 159
Pickled pineapple 52
pies
   Chicken and sweetcorn pie 22
   Zucchini, bacon and cheese
     pies 191
pilaf
   Mum's rice pilaf 140

pineapple
   Ham and pineapple pizza 52
   Pickled pineapple 52
Pita bread 10
pizza
   Ham and pineapple pizza 52
Pommes fondants 119
Popcorn prawns with salt-and-
  vinegar dipping sauce 127
pork
   Compressed apple with
     slow-roasted pork belly 6
potatoes
   Braised chicken with potato,
     tomatoes and cinnamon 24
   floury and waxy 115
   Golden thread prawns with
     cocktail sauce 124
   Hot chips with taramosalata 116
   Potato fondants 119
   Potato gnocchi 120
prawns
   Golden thread prawns with
     cocktail sauce 124
   Popcorn prawns with salt-and-
     vinegar dipping sauce 127
   Prawn risotto 128
   Prawn stock 128
   Prawns wrapped in kataifi 100
   preparing 123
puddings
   Chocolate rice pudding 144
Pumpkin cappuccino 152
Pumpkin risotto my way 143

Q

Quail wrapped in vine leaves 175

R

Raspberry ice cream 72
Real chicken parma 21
recipes, following 195, 198
rhubarb
   Apple and rhubarb puree 2
rice
   Chocolate rice pudding 144
   Mum's rice pilaf 140
   varieties 139

risotto
    Prawn risotto 128
    Pumpkin risotto my way 143
Roasted beetroot and yoghurt
    salad 64

S

safety in the kitchen 195–8
salads
    bread in 59
    Cypriot grain salad 63
    flowers in 59
    Greek salad cornets 172
    Green bean and feta salad 167
    Parsley salad 135
    Roasted beetroot and yoghurt
        salad 64
    Sweetcorn salad with labne 164
    Tomato salad 103
    Watermelon and feta salad 60
    Zucchini flower salad 192
Salt-and-vinegar dipping sauce 127
saucepan safety 196
sauces
    Bechamel sauce 112
    Cocktail sauce 124
    Homemade barbecue sauce 18
    Meat sauce for pasta 112
    Salt-and-vinegar dipping
        sauce 127
    Tartare sauce 100
    see also mayonnaise
seafood
    Crumbed calamari 48
    see also prawns
sharp things 195–6
Sherry vinaigrette 164
skewers
    Fruit skewers with fairy floss 104
    Lamb doner kebabs 84
    Lamb kebabs with tomato
        salad 103
    Prawns wrapped in kataifi 100
souffles
    Chocolate marshmallow
        souffles 40
soup 147

Chicken and sweetcorn soup 151
    Mum's lentil soup 148
    Pumpkin cappuccino 152
Star anise mayonnaise 44
stock 147
    Chicken stock 201
    Prawn stock 128
sugar, types of 155
sweetcorn
    Chicken and sweetcorn pie 22
    Chicken and sweetcorn soup 151
    Sweetcorn salad with labne 164
syrup, lemon 183

T

Taramosalata 28
Tartare sauce 100
tarts
    Apple tarts with frangipane
        cream 5
toasters 198
toffee
    Peanut butter and strawberry
        brittle 159
tomatoes
    Braised chicken with potato,
        tomatoes and cinnamon 17
    Ham, tomato and cheese
        jaffles 132
    Tomato salad 103
Triple chocolate muffins 156
Turned vegetables 168

U

Upside-down pavlova 160

V

Vanilla-bean ice cream 69
vegetables
    Green bean and feta salad 167
    seasonal 163
    Sweetcorn salad with labne 164
    Turned vegetables 168
    see also specific vegetables
Velik, Caroline 72
vine leaves
    Quail wrapped in vine leaves 175

W

Watermelon and feta salad 60
Whole egg pasta dough 108
wraps 171

Y

yeast 9
yoghurt
    Homemade yoghurt with
        honey and walnuts 180
    Labne 164, 184
    origins 179
    Roasted beetroot and yoghurt
        salad 64
    Yoghurt and lemon syrup
        cake 183
    Yoghurt snow 184

Z

zucchini
    buying and storing 187
    Zucchini, bacon and cheese
        pies 191
    Zucchini fritters 188
zucchini flowers 187
    Zucchini flower salad 192

LANTERN

Published by the Penguin Group
Penguin Group (Australia)
250 Camberwell Road, Camberwell, Victoria 3124, Australia
(a division of Pearson Australia Group Pty Ltd)
Penguin Group (USA) Inc.
375 Hudson Street, New York, New York 10014, USA
Penguin Group (Canada)
10 Alcorn Avenue, Toronto, Ontario, Canada M4V 3B2
(a division of Pearson Penguin Canada Inc.)
Penguin Books Ltd
80 Strand, London WC2R 0RL, England
Penguin Ireland
25 St Stephen's Green, Dublin 2, Ireland
(a division of Penguin Books Ltd)
Penguin Books India Pvt Ltd
11 Community Centre, Panchsheel Park, New Delhi – 110 017, India
Penguin Group (NZ)
Cnr Airborne and Rosedale Roads, Albany, Auckland, New Zealand
(a division of Pearson New Zealand Ltd)
Penguin Books (South Africa) (Pty) Ltd
24 Sturdee Avenue, Rosebank, Johannesburg 2196, South Africa

Penguin Books Ltd, Registered Offices: 80 Strand, London, WC2R 0RL, England

First published by Penguin Group (Australia), a division of Pearson Australia Group Pty Ltd, 2011

1 3 5 7 9 10 8 6 4 2

Text copyright © George Calombaris 2011,
except Maggie Beer's Sour-cream Pastry (p 22) © Maggie Beer

Photography copyright © Mark Chew 2011

The moral right of the authors has been asserted

All rights reserved. Without limiting the rights under copyright reserved above, no part of this publication may be reproduced, stored in or introduced into a retrieval system, or transmitted, in any form or by any means (electronic, mechanical, photocopying, recording or otherwise), without the prior written permission of both the copyright owner and the above publisher of this book.

Design by Daniel New and Evi Oetomo © Penguin Group (Australia)
Styling by Caroline Velik
Typeset in Caecilia 9.75/13.75pt by Post Pre-press Group, Brisbane, Queensland
Colour reproduction by Splitting Image Colour Studio Pty Ltd, Clayton, Victoria
Printed and bound in China by 1010 Printing International Ltd

National Library of Australia
Cataloguing-in-Publication data:

Calombaris, George.
Georgie Porgie: for kids aged 8 to 80 / George Calombaris; photography by Mark Chew.
9781921382567 (pbk.)
Includes index.
Cooking.
Chew, Mark.
641.5

penguin.com.au